PAYMENTS LAW
IN A NUTSHELL®

SECOND EDITION

by

MARY BETH MATTHEWS
Sidney Parker Davis Jr.
Professor of Business and Commercial Law
School of Law
University of Arkansas Fayetteville

STEVE H. NICKLES
C.C. Hope Chair in Financial Services and Law
School of Law and Babcock
Graduate School of Management
Wake Forest University

WEST ACADEMIC PUBLISHING

Mat #41533686

444 Cedar Street, Suite 700
St. Paul, MN 55101
1-877-888-1330

Printed in the United States of America

ISBN: 978-0-314-29031-1

David, Zach, Eli and Elizabeth,
MBM

M. Ellen, Ellen M., and Jean
SHN

OUTLINE

PART IV. PAYING WITH CREDIT

PART V. PAYING WITH ELECTRONIC TRANSFERS OF FUNDS

TABLE OF CASES

References are to Pages

TABLE OF STATUTES

References are to Pages

TABLE OF UNIFORM COMMERCIAL CODE

References are to Pages

TABLE OF REGULATIONS

References are to Pages

PAYMENTS LAW
IN A NUTSHELL®

SECOND EDITION

PART I

PAYING WITH CASH

CHAPTER 1
CURRENCY

Money is any medium of exchange. Money may be something that is itself valuable, such as jewels or precious metals. It may be something that is not itself valuable but is only **symbolic** and backed by something that is intrinsically or otherwise valuable.

The **symbolic money** most familiar to American law students is United States **currency**: coins and folding money, which is the meaning of currency and cash for purposes of this chapter. It has been defined by one online glossary as "[a]ny form of money that is in public circulation. Currency includes both hard money (coins) and soft money (paper money). Typically currency refers to money that is legally designated as such by the governing body, but in some cultures can refer to any object that has a perceived value and can be exchanged for other objects."[1] People willingly accept American currency as payment without discount because this American cash is backed by federal law declaring it legal tender (31 U.S.C.A. § 5103) and—really and ultimately—by the strength of and confidence in the United States government.

Currency is the most basic, simplest **payment system**, which loosely means an accepted way of paying debts. **Payment** means satisfying a debt such

---

[1] *Currency,* InvestorWords.com—Online Investing Glossary, http://www.investorwords.com/1240/currency.html (last visited Sept. 26, 2014).

that the obligor has no further legal liability for the debt once the payment is made and no further interest in the currency, credit, or other money used to effect the payment.

As a payment system, currency raises few issues because it is so simple; but these issues are fundamentally important and shared by other, more complex systems. How the issues are resolved by the different payment systems determines, to a large extent, the organization and substance of payments law and is the focus of the study, practice, and business of payments. Currency sets the base line.

1. WHEN MUST THE OBLIGEE ACCEPT CASH AS PAYMENT?

In the real lives of normal people, everybody wants cash; and in this country and many other places, most people accept American currency as a means of payment. It's only in law school that we ask: under United States law can somebody ever refuse dollars as payment?

The answer is maybe. Federal law says: "United States coins and currency (including Federal reserve notes and circulating notes of Federal reserve banks and national banks) are legal tender for all debts, public charges, taxes, and dues." 31 U.S.C.A. § 5103. This statute means in part that American cash is a form of payment that can be offered and accepted to satisfy debts, not that cash is the only or default means of acceptable payment.

The older default or general rule is that payment is due in legal tender, i.e., cash. Even that rule might be subjected to a rule of reasonableness, however. *Nemser v. New York City Transit Authority*, 530 N.Y. Supp. 2d 493 (Sup. Ct. 1988) (bus system entitled to require tokens because "the absolute language of the legal tender statute is clearly modifiable by the necessary consideration of what is reasonable under the circumstances.") The more modern rule makes acceptable payment or an offer of payment in cash *or in any manner current in the ordinary course of business*. Restatement (Second) of Contracts § 249 (1981) (emphasis added); see also Uniform Commercial Code (UCC)[2] 2–511(2). There are two really important exceptions.

First, the parties to the payment can agree otherwise and thereby require an exclusive, specific means of payment, including cash, stock, real estate, an executory promise, or anything else they decide on. However, what the agreement provides respecting means of payment is a question of contract interpretation. Thus, it's possible that a contract calling for payment in "cash" can include, for example, payment by check; and a requirement of payment in money, without more specificity, allows payment by any manner current in the ordinary course of business. Restatement (Second) of Contracts § 249 (1981). Also, even if there is no prior agreement as to the means of payment, "payment can be made in any medium which the party obligated

---

[2] All references are to the 2014 Official Text, unless otherwise indicated.

offers, and the party to whom payment is due, accepts." *Lamb v. Thieme*, 367 N.E.2d 602, 603 (Ind. App. 1977).

Second, if the parties' agreement is silent on the means of payment and the obligor offers something other than currency, the obligee can demand payment in legal tender. In this event, however, the obligee but must give the obligor any extension of time reasonably necessary to procure the money. Restatement (Second) of Contracts § 249 (1981).

2. WHEN IS PAYMENT MADE?

"[T]he giving in payment is effected by the transfer and acceptance of property and has the effect of extinguishing and discharging the original demand." *Taylor v. Taylor*, 24 So.2d 74, 75 (La. 1945). In other words, "[a] debtor can be considered to have paid a creditor only if he has delivered, and the creditor has received, money, or other valuable thing, in the amount of the debt." *Feldman v. New York City Health & Hospitals Corp.*, 445 N.Y.S.2d 555, 559 (N.Y.A.D.1981). So, payment by currency or otherwise usually "contemplates manual delivery of the sum due or the placing of it within the control of the payee if and when contingencies to its payment are met." *Enriquillo Export & Import, Inc. v. M.B.R. Industries, Inc.*, 733 So.2d 1124, 1126 (Fla. App. 1999).

The effect of making payment is to satisfy, extinguish, or discharge the debt that was paid. Suppose the obligee refuses the payment that is properly, unconditionally tendered? The effect is not to discharge the principal debt. Typically, at most, the obligor escapes liability for further interest and certain, related costs; and sometimes the further effect is to discharge any sureties for the debt and any lien on property securing the debt.

3. WHEN CAN AN OBLIGOR RECOVER PAYMENT ALREADY MADE?

Suppose a seller delivers goods to a buyer, and the buyer pays the seller in currency. Soon after beginning to use the goods, the buyer discovers the goods are defective and the seller has thereby breached a warranty of quality that was part of the sales contract. Can the buyer recover the money she paid the seller?

Be careful! Undoubtedly, the seller is personally liable to the buyer for damages under UCC Article 2. So, buyer can sue the seller for a money judgment.

Having a right to recover damages, however, is not the same as having a right to the money that the buyer paid the seller. I know what you're thinking: it's a law professor's distinction without a difference. Wrong. There's a very big difference if the seller is insolvent and files bankruptcy. In this event, the buyer's claim for damages is an unsecured debt that bankruptcy will discharge.

On the other hand, if the buyer has a right to recover the money paid the seller, which is a right of restitution, then the buyer may have a property claim to (or property interest in) the money. To this extent, the buyer is a secured creditor and arguably can recover fully ahead of everybody else in the seller's bankruptcy.

However, disappointed obligors who have already paid their obligees are not likely to succeed in pursing this right of restitution because:

- Restitution of payments already made is a very, very narrow and rarely applied remedy. Generally speaking, the remedy is available only when payment results from fraud or certain mistake of law or fact, but not including the ordinary mistaken belief by the obligor that she got what she bargained for. See generally Restatement (Third) of Restitution and Unjust Enrichment, ch.1–2 (2011).
- Moreover, the obligor cannot chase money that even the tackiest obligee has paid to a bona fide purchaser.
- Finally, even if there is a right to restitution of money that the obligee still holds, not all courts deciding the obligee's bankruptcy case will recognize or enforce the obligor's "property" claim or interest based on state law of restitution. *In re Omegas Group, Inc.*, 16 F.3d 1443, 1447 (6th Cir. 1994).

4. WHAT HAPPENS WHEN CASH IS LOST OR STOLEN?

Suppose you take a vacation in Hawaii following news that you passed the bar exam. You visit the Kilauea volcano. Feeling confident that you're bullet proof, you hike to the very edge of the rim and look down into hell. Unfortunately, the wad of folding money (that is the proceeds of your signing bonus from the law firm) falls out of your pocket and drops (it's very heavy) into the inferno. Can you get your money "back" from the United States Government? No.

Now, suppose you got the top score on the bar exam. You feel completely invincible and climb down after the cash. You find it and escape, but the cash is badly burned. Can you swap it for new cash from the government? Maybe.

Federal law provides that "[l]awfully held mutilated paper currency of the United States . . . may be redeemed at face amount if sufficient remnants of any relevant security feature and clearly more than one-half of the original note remains." 31 C.F.R. § 100.5. But, "[n]o relief will be granted on account of lawfully held paper currency which has been totally destroyed." Id. § 100.6.

Suppose that while on the volcano floor you also find wads of bills inadvertently dropped by other people. You rescue this money, too. Can you keep it if the other people find out about the rescue and want the money back? Probably not, unless there is some bizarre law of accidental abandonment or such that gives you a better claim. The money belongs to the people who dropped it. It is their property. They own it. You've got no property interest (again, absent some bizarre law of lost and found).

If the other people don't know that you found their money, should you tell them? (Ask your Mother.)

Okay. Suppose you climb down into the volcano, find your money, and rescue it. Later, a tacky person (TP) steals it from your hotel room. Can you recover it from TP? Yes. It was and remains your property. A thief gets no interest in property she steals. You win.

But, suppose TP uses the money to pay her $30,000 hotel bill. Can you recover the money from the hotel? Probably not. The general rule that applies to all property is that a transferee gets only the rights of the transferor, nothing more. It's called the principle of **derivative title**. The hotel's transferor was TP, who had no rights to the money. So, by this principle the hotel gets no rights, and you win.

Sadly for you, the principle of derivative title has lots of exceptions and many of them protect many (though not all) good faith purchasers, which probably includes the hotel to which TP paid your money. The exception applicable here is reported in the old but still very important and controlling case, Miller v. Race, 97 Eng. Rep. 398 (K.B. 1758) (a really important precedent in payments law).

In the *Miller* case, Finney mailed a Bank of England bearer note, which was redeemable by anyone in possession and functioned as paper currency. The stage was robbed. (Remember: your Mother warned you about sending cash through the mail!) The thief got Finney's money and used it to pay an innkeeper who "took it, bona fide, in his business from a person who made an appearance of a gentleman." There was "no pretense or suspicion of collusion with the robber." Well, when Finney learned of the robbery, he contacted the Bank, reported the facts to a Mr. Race who worked for the Bank, and demanded that Race not pay or redeem the note against Finney's account. Race complied. So, the innkeeper sued Race.

Lord Mansfield reasoned that cash, like other property, can be tracked, followed, and claimed by its owner. Unlike other property, however, cash "cannot be recovered after it has passed in currency," which means "in case of money stolen, the true owner cannot recover it, after it has been paid away fairly and honestly upon a valuable and bona fide consideration." Finney lost on the policy that "it is necessary, for the purposes of commerce, that . . . [the] currency [of cash] should be established and secured." His only remedy (absent insurance) was to sue the thief for the tort of conversion; but, in modern terms, Finney would bear the risk of the thief's insolvency.

The result is different if Finney had sued the thief *before* the money "has passed in currency," i.e., before the thief had paid the money to somebody else. In this event "an action may be brought for the money itself."

In sum, Finney could recover the money from the thief if the thief hadn't spent it, and sue the thief for conversion if the thief has already spent the money. (The problem, of course, is that thieves generally are financially unavailable.) Or, if Finney had dropped the money down the mouth of a volcano and someone found it, "[a]n action may lie against the finder, it is true . . . [b]ut not after it has been paid away in currency."

The result is also different if the innkeeper had not come by the money "fairly." In this case, the innkeeper is accountable for the money itself or liable for its value.

However, the most important lesson of *Miller v. Race* is: when stolen money has been paid away in the usual course of affairs to someone who gives value in good faith, the true owner loses her property interest in the money. The good faith purchaser wins.

PART II

PAYING BY CHECK

Okay. You read the previous chapter. Government-backed currency (real cash $$$$$) is hugely common, and you probably have a lot of experience using it as a means of payment. There are real problems with currency, however. The risk of loss is high. You can recover from the thief if you can find her, she is solvent, and you can afford the price of recovery. Also, the costs of managing currency are high. All those wads of bills and especially the coins in your pocket or purse are heavy. Plus, your Mother told you never to send currency through the mail; and you typically don't do so even if you are willing to accept the risk of loss and even if the distant payee would accept cash.

Instead, you open a checking account, deposit your currency and other money there, and (unless you use your debit card instead) spend the money by writing checks on the account.

How do checks work as a payment system? Basically you swap the money you deposit for debt the bank owes you. The bank does not keep your money in a bag with your name on it. The money you deposit belongs to the bank, and you get—in return for your deposit—a credit balance to your checking account. The bank then reduces the debt it owes you, i.e., your account balance, by paying the bank's money to people whom you order the bank to pay. You give these orders by writing checks against your account.

You are not alone in putting your money in a bank account and paying for stuff using checks written against the account. Although the number of payments by debit card in 2012 more than doubled the number of payments by check,[1] there are still huge numbers of checks written. An estimated 32.8 billion checks were paid in the United States in 1979, 49.5 billion in 1995, but only 18.3 billion in 2012. The use of checks peaked sometime in the mid-1990s, as retail electronic payments and other means of retail payment gained ground. The number of checks paid actually declined 6.6 percent per year from 2000 to 2012.[2]

There are six general areas of concern with respect to checks as a means of payment:

1. **Rights and duties between you and the person to whom you give a check (and other people who are transferees of this person).** A check is a very special piece of paper. You are liable on the check simply because you sign it, and your liability runs to possibly a large number of people: the payee and strangers who get the check after the payee. This group of people is known as persons entitled to enforce the check. And when your check is used to pay for property or services or to satisfy other debt, the underlying obligation that you are paying or

---

[1] The 2013 Federal Reserve Payments Study—Recent and Long-Term Trends in the United States: 2000–2012, 15 (Exhibit 2), available at http://www.frbservices.org/files/communications/pdf/general/2013_fed_res_paymt_study_detailed_rpt.pdf.

[2] Id. at 46.

satisfying is affected but usually does not disappear. It sleeps. What happens to your liability on the underlying obligation and on the check itself depends on whether your bank pays the check or does not pay, i.e., dishonors, the check. All of these issues and more are governed by UCC Article 3 because Article 3 governs negotiable instruments, and a check is a form of negotiable instrument.

2. How a check is collected. When you give someone a check the person does not immediately turn around and tell you to pay it. The whole idea is that the person will take it to your bank and your bank will pay it for you. The process of getting the check to your bank for payment is known as the check collection process, which is governed by UCC Article 4. Most important, Article 4 defines the process of how and when a check is dishonored or paid, and so Article 4 determines the state of your liability on the check and the underlying obligation for which the check was given and taken.

3. Rights and duties between you and your bank with respect to your checking account. The substance of whether your bank should pay or can dishonor a check is mainly governed by the terms of the contract you make with your bank when you open the checking account. This contract is called the deposit agreement. This agreement spells out the reciprocal rights and duties between you and the bank with respect to the checking account, including when the bank can charge your account for checks the bank pays and when the bank should dishonor checks written against your account. UCC Article 4 also applies here, mainly by outlining the baseline rights and duties associated with the deposit relationship between you and your bank.

4. Risks and losses from check fraud between you and your bank. The biggest legal problem that arises in the relationship between you and your bank with respect to your checking account is how to allocate the risks and losses of check fraud. Somebody steals your checkbook and buys all kinds of stuff you did not want and never see. Sure. The thief is liable but is also financially unavailable. Who takes the hit between you and your bank. Or, your Grandmother sends you a graduation check and somebody steals the check, cashes it, and blows the money. Again, the thief is liable but. . . . Who takes the hit among you, your bank, and—surprisingly—Grandma? These and related issues of check fraud are governed by standard principles of Articles 3 and 4; but the combination of these principles is so potent and relatively complex that the safer course of study is to segregate cases of check fraud and explain apart from everything else how the UCC resolves them.

5. Shifting check fraud losses. Whoever gets stuck initially with losses caused by check fraud against your account, the loser will naturally want to pass the loss to someone else. Again, the ways and means of shifting these losses among other players in the check collection process are more easily studied by focusing on these issues separately.

6. Bank checks. Cashier's check, certified checks, and teller's checks are known, as a group, as bank checks because, unlike ordinary checks, banks sign and therefore become liable on them under Article 3. Articles 3 and 4 govern the contract, property, and collection aspects of bank checks but treat them differently in very important respects.

These six areas of concern are addressed separately and sequentially in the next six chapters of this book.

CHAPTER 2

LIABILITY ON CHECKS UNDER ARTICLE 3

A **check** is a subtype of **negotiable instruments** that are governed by UCC Article 3. There are two basic types of instruments: **notes** and **drafts**. A **note** is a negotiable instrument that is an explicit promise to pay. A **draft** is a negotiable instrument that explicitly orders someone else (known as the **drawee**) to pay and implicitly promises to pay if the drawee does not pay. The person who creates or authors the draft is the **drawer**. The technically correct verb form is "to **draw**" the draft. A drawer draws the draft and thereby gives the explicit order to the drawee to pay the draft and implicitly promises to pay the draft herself if the drawee does not pay it. A **check** is the most common form of draft. A check is a negotiable instrument in the form of a draft that orders a bank (as drawee) to pay on demand.

Under Article 3, a negotiable instrument—including a check—creates rights and liabilities that certain people can legally enforce. The rights and liabilities are reified—embodied—in the instrument itself. A check—with these rights and liabilities—is property and thus transferable. Article 3 explains who is liable on a check, when, and how. The statute also explains how a check—as property—is transferred and with it the rights of enforcement. Defenses to enforcement are described, too, and the special protections against certain defenses that

Article 3 gives to a very special person with rights to enforce: a holder in due course.

1. IMPORTANCE OF LIABILITY UNDER ARTICLE 3

Let's get this straight right now so you're not confused and understand the importance of liability *under Article 3*. Suppose you make a contract with BarBri to take the bar review course. (True, you don't really need the course, but why risk it.) The contract is governed by the common law. BarBri promises to let you attend the lectures, get you copies of the books, etc. You promise to pay the price of the course. You don't need to sign a note, check, or any other kind of negotiable instrument to make you liable to BarBri. If you don't pay, you're liable under the common law.

When you pay, you may use a check. Signing and giving BarBri a check for the price of the course makes you liable, too, on the check. If your bank pays the check, everybody is happy; and, legally, your liability on the check is discharged and also your liability on the underlying transaction, which is the common-law contract.

The story is very different if (hopefully not!) your check bounces, i.e., your bank fails to pay the check and thereby dishonors it. In this event, you're liable on the underlying contract and also on the check. BarBri gets to choose whether to sue you on the contract or on the check. It's a lot easier to sue on the check; and your liability on the check is established and governed by Article 3 and so, too, your defenses.

Your liability is not limited to BarBri only. BarBri owns the right to enforce the check and can transfer this right to anybody else. If your check bounces (technically, is "**dishonored**"), BarBri's transferee or a further, remote transferee can sue you and enforce your liability even though this person is a complete stranger and was in no way involved in the underlying contract between you and BarBri.

It's even possible—and often happens on law school and bar examinations—that a person can acquire the right to enforce the check by stealing it or taking the check through a thief. We are not making this up. It's really true.

It's only true, however, if Article 3 applies, which requires that the writing you signed meets the Article 3 requirements of a check.

2. REQUIREMENTS OF A CHECK

The Article 3 rules of liability and property only apply to a writing that is a **negotiable instrument** as Article 3 defines it. To be a check under Article 3, and therefore to trigger the Article 3 rules that apply to checks, the writing must satisfy the general requirements of form that apply to all negotiable instruments and must also take a more specific form that distinguishes a check from other kinds of negotiable instruments. Put another way for emphasis: Article 3 applies to nothing that is not a negotiable instrument, and nothing is a check under Article 3 that does not satisfy the Article 3 requirements of a negotiable instrument.

The requirements of a negotiable instrument under Article 3 are known as the **requisites of negotiability**. They define "negotiable instrument," a/k/a "instrument," and thus determine if Article 3 applies or not. A writing that satisfies these requisites is said to be negotiable and is governed by Article 3. A writing that does not satisfy these requisites is not negotiable; is not an instrument; and is not within the scope of Article 3.[1]

Now, there is a **practical truth** that should be stated for purposes of honest disclosure and proper perspective. The typical check form, when typically completed, always satisfies these requisites of negotiability. In practice, the issue of the negotiability of a check almost never arises. Instead, issues of negotiability in recent years have arisen largely in regard to promissory notes. The recent mortgage foreclosure crisis has actually forced courts to inquire into archaic issues of negotiability in order to determine the right to enforce a mortgage note,

1 In this event nothing in Article 3 applies. On the other hand, the inapplicability of Article 3 to a writing that is not an instrument does not necessarily spell unenforceability of the writing or the commitments beneath it. Inapplicability means only that the legal significance and consequences of the writing or underlying commitments are determined by other law. Most significantly, therefore, no transferee of the writing could acquire the extraordinary rights that Article 3 gives a transferee who is a holder in due course.

On the other hand, the inapplicability of Article 3 does not mean that nothing else in the UCC applies. Especially important is that something that serves the purpose of a check but that is not a check or other instrument under Article 3 may nevertheless be governed in some respects by UCC Article 4, which applies more widely to items, not just Article 3 checks.

and the availability of defenses against it.[2] In the law school classroom, however, your teacher will suggest many variations from reality that make you apply the requisites of negotiability. So, to satisfy your teacher's surreal imagination and to deepen your general education, some detail is provided here about the requisites of negotiability as applied to checks.[3]

The requisites of negotiability, which apply to all kinds of negotiable instruments, are spelled out in section 3–104(a). It provides:

> "[N]egotiable instrument" means an unconditional promise or order to pay a fixed amount of money, with or without interest or other charges described in the promise or order, if it:
>
> > (1) is payable to bearer or to order at the time it is issued or first comes into possession of a holder;
> >
> > (2) is payable on demand or at a definite time; and
> >
> > (3) does not state any other undertaking or instruction by the person promising or ordering payment to do any act in addition to the payment of money, but the promise or order may contain (i) an undertaking or power

2 See, Kurt Eggert, Not Dead Yet: The Surprising Survival of Negotiability, 66 Ark. L. Rev. 145 (2013).

3 The discussion here, about the negotiability of checks, is generally applicable to the issue of the negotiability of notes, but some requisites apply differently to notes and checks. So, be careful in applying this discussion to notes.

to give, maintain, or protect collateral to secure payment, (ii) an authorization or power to the holder to confess judgment or realize on or dispose of collateral, or (iii) a waiver of the benefit of any law intended for the advantage or protection of an obligor.

There is also a hidden requirement of a **writing**. It is part of the definition of the necessary "promise or order." 3–103(a)(8) & (12). So, all these requirements of negotiability must be satisfied by a **written** instrument. There is no such thing as an oral negotiable instrument.[4]

A **check** is a subset of these requirements. It is a negotiable instrument that is distinguished by satisfying all of these requirements in a writing that

- orders
- a bank
- to pay on demand.

Put another way:

- It is the **ordering of payment** that distinguishes the writing as a draft, as opposed to a note.

[4] If the state has adopted the **Uniform Electronic Transactions Act,** an electronic note in the form of a "transferable record" can be created under § 16, which can be given rights similar to holder in due course protection under Article 3—although created by other law. However, that transferable record is subject to a lot of restrictions to prevent duplication or fraud.

- It is the ordering of **a bank** to pay **on demand** that distinguishes the writing as a check, as opposed to an ordinary draft.

The negotiability of a check, whether or not the Article 3 requirements are satisfied, is determined by the face of the writing: the language that appears there must satisfy the requisites of negotiability. The provisions that 3–104(a) requires must appear on the face of the writing, and the provisions that the statute prohibits must not appear there. On the other hand, if a writing is negotiable on its face, the presence of a separate agreement (oral or written) does not affect negotiability, not even when the terms of the agreement would prevent negotiability if they were part of the writing itself. See 3–117 (by implication).

Thus, it is usually possible to determine very quickly if a writing is negotiable simply by having the writing in hand and 3–104(a) in mind, except that 3–104(a) is amplified and supplemented by the balance of the provisions in part 1 of Article 3. In effect, these provisions define the 3–104(a) requisites of negotiability, and these definitions are often more generous, tolerant and lenient than the plain language of 3–104(a) itself. Any decision about negotiability, especially that a writing is not negotiable, is not complete without checking these supplemental provisions. They mainly inform the following discussion which focuses, in turn, on each of the nine separate (but related) requirements that 3–104(a) describes.

A. WRITING

The core requirement of a negotiable instrument that is a check is an **order to pay money**; and an order, by its own definition, must be **written**. Commercial paper is usually executed on printed, paper forms, but this kind of writing is not necessary for negotiability. **Written** or **writing** includes any "intentional reduction to tangible form." 1–201(b)(43). Therefore, the requirement of a writing can be met by engraving, stamping, lithographing, photographing, typing, or longhand writing in pencil or ink on anything tangible, or by any similar process or any combination of them. There are stories of instruments painted on cows and coconuts.

There is, however, an important limit: the form of the writing must be **tangible**. In this respect, the meaning of writing for purposes of Article 3 is less than the meaning of record elsewhere in the law. So, for example, a promise is not written if typed on a computer and saved to disk. The file may be a record under some other law but is not a **writing** under Article 3 which requires **tangible form**.

B. SIGNED BY DRAWER

The order that negotiability requires for a check means a written instruction or undertaking that is **signed** by the person who orders the bank to pay. This person is the **drawer**. The bank whom the drawer orders to pay is called the **drawee**.

The meaning of "signed" is very broad, including "any symbol executed or adopted with present intention to adopt or accept a writing." 1–201(b)(37). Normally, a person using a pen to write her name in longhand meets this requirement. It may also be met by the person using a symbol that she affixes to the instrument by hand, machine or in any other manner. A smiley face drawn or stamped on a writing can be a signature as well as a rubber stamped signature or a name or number that a computer prints on paper.

> The symbol may be printed, stamped or written; it may be by initials or by thumbprint. It may be on any part of the document and in appropriate cases may be found in a billhead or letterhead.

1–201, comment 37. It may be a symbol the party adds to the writing or a symbol that is already there. Thus, a computer-produced check with a facsimile signature is a signed instrument; and a person can be found to have signed a writing because she wrote on paper preprinted with her name.

In short, the decisive issue is never the kind or nature of graphic mark or the physical means of placing it on the writing. Any symbol however done will do. The decisive issue "always is whether the symbol was executed or adopted by the party with present intention to adopt or accept the writing." Id.

No symbol is a signature that lacks the purpose of authentication. Not even a person's name on a writing is, by itself, a signature. This explains why name and signature are not synonymous terms. A name is not a signature on a writing without the present intention to adopt or accept the writing. So, the drawee on a check, i.e., the bank ordered to pay, has not signed the check simply because the bank is named on the check as the drawee.

On the other hand, a person's signing a writing using someone else's name is a signature so long as the signer does so with the requisite intent to adopt or accept the writing. The other person's name is as good a symbol as a smiley face or a thumbprint.

C. ORDER A BANK

Fundamentally, a check requires a signed writing that orders, i.e., **instructs** a **bank** to pay money. The bank that is ordered to pay is known as the **drawee**. A **bank** is "a person engaged in the business of banking, including a savings bank, savings and loan association, credit union, or trust company." 3–103(c); 4–105(1).

It is not sufficient that the bank is authorized to pay: the writing must also instruct the bank to pay. The usual way of expressing the order is to use the imperative form of the verb "Pay." "Pay to the order of Steve" is clearly an order. The reason is not the use of the word "order," which satisfies the altogether different requirement that the writing is payable to order or bearer. The order to pay is inferred from the instruction that the drawee "Pay." Thus, the requirement of an order is met even if the writing provides "Pay Bearer."

An instruction may be an order even though it is couched in courteous form such as "please pay" or "kindly pay." On the other hand, there must be more than an authorization or request to pay. Such uncertain language as "I wish you would pay" is not an order.

Moreover, an order in a check must identify with reasonable certainty the bank which is ordered to pay, i.e., the drawee. A check usually meets the requirement because the drawee bank's name is encoded on the face of the check form along the bottom (with other electronic routing information) and printed in human readable language in the lower left-hand corner of the form.

Note again that, although the drawer of a check does not expressly promise to pay the instrument, the law obligates her to pay the instrument upon dishonor. 3–414(b). In short, the drawer of a check that is dishonored by the drawee bank may be liable on the instrument even though the check itself contains no express promise to pay. This liability is discussed later in this chapter.

D. UNCONDITIONAL

Generally speaking, an order is unconditional unless the writing states:

- an express condition to payment,
- that the promise or order is subject to or governed by another record, or
- that rights or obligations with respect to the promise or order are stated in another record.

3–106(a). In other words, if the check contains none of these provisions, it is unconditional. The check is therefore negotiable if the other 3–104(a) requisites of negotiability are satisfied. On the other hand, if it contains even one of the three kinds of provisions that 3–106(a) describes, the writing is conditional, negotiability is impossible, and the writing is not a check.

E. MONEY

The unconditional order to pay that negotiability requires of a check is an order to pay *money*. An instrument is payable in money if it is stated as payable in "a medium of exchange currently authorized or adopted by a domestic or foreign government. The term includes a monetary unit of account established by an intergovernmental organization or by agreement between two or more countries." 1–201(24). Money, therefore, is not limited to United States dollars. If the instrument is payable in foreign money, the amount "may be paid in the foreign money or in an equivalent amount in dollars calculated by using the current bank-offered spot rate at the place of payment for the purchase of dollars on the day on which the instrument is paid." 3–107.

F. FIXED AMOUNT

The money payable must be a *fixed amount:* a total which the holder can determine from the instrument by any necessary computation at the time the instrument is payable, without reference to any outside source.

G. PAYABLE ON DEMAND

For a check, negotiability requires that the writing "is payable on demand." 3–104(a)(2).

An instrument is "payable on demand" if it:

- states that it is payable on demand or at sight,
- otherwise indicates that it is payable at the will of the holder, or
- does not state any time of payment.

3–108(a). Most instruments that are payable on demand are so payable for the last reason: they make no express provision for time of payment.

H. PAYABLE TO ORDER OR TO BEARER (*WORDS OF NEGOTIABILITY*)

Negotiability requires that a check is "payable *to bearer* or *to order* at the time it [the instrument] is issued or first comes into possession of a holder." 3–104(a)(1). Words that satisfy this requirement are called **words of negotiability**. These words are the most common earmarks of negotiability. They most clearly indicate the intention of the drawer to issue an instrument that is negotiable and subject to all the incidents attaching to this form of contract and property. They alert the prospective drawer, more certainly than anything else, of the possibility that if the instrument is negotiated to a holder in due course, the effect is to cut off any claims and defenses of the drawer against the payee.

"To order" and "to bearer" are alternative forms of the words of negotiability. In determining if a writing is a negotiable instrument, it makes no difference whether it is payable to order or to bearer so long as it is payable to one or the other. The difference is important in deciding how the instrument is negotiated so that the transferee becomes a holder and is entitled to the rights of that status, which can include the rights of a holder in due course. An instrument that is payable to order (a/k/a *order paper*) is negotiated by transfer of possession and indorsement. An instrument payable to bearer (a/k/a *bearer paper*) is negotiated by transfer of possession alone. 3–201(b). Much more is said about negotiation and due-course status in other sections later in this chapter.

1. Payable to Order

Typically, an instrument is payable to order, which means it is not payable to bearer and is payable:

- to the order of an identified person, or
- to an identified person or order.

3–109(b). This meaning covers the most common form of the words of negotiability: "Pay to the order of Jane Doe." It also covers the typical variation, "Pay Jane Doe or order." An instrument that uses this form is payable to order even if Ms. Doe is fictitious. 3–109 comment 2.

In general, in all kinds of instruments except checks, the word "order" (or, perhaps, a very close equivalent) is essential to create an instrument payable to order. It makes clear that the maker intends payment to transferees as well as the identified person. It empowers this person, through the process of negotiation, to redirect the obligation that runs to her, as payee, to someone else she designates or to anyone who holds the instrument. So, generally, an instrument is not payable to order that provides only, "Pay Jane Doe" because the magic "order" word is missing. Neither is it payable to bearer. The writing therefore lacks words of negotiability, is not a negotiable instrument, and—contrary to former law—is entirely beyond Article 3.

The single **exception applies to a check**. A writing that satisfies all of the requisites of negotiability, and that otherwise falls within the definition of "check," is negotiable and is a check even if it lacks the word "order" in describing to whom it is payable. Section 3–104(c). Therefore, a check providing "Pay Jane Doe" is fully negotiable; is covered by Article 3; is presumably treated as payable to order; and, with the necessary indorsement, a transferee of it can become a holder in due course, even though the check technically lacks words of negotiability.[5]

---

[5] This exception for the 3–104(c) check is very narrow. Any other would-be draft or other form of instrument that is payable only to an identified person, and not also her order, is not negotiable. This order language is not supplied by the "order to pay" that distinguishes the draft from a note and that is implied by the direction "Pay." The "order to pay" in a draft satisfies a

2. Payable to Bearer

An instrument that is not payable to order is not, automatically, payable to bearer. The two forms of the words of negotiability—order and bearer—are alternatives of the same requirement and either of them can be used in creating a negotiable instrument, but each of them has its own peculiar meaning. Failing one does not satisfy the other by default; and if the writing does not use one form or the other, as Article 3 defines them, the words of negotiability that 3–104(a) requires are lacking, the writing is not an instrument, and nothing in Article 3 applies.

"Payable to bearer" means that a promise or order:

- states that it is payable to bearer or to the order of bearer or otherwise indicates that the person in possession of the promise or order is entitled to payment;
- does not state a payee; or
- states that it is payable to or to the order of cash or otherwise indicates that it is not payable to an identified person.

3–109(a). The unofficial essence of payable to bearer is that anyone who possesses or holds the instrument can enforce it, which negatively implies that payment

---

requirement of negotiability that is different from the requirement of words of negotiability. The former identifies the nature and purpose of the instrument and the issuer's undertaking. The latter signals transferability. A negotiable draft requires both an order to pay that, additionally, is payable to order or bearer, except for the 3–104(c) check.

is not limited to a particular person or people. The issuer intends payment to anybody with the instrument. Thus, an instrument that expresses this intent in so many words is, officially, payable to bearer. 3–109(a)(1). The most common expressions of this intent, which meet the test of "payable to bearer", are:

"Pay to Bearer,"

"Pay to the order of Bearer,"

"Pay to Cash," or

"Pay to Cash, or Order,"

as long as "Bearer" or "Cash" is not used to identify a person.

I. NO OTHER UNDERTAKING OR INSTRUCTION

The final requirement of negotiability for a check is that beyond the drawer's order to pay money, the instrument itself must not contain "any other undertaking or instruction" by the drawer "to do any act in addition to the payment of money," with a few exceptions that Article 3 describes.[6] The principal exceptions are incorporated into 3–104(a) itself.

---

6 Recent cases in regard to promissory notes have been willing to find that such clauses as a right to prepay [*In re Kain*, 2012 WL 1098465 (Bankr. D.S.C. 2012)] or a requirement to pay taxes and maintain insurance on stated collateral [*Kelley v. McGrail*, 31 Conn. L. Rptr. 326; 2002 WL 2414447 (Sup. Ct. Conn. 2002) (unpublished opinion)] do not violate this requirement.

Negotiability is not affected if the writing also contains:

- an undertaking or power to give, maintain, or protect collateral to secure payment,
- an authorization or power to the holder to confess judgment or realize on or dispose of collateral, or
- a waiver of the benefit of any law intended for the advantage or protection of an obligor.

3–104(a)(3)(i–iii).

3. SIGNATURE ON A CHECK CREATES LIABILITY

"Obligation on an instrument depends on a signature that is binding on the obligor." 3–401 comment 1. This principle is two sided. It means that no person is liable on an instrument unless she signed it, either personally or through someone else whose signature binds her. See 3–401(a). Conversely, a person who signs an instrument, or is bound by someone else's signature, is prima facie liable because of the signature. The rule is that in an action with respect to an instrument on which the signature of the defendant is valid and binding, the plaintiff is entitled to recover simply by producing the instrument, unless the defendant establishes a defense. 3–308(b). The plaintiff's prima facie case depends on nothing else. It is the signature on the instrument that creates the defendant's liability.

People who sign checks typically sign either as the drawer of the check or as an indorser of the check. The **drawer** is the person who creates or issues the check and thereby orders her bank (the **drawee**) to pay on demand whomever the drawer identifies, either an identified person or bearer. Anybody else who signs the check, except in the role of a co-drawer, is an **indorser**. 3–204(a).

The bank named as drawee of the check does not, as drawee, sign the check. The bank's name is there but not the bank's signature. If a bank signs a customer's check for the purpose of incurring liability on the check, the purpose is for the bank to **certify** the check. 3–409(d). By doing so the bank **accepts** the check and is liable as an **acceptor**. *Certifying checks is extremely rare these days.* If a bank decides to incur liability on a check, the bank will issue its own check drawn by itself on itself. It is called a **cashier's check**, and the bank is both drawer and drawee. 3–104(g). See Chapter 7 *infra*, where cashier's checks and certified checks are discussed.

The discussion here focuses on the terms and conditions of the liability of people who sign very common, ordinary checks drawn by natural people or businesses on or against their checking accounts at drawee banks. At this point the chapter explains what it means for a person to have signed a check and thereby incur the liability that Article 3 imposes as a consequence of signing a negotiable instrument.

A. MECHANICS OF SIGNATURE

To sign a writing means to execute or adopt "any symbol * * * with present intention to adopt or accept a writing." 1–201(b)(37). The earlier discussion in this chapter about the requisites of negotiability considers the requirement that the drawer must sign the check. What is said there about the mechanics of signing and signature applies equally here to a signature of a person (as principal or agent) in any capacity on a check or any other kind of negotiable instrument.

B. MEANS OF SIGNATURE: BY AN AGENT OR REPRESENTATIVE

1. Principal's Liability

The signature that obligates a person on an instrument can be put there by the person herself or by the signature of an agent or representative. In the latter case, there are two basic requirements to obligate the person represented (i.e., the principal). First, the representative must herself sign the instrument. 3–401(a). Article 3 requires no special form, and nothing in Article 3 turns on whether she uses her name or the principal's name.

Second, the representative's signature must be binding on the principal. Id. This turns on other law, usually ordinary and local agency law. The rule is that "the represented person is bound by the signature to the same extent the represented person would be bound [by agency law] if the signature were on a simple contract." 3–402(a). The effect is that to this extent, "the signature [of the representative] is the authorized signature of the represented person." 3–402 comment 1; see also 3–402(a). Whether or not the principal is named in the instrument is unimportant, as far as Article 3 is concerned, to the principal's own liability on the instrument. Therefore, even an undisclosed principal can be liable on an instrument that only her agent signed even in the agent's own name if, under the same or similar circumstances, agency law would obligate the principal on a simple contract.

2. Agent's Liability

Even when an authorized representative is acting for someone else, her signature on the instrument may appear to be solely for her own benefit and can mislead third parties who know nothing different. Therefore, when an authorized representative signs her name to an instrument, even while acting for the principal and with the principal's specific authority, *the representative is herself prima facie liable* unless:

- the form of the signature shows unambiguously that the signature is made on behalf of the represented person, and
- the represented person is identified in the instrument.

3–402(b)(1). By this rule the representative is freely and entirely safe only if both conditions are met, as by signing "P, by A, Treasurer." 3–402 comment 2. In this case she avoids liability as a matter of law.

If the form of the representative's signature fails *either* of these conditions or both of them, she is liable on the instrument unless she "proves that the original parties did not intend the representative to be liable on the instrument." 3–402(b)(2). In effect, it is a defense to liability that the representative acted for someone else and that her signature was not intended to be personally binding. She can assert this defense against anyone, except a holder in due course who "took the instrument without notice that the representative was not intended to be liable on the instrument." Id. It makes no difference to the availability or applicability of the defense that the instrument shows nothing but the representative's signature in her own name and is entirely silent as to both the principal's identity and the representative's capacity. Even in this case, except as against the innocent holder in due course, the representative is free to prove the defense that the original parties did not intend to bind her on the instrument.

An **exceptional rule** that better protects the agent applies to checks. By law, the authorized agent is not liable to anyone on a check that she draws on the principal's account, *even if the agent neglects to indicate her agency status*, so long as the check identifies the principal. 3–402(c). The reason is that such a check effectively identifies somebody else as the owner of the account and thus the true obligor. Therefore, "nobody is deceived into thinking that the person signing the check is meant to be liable." 3–402 comment 3.

3. Unauthorized Agent

With two exceptions, an unauthorized signature binds no one and is entirely ineffective. 3–403(a). An *unauthorized signature* includes both an outright forgery and also a signature made without actual, implied, or apparent authority. 1–201(b)(41). The rule that such a signature is ineffective applies even if the signer represents a principal for other purposes, and even if the principal's name is used by the unauthorized signer.

The exceptions are, first, that an unauthorized signature binds the unauthorized signer herself by operating as her signature "in favor of a person who in good faith pays the instrument or takes it for value." 3–403(a). This is true even if the unauthorized signer uses someone else's name, such as the name of the person she purports to represent. It makes no difference whether or not the signer believes, when she signs, that she is acting for and with the authority of someone else. An innocent and a forger are themselves equally bound by their unauthorized signatures.

Second, because of extraordinary rules that reach even cases of outright forgery, a person's unauthorized signature can sometimes bind her for reasons of ratification and culpability, such as negligence that contributed to the forgery. These rules are discussed later in the context of check fraud. See Chapters 5 and 6 *infra*.

4. TERMS AND CONDITIONS OF LIABILITY

A person's signature on a check subjects her to prima facie liability on the instrument, but the nature of this liability is not the same for every signer. Article 3 imposes terms of and conditions on liability which vary with the capacity in which the person signed the instrument. *Capacity* refers to the role the signer plays with respect to the instrument itself, which in the case of a typical check is drawer or indorser. Put another way, a person's signature on a check creates liability. The person's capacity defines and limits this liability.[7]

A. LIABILITIES OF PERSONS WHO NORMALLY SIGN CHECKS

1. Drawer

The **drawer** of a check is the person who creates or issues the instrument, usually by signing in the lower, right-hand corner of the check. In so doing, the drawer does not expressly promise to pay the instrument. She does not even expect to pay it personally. Instead, the drawer orders someone else—her bank, the drawee—to pay the check. 3–103(a)(5). It is only if the drawee refuses or fails to pay the instrument upon presentment (i.e., the drawee dishonors the check) that the drawer expects to pay it directly.

---

[7] So defined, a person's liability on an instrument that results from her signature is commonly known among law professors as the person's "*contract of liability*" with respect to the instrument.

Consider the ordinary check. The drawer in effect says to the bank, "Pay the amount of this check to the holder when she presents it and charge my account." In effect, she says to the payee, "Take this check to the bank and ask for payment and if it does not pay, come back to me and I will." This conditional promise is not stated in the check she signs, which contains no promise but only an order expressed by the word "Pay" addressed to the drawee. Rather, the drawer's promise is implied in the draft because of the contract of liability that a drawer makes by force of Article 3:

> *If an unaccepted draft [such as a check] is dishonored, the drawer is obliged to pay the draft (i) according to its terms* at the time it was issued or, if not issued, at the time it first came into possession of a holder, or (ii) if the drawer signed an incomplete instrument, according to its terms when completed, to the extent stated in Sections 3–115 and 3–407.

3–414(b) (emphasis added). In every case, the drawer's obligation runs to a "**person entitled to enforce**" the instrument or to an **indorser** who paid it. Id.

If the drawee bank pays the check, which usually happens, the drawer's liability on the check—and on the underlying obligation for which the check was given and taken—are discharged. If the drawee bank does not pay the check, which is dishonor, the drawer is liable and must pay herself, directly and personally. If she refuses, the payee or other person entitled to enforce the check can sue the drawer, establish the liability in court, and pursue the appropriate collection remedies against the drawer.

As a general rule, a drawer may avoid contract liability on an *ordinary draft* by adding words to her drawer's signature that disclaim liability to pay the draft. 3–414(e). The most commonlyused disclaimer are the words "without recourse." *A drawer of a check, however, is not permitted to disclaim her liability.* Id. "There is no legitimate purpose served by issuing a check on which nobody is liable." 3–414 comment 5.

2. Indorser

An **indorser** of a check is someone who signs the instrument in order to negotiate it, restrict payment, or just to incur liability on the instrument. 3–204(a). Her signature is known as an *indorsement,* id., which usually is placed on the back of the check but can be placed on the front of the check in the margin or elsewhere. An instrument is most commonly indorsed for the purpose of negotiating an order instrument so that the transferee becomes a holder, which is discussed later in this chapter.

An indorser's liability on a check, like a drawer's liability, is conditioned on *dishonor* by the drawee bank. 3–415(a). Unlike a drawer, an indorser is also generally entitled to *notice of dishonor*. Her contract of liability is conditioned on notice, 3–503(a), and lack of notice is a defense to liability. 3–415(c). An indorser does not say, "I will pay." Rather she says, "I will pay if the instrument is dishonored and any necessary notice of dishonor is given." Assuming that these conditions are satisfied, she agrees to be liable according to the terms of the instrument at the time of her indorsement. 3–415(a). This obligation "is owed to a person entitled to enforce the instrument or to a subsequent indorser who paid the instrument * * *." Id.

Several people may indorse the same instrument, which most commonly happens when a check is transferred by the original holder to somebody else who then transfers the check further and so on, with each person indorsing the check as it moves along. The last person in the chain presents the check to the drawee bank for payment. If the check is paid, everybody's liability on the check and underlying obligations are discharged.

If the check is dishonored, however, the person last in line who is entitled to enforce the instrument—and to whom the check is bounced back by the drawee bank—may immediately proceed against the drawer or, upon proper notice of dishonor, against any one of the indorsers without proceeding against the person who indorsed the check to her.

If the person last in line decides to collect from an indorser in the middle of the chain of transfer, it then becomes important to determine if the targeted, middle indorser who pays has any rights against the other indorsers or anyone else. Generally, indorsers are liable to one another in the order in which they indorse, that is, each indorser is liable to every subsequent indorser. Thus, an indorser who pays can recover from people who indorsed before her, and any indorser can recover directly from the drawer.

Any indorser can disclaim her contract of liability on the instrument by **qualifying** her indorsement, which means adding to her signature words such as "without recourse" or the like. 3–415(b). These words usually precede, but may follow, the signature. Although a *qualified indorser* incurs no contract liability on the instrument, she incurs liability on warranties, as do indorsers who do not qualify their indorsements and persons who transfer an instrument without any indorsement whatsoever. Warranty liability is discussed later in the contexts of check collection and check fraud. See Chapters 3, 5, and 6 *infra*.

An indorsement that is not qualified is **unqualified**. (Every indorsement is either qualified or unqualified.) Typically, an indorsement is unqualified. Moreover, someone who gives value for an instrument is entitled to the transferor's unqualified indorsement. 3–203(c).

B. USUAL NON-LIABILITY OF THE DRAWEE

The bank that is a drawee of a check does not sign the typical check in the typical case.[8] The bank's name is there but not the bank's signature. So, the drawee bank has no liability on the check itself under Article 3 no matter what happens unless and until the bank *accepts* the instrument. 3–408. The drawee accepts by signing the draft for the purpose or intent

8 Again, in the atypical, very rare case, a drawee signs a customer's check to accept the instrument and thereby certify it. See Chapter 7 *infra*. Certification is not part of normal, everyday practice and practically never happens.

of agreeing to pay it, and she usually does so by signing vertically across the face of the instrument. 3–409. This signature is an *acceptance* which obligates the drawee as an *acceptor*. A bank's acceptance of a check has a special name, *certification*. A check that a bank certifies is, amazingly, a *certified check*. See Chapter 7 *infra*.

The truth is, however, that *the drawee bank never accepts a check in the typical case*. As the check moves through banking channels in the collection process (see Chapter 3 *infra*), the drawee and other banks may stamp, write or spit on, mark, and mutilate the check. None of these acts is acceptance that amounts to certification. So, in the typical case of the typical check (which happens a jillion times a day), neither the drawee bank nor any other bank in the collection process signs the check in such a way or purpose as to become liable on the check as an acceptor or—for that matter—as an indorser. There may be liability for other reasons but not for the reason that the bank incurred liability as a signatory.

The bank may incur liability apart from the check, notably under Article 4 for violating the rules described there governing the collection of checks, see Chapter 3 *infra*, and also governing the relationship between itself and its customers with respect to customers' checking accounts. See Chapter 4 *infra*.

C. CONDITIONS OF LIABILITY: PRESENTMENT, DISHONOR, AND NOTICE

The liability of a drawer or indorser of a check is conditioned on *dishonor* of the instrument by the drawee. Dishonor usually involves *presentment* of the check for payment to the drawee bank. An indorser's liability is further conditioned on *notice of dishonor*. The explanation is that drawers and indorsers normally are not expected to pay unless the drawee bank fails to do so. Thus their liability is delayed until the bank is asked to pay and, instead of paying the check, dishonors it. **In this sense** it is commonly said that the liabilities of drawers and indorsers are **secondary liability**.

Postponing liability is not the only consequence of not meeting these conditions. Failure or delay in presentment or notice of dishonor can entirely discharge the liability of an indorser or a drawer. The further effect is to discharge, pro tanto, the person's obligation on the transaction underlying the instrument.

In concept, the conditions of secondary liability of the parties to a check are easy to understand: presentment involves requesting payment of the expected drawee bank; dishonor is the bank's refusal of the request; and notice of dishonor is alerting the indorser whose own liability on the instrument is now triggered.

5. DISCHARGE OF LIABILITY ON INSTRUMENTS

A. MEANING AND MODES OF DISCHARGE

"Discharge" means that an obligor is released from liability on the instrument for reasons of Article 3 or contract law. To be clear about the effect of discharge, keep in mind a few basic, fundamental propositions about it.

- First, the "instrument," itself, is not discharged. Rather, the liability of one or more parties on the instrument is discharged. The common expression, which far overstates the result, is that the parties themselves are discharged.
- Second, the liability of different parties may be discharged at different times.
- Third, a party may be discharged with respect to one person while remaining liable to someone else.
- Fourth, discharge of liability on an instrument is not always final. Liability that has been discharged can sometimes be revived. See, e.g., 3–418(d).
- Fifth, the discharge of any party is not effective against a subsequent holder in due course unless she has notice of the discharge when she takes the instrument. To reiterate for emphasis, such notice does not stop her from becoming a holder in due course but does subject her to the party's discharge defense.
- Finally, discharge of liability on a check can occur in several different, alternative ways. The major ways are:

  1. Payment (3–602);

2. Alteration (3–407);
3. Cancellation or renunciation (3–604); and
4. Any other act or agreement which would discharge an obligation to pay money under a simple contract.

B. PAYMENT OF THE INSTRUMENT

1. Requirements of the Discharge

A person who signs an instrument becomes liable to pay it. It is natural, therefore, that her payment of the instrument should end her liability on it. The law confirms and reaches this outcome by way of discharge, by providing that "[t]o the extent of a payment * * * the obligation of the party obliged to pay the instrument is discharged * * *." 3–602(c). Also, by separate rule, payment of the instrument usually discharges the underlying obligation. 3–310(b–c).

Three very important limits are built into the rule that payment of an instrument discharges liability on it. First, the discharge is pro tanto only, "to the extent" of payment. Second, the discharge only affects the liability of the party who pays the instrument. For this reason, payment alone does not extinguish the whole instrument or discharge any other party's liability on it. Former law agreed but also applied a supplemental rule that discharged everybody on the instrument when any party was discharged who herself had no right of recourse on the instrument. 3–601(3)(b) (1989 Official Text).

Thus, when a check was paid by the drawee bank for the drawer, an indorser was discharged. The current Article 3 lacks this rule, but the result is the same. An indorser's liability is conditioned on dishonor. 3–415(a). Because of the drawee's payment, the indorser's liability never will mature.

The third and final limit of 3–602(a) is that the actual payment must match the statutory definition of "payment" that applies here, which requires that payment is made:

- by or on behalf of a party obliged to pay the instrument, and
- to a person entitled to enforce the instrument.

3–602(a). Whenever someone other than a party gives value for the instrument, it is a purchase rather than "payment" and there is no discharge by this rule unless she acts for a party to the instrument. REMEMBER: a drawee bank paying a check typically acts for its customer, the drawer. This relationship results from the deposit agreement between the drawee and drawer with respect to the drawer's checking account at the bank. See Chapter 4 *infra*. So, though the drawee itself is not liable on the check, the drawee's payment acting for its checking account customer is payment "on behalf of" the drawer, who is obliged to pay the instrument.

There is also no payment and no discharge if a right person pays the wrong person. The rule requires payment to a person entitled to enforce, who is usually the holder of the instrument. See 3–301.

Interestingly, the mechanics of "payment" for any kind of instrument are not fully described. The medium obviously is money; but procedural aspects are not specified, including the means of payment and the point at which payment is accomplished. These matters are important because they affect how and when the risks shift with respect to the funds.

In the case of a check, though, there are detailed rules in Article 4 on the mechanics of payment when a check is presented to the drawee bank for payment. Remember: the drawee bank is ordered to pay. This bank is not obligated on the check but is acting on behalf of the drawer. If the bank pays, the drawer is discharged.

How and when payment of a check occurs by the drawee bank are questions answered by Article 4 because this statute governs the collection of checks (and other items), including the presentment and dishonor or payment of a check.

Remember: Article 3 points to Article 4 on how the dishonor of a check occurs. Basically, if a bank does not dishonor in line with the requirements of Article 4, the effect is payment for purposes of Article 3. See Chapter 3 *infra*.

If the drawee bank dishonors the check, the liability of the drawer and any indorser is triggered. How each of them pays and thereby effects discharge of her liability on a dishonored check is left to the vagaries of and gloss added to 3–602 and related provisions.

2. Third-Party Claims

Significantly, while 3–602(a) requires payment to a holder or other person entitled to enforce the instrument, the rule does not require this person to be the exclusive owner. The rule does not require her to have any interest whatsoever beyond having a right to enforce under the rules of Article 3. "The right to enforce an instrument and ownership of the instrument are two different concepts." 3–203 comment 1.

For this reason, a situation may arise in which the check is in the hands of a person entitled to enforce the instrument who wants payment; but a third person objects, claiming that she owns the instrument or part of it or that she owns a better interest or superior possessory right than the person entitled to enforce the instrument. Paying the claimant is risky even if her claim is true. A holder in due course would take free of the claim and not be subject to the obligor's defense of having honored it. On the other hand, because of 3–602, the obligor would be safe in paying the holder. The obligor's knowledge of the third person's claim, in itself, does not jeopardize the discharge that 3–602(c) would give her if she paid the holder. The discharge applies "even though payment is made with knowledge of a claim to the instrument * * * by another person." 3–602(c). The third person's remedy is a court order blocking payment and giving her possession of the instrument.

Discharge is denied if payment is made in the face of certain other circumstances that are beyond bare knowledge of a third person's claim. Specifically, the discharge is denied if:

(1) a claim to the instrument under Section 3–306 is enforceable against the party receiving payment and

(i) payment is made with knowledge by the payor that payment is prohibited by injunction or similar process of a court of competent jurisdiction, or

(ii) in the case of an instrument other than a cashier's check, teller's check, or certified check, the party making payment accepted, from the person having a claim to the instrument, indemnity against loss resulting from refusal to pay the person entitled to enforce the instrument; or

(2) the person making payment knows that the instrument is a stolen instrument and pays a person it knows is in wrongful possession of the instrument.

3–602(e)(1–2). The knowledge that (e)(2) covers is much more than merely knowing of a third person's claim; in truth, it is knowing that the possessor has no right, which is true of any thief or anyone who holds through a thief.

The exclusion in (e)(1)(ii) for bank checks is part of a scheme to encourage payment of these instruments, or to discourage dishonor of them. See also 3–411. The bank's payment to a holder effects a discharge even though the claimant has provided indemnification, but the bank is liable to the claimant for breaching any agreement not to pay the instrument. More is said later about bank checks. See Chapter 7 *infra*.

With respect to both 3–602(e)(1)(i) and (ii), they apply to deny the discharge only if the third person's claim is good against the person who is paid, which will not be true if this person is a holder in due course who took free of the claim. The obligor who pays in this case nevertheless faces liability apart from the instrument if the injunction ran personally against her, or if her payment to the holder violated an indemnity agreement with the claimant.

3. Distinguishing Payment of the Underlying Obligation

It is important to understand that the discharge of 3–602 is based on payment of the instrument, not payment of the underlying obligation. They are not the same. Paying the instrument also results, by separate rule, in discharge of the underlying obligation. See 3–310. The converse is not true. *Paying the underlying obligation, technically, does not discharge liability on the instrument.* By most accounts, this lack or absence of discharge is important.

Suppose, for example, that S takes B's check for the price of goods and immediately negotiates the instrument to T. For some bizarre reason, B directly pays S the price before the check is presented to the drawee bank for payment. When T presents the check for payment, the drawee bank dishonors the instrument.

T therefore sues B on the check. B does not have the 3–602(a) defense of discharge by payment. B paid S, but S was not then a person entitled to enforce the instrument. This right already had passed to T. The common understanding is that B must pay T even if T lacks the rights of a holder in due course. The reasoning is that when a negotiable instrument is assigned, the risk of paying the right person is on the obligor. The risk is on her even though she has not been notified of the assignment, which is different from the common-law and Article 9 rule that applies in the case of an ordinary contract right. The reasoning is that in the case of an instrument, "the right [to payment] is regarded as intimately connected with the writing and performance rendered to a party that does not produce the writing is rendered at the obligor's peril, regardless of the lack of notification." E. Allan Farnsworth, 3 FARNSWORTH ON CONTRACTS § 11.7 at 103 (4th Ed. 2004).

Possibly, however, this analysis is technically flawed and B should win. It is true that B's payment did not discharge her on the instrument. The payment nevertheless satisfied her underlying obligation to S. Satisfying this debt would have been a defense for her if S sued on the sales contract. T's rights on the instrument, if she is not a holder in due course, are subject to "a defense of the obligor that would be available if the person entitled to enforce the instrument were enforcing a right to payment under a simple contract." 3–305(a)(2). On this basis, B could argue that her payment of the sales contract is a defense good against T, and that her lack of discharge on the instrument is unimportant. This argument appears sound, but opposes commonly accepted doctrine. In any event, the argument rightly fails and B flatly loses if T is a holder in due course.

C. FRAUDULENT ALTERATION

1. Meaning of Alteration

" 'Alteration' means (i) an unauthorized change in an instrument that purports to modify in any respect the obligation of a party, or (ii) an unauthorized addition of words or numbers or other change to an incomplete instrument relating to the obligation of a party." 3–407(a).

2. Rule of Discharge

An alteration of an instrument that is "fraudulently made discharges a party whose obligation is affected by the alteration unless that party assents or is precluded from asserting the alteration." 3–407(b). A non-fraudulent alteration is benign, but the instrument is enforceable only to the extent of its original, unaltered terms. Id.

3. Effect on Holder in Due Course

A discharge because of fraudulent alteration is not effective against a holder in due course who takes the instrument without notice of the discharge. Nevertheless, with one exception, such a holder can enforce the instrument only to the extent of its original, unaltered terms. 3–407(c). The exception is that in the case of an incomplete instrument altered by unauthorized completion, the holder in due course can enforce the instrument as completed. Id.

D. CANCELLATION OR RENUNCIATION

The holder of an instrument may discharge any party's obligation on an instrument by *cancellation* or *renunciation*. 3–604(a). The former is "an intentional voluntary act, such as surrender of the instrument to the party, destruction, mutilation, or cancellation of the instrument, cancellation or striking out of the party's signature, or the addition of words to the instrument indicating discharge * * *." Id. Renunciation occurs differently, "by agreeing not to sue or otherwise renouncing rights against the party by a signed record." Id. Neither cancellation nor renunciation requires consideration, id., but they must be (1) by a person entitled to enforce the instrument and (2) intentional. This means, for example, that surrender or mutilation of an instrument by mistake or because of fraud is not an effective cancellation. No discharge results.

Although canceling an indorsement discharges the indorser's liability on the instrument, it does not "affect the status and rights of a party derived from the indorsement." 3–604(b). The cancellation does not negate a negotiation of the instrument that depended on the indorsement. It does not create a missing necessary indorsement that, *nunc pro tunc*, undermines holder status.

E. DISCHARGE BY AGREEMENT OR OTHER ACT

The reasons for discharge that Article 3 describes are geared to the character of a negotiable instrument as a special form of contract. Fundamentally, however, an instrument is and remains a contract; and the common-law rules of discharge that govern simple contracts apply equally to instruments. 3–601(a). Thus, an agreement to discharge liability on an instrument is enforceable under Article 3 to the extent that contract law would enforce it, even in the absence of renunciation, cancellation, payment, or any other discharge provided by Article 3 itself.

F. ARTICLE 3 DISCHARGE AS A DEFENSE AGAINST HOLDER IN DUE COURSE

Normally, notice of a defense to an instrument prevents a person from becoming a holder in due course of it. 3–302(a)(2)(vi). Notice of an Article 3 discharge of liability on an instrument does not have this effect; but any party's "[d]ischarge is effective against a holder in due course * * * if the holder had notice of the discharge when holder in due course status was acquired." 3–601 comment. Subject to this person's defense, the holder in due course can enforce the instrument against any other party and in doing so is immune to personal defenses, including any party's discharge of which the holder was unaware. "Discharge of the obligation of a party is not effective against a person acquiring rights of a holder in due course of the instrument without notice of the discharge." 3–601(b).

6. HOW AN INSTRUMENT AFFECTS THE UNDERLYING OBLIGATION

A. TYPICAL CASE—SUSPENSION AND DISCHARGE OR REVIVAL

In the typical case, the drawer of a check issues the instrument because of an underlying transaction, specifically to evidence or effect payment of an obligation that the transaction creates. "Issue" is the "first delivery of an instrument by the maker or drawer * * * for the purpose of giving rights on the instrument to any person." 3–105(a). (See the related discussion later in this chapter.) An obligee, however, is not ordinarily required by law to take an instrument that is issued for an underlying obligation; but the parties commonly agree on the use of an instrument and, for this reason, the payee takes the instrument that is issued to her. The overall effect between the parties, especially on the underlying obligation, is important to understand.

To begin, by getting possession of the instrument, the payee to whom the instrument is issued becomes a "holder," 1–201(b)(21)(A). She thereby acquires rights with respect to the instrument, most significantly including the right to enforce it against the issuer, 3–301, but normally does not lose rights against the issuer on their underlying deal. The issuer's liability on the instrument does not ordinarily replace her underlying obligation. This obligation usually continues; but the holder-payee-obligee gets no windfall, no possibility of double recovery.

The explanation is that the usual effect of taking the instrument is to *suspend* the underlying obligation pro tanto, i.e., "to the same extent the obligation would be discharged if an amount of money equal to the amount of the instrument were taken * * *." 3–310(b). In the case of an ordinary check, the suspension continues until the instrument is paid or dishonored. 3–310(b)(1). Payment of the instrument serves a double purpose. It discharges the maker or drawer's liability on the instrument itself, 3–602(c), and also on the underlying obligation. 3–310(b)(1–2).

If the instrument is dishonored, the underlying obligation is revived. Then, the payee-obligee "may enforce *either* the instrument or the obligation." 3–310(b)(3) (emphasis added). She is likely to choose enforcing the instrument because doing so is procedurally easier than suing on the underlying obligation. See 3–308. Principally, she makes her case on the instrument by producing it. The prima facie case requires nothing more.

If the obligee loses the instrument, or it is stolen or destroyed, she is not free to pursue the underlying obligation. Rather, "the obligation may not be enforced to the extent of the amount payable on the instrument, and to that extent the obligee's rights against the obligor are limited to enforcement of the instrument." 3–310(b)(4) (second sentence). Special rules govern the enforcement of a lost, destroyed, or stolen instrument that aim to protect the obligor against a claim to the instrument that may appear at some later time. See 3–309.

Enforcing an instrument obligates the holder to observe Article 3's statute of limitations, 3–118, and to meet any applicable requirements of presentment, dishonor, and notice that Part 5 of Article 3 imposes. Also, enforcement of the instrument is generally subject to defenses and counterclaims that are produced by the underlying transaction. 3–305(a)(2). Enforcement is even subject to a claim in recoupment of the obligor against the original obligee that arose from the same transaction as the instrument. 3–305(a)(3). In short, the payee-obligee is generally in the same position as if she had sued on the underlying obligation. In sum, as between the immediate parties, there is not much substantive advantage in suing on the instrument.

Of course, defenses and the like of the underlying transaction are rooted in the terms of the parties' underlying contract. If the instrument controls as the exclusive source of rights and duties, there is a fundamental advantage in suing on the instrument, which is to suppress the terms of the wider contract that could provide a defense. In truth, however, the instrument blends with other writings of the parties' transaction that are not barred by the parol evidence rule. The instrument is construed with the other writings, not apart from them, in determining the rights, duties, and defenses to the underlying contract and the instrument itself. 3–117.

B. WHEN PERSON ENTITLED TO ENFORCE THE INSTRUMENT IS NOT THE ORIGINAL OBLIGEE

Suppose that M issues a check to P that P indorses over to T. In both cases the instrument is taken for an underlying obligation. The effects on the relationship between M and P are already known, and the effects between P and T are essentially identical. The underlying obligation of P to T is suspended until paid or dishonored by M. 3–310(b)(1). In the latter case, T can sue P as indorser or on the underlying obligation P owes T, which will have been revived by the dishonor. 3–310(b)(3). T could also sue M as drawer, but not on M's underlying debt to P. T is neither a party to this debt nor an assignee of it. She thus has no rights with respect to the debt.

M's payment of the check would discharge her liability on the instrument and, pro tanto, her underlying obligation to P. The payment by M should have the same effects for P, but confirming these effects for P is not neatly done. Article 3 is clear in discharging M on the instrument, and also in discharging P on her underlying obligation when P is discharged on the instrument. 3–310(b)(3) (second sentence). The problem is finding a rule that discharges P on the instrument when M pays it and is discharged.

The best solution is the practical answer that M's payment precludes dishonor so that this condition to P's liability on the instrument is never met. The technical effect is only to bar enforcement of liability rather than erase the liability that is created by P's signature on the instrument. There is no discharge of liability on the instrument and therefore nothing that triggers the rule that such a discharge also discharges the underlying obligation. Nevertheless, because dishonor is necessary to trigger liability on the instrument and to resurrect liability on the underlying obligation, payment preventing dishonor is as good as discharging these liabilities.

It is a different and easier case to explain if, instead of the check to T being paid, the check to T is dishonored. Suppose, then, that T notified P of the dishonor. P satisfied her indorser liability to T, "paying" and then reacquiring the instrument from T. The effects of P's payment would be to discharge P on the instrument, 3–602(a), and also discharge P, pro tanto, on her underlying debt to T. 3–310(b)(3) (second sentence). P could then recoup by suing M as drawer of the check, or by suing M on M's underlying debt to P. Id. (first sentence).

C. WHEN TAKING AN INSTRUMENT DISCHARGES THE OBLIGATION

In two exceptional situations, taking a check or other instrument for an underlying obligation discharges the obligation instead of only suspending it.

1. Agreement

Taking an instrument discharges the underlying debt when the parties to the deal agree to this effect. 3–310(b) ("Unless otherwise agreed * * * "). Such an agreement, which is very rare, is effective to discharge the underlying obligation regardless of the nature or kind of instrument that is taken, even if it is an ordinary note or check of the person who is the issuer of the instrument and the underlying obligor.

2. Bank Instruments

The other situation in which taking an instrument discharges the underlying debt is much more common. It is when the instrument is a certified check, cashier's check, or teller's check, or any other instrument on which a bank is liable as maker or acceptor. 3–310(a); see Chapter 7 *infra*. This rule follows the common business understanding that such an instrument is the equivalent of cash. The obligor who remits the instrument thus satisfies the underlying debt and is freed of liability for it. Also, she ordinarily lacks any liability on the instrument itself. Thus, in the unlikely event the bank does not pay the instrument, the obligee cannot look to the obligor on any basis or theory.

There are exceptions to this exception. Even though a bank instrument is used, the parties can keep alive the underlying debt by agreeing to do so. Id. ("Unless otherwise agreed * * * "). Also, even if they make no such agreement so that the debt is discharged, the obligor may indorse the instrument and thereby become secondarily liability on it behind the primary liability of the bank as "drawer-maker" (3–412) or acceptor.

D. ACCORD AND SATISFACTION

Sometimes, in an attempt to settle a disputed claim, the person against whom the claim is asserted issues a check to the claimant for an amount less than the full amount the claimant demands. The check is commonly known as a "*full-payment check*" which, when successfully used, results in discharging the claim upon payment of the check. In contract terms, it is known as an "accord and satisfaction." Success would depend on the common law, but Article 3 provides its own rules of accord and satisfaction when instruments are used. These rules are collected in 3–311 and, for the most part, follow the common law.

The general rule is that the full-payment check fully discharges the claim for which it is given if these requirements are met:

- the check was tendered in good faith to the claimant as full satisfaction of the claim,
- the instrument or an accompanying written communication contained a conspicuous statement warning that the instrument was tendered in full satisfaction,
- the amount of the claim was unliquidated or subject to a bona fide dispute, and
- the claimant obtained payment of the check.

3–311(a–b). The discharge results even if the claimant expresses orally or in writing, on the instrument or elsewhere, that she rejects the settlement or that she still demands the balance of her claim.

There are two small exceptions. First, if the claimant is an organization, no discharge results unless the check is sent to the organization's office that handles disputed debts, so long as the other person had prior warning to send full-payment checks there. 3–311(c)(1). Second, whether or not the claimant is an organization, a discharge can be undone by the claimant tendering repayment of the full-payment check within 90 days after the check was paid. 3–311(c)(2). This exception is designed for claimants who were unaware that the check was for full payment, not for claimants who have second thoughts about settling.

Both exceptions are subject to a limitation. Neither exception applies, and the discharge stands, if the claimant actually knew within a reasonable time before trying to collect the check that it was tendered in full satisfaction of the claim. 3–311(d).

WARNING! There is no 3–311 discharge in the first instance unless the statute applies, which assumes that the instrument was negotiable so that Article 3 is applicable and that the four requirements for 3–311 discharge were met. When 3–311 is inapplicable for any reason, other law applies to determine if there was a valid accord and satisfaction. The other applicable law will almost certainly be common law, which is very unlikely to provide a discharge on facts that would fail the requirements of 3–311.

7. SUING ON CHECKS

A. INSTRUMENTS AS PROPERTY

Checks and other instruments are, first, contracts in the sense that they embody enforceable promises—whether explicit or implicit—to pay money. Accordingly, earlier sections of this chapter focus on the contract liability of parties to instruments.

Instruments are also property. Their ownership is assignable, and enforceability is transferable. Significantly, ownership of an instrument and the right to enforce it are not the same or inseparable. They often coincide, but they can split so that someone other than the owner of an instrument can enforce it, sometimes even when the instrument was stolen from the owner.

Typically, the right to enforce an instrument is deliberately transferred rather than stolen. *Transferring an instrument* vests in the transferee, derivatively, any right of the transferor to enforce the instrument. Normally, the transfer is part of a larger process of *negotiating* the instrument, which gives the transferee a fresh and independent right of enforcement. She enforces in her own name rather than through the transferor.

A transfer also involves duties because the law normally implies *warranties* that bind transferors of instruments. *Warranty liability* is different from contract liability on an instrument. Warranty liability usually is in addition to contract liability, but the former is not dependent on the latter and can exist without contract liability. Even a person who has not signed an instrument may incur warranty liability if she transfers the instrument or presents it for payment.

In effect, transferors guarantee certain qualities about the instruments they convey and back this guarantee with their personal liability. So do the people who present instruments for payment. The transfer warranties differ somewhat from the presentment warranties, but both sets are alike in assuring a right to enforce the instrument. For the most part, issues about warranty liability arise in cases of check collection and check fraud and are mostly saved for discussion in later chapters dealing with check collection and fraud. See Chapters 3 and 5 *infra*.

A right to enforce, however, is not payment. Between the two are the risks that the obligor will be insolvent or can assert defenses that reduce or eliminate her obligation to pay the instrument. There is also the risk that a third party will intervene and assert an overriding claim of ownership. The transferee of an instrument—even if she is a holder—is generally subject to a fundamental principle of property law, *derivative title*. As applied to contract rights, it is normally expressed as the familiar rule that an assignee stands in the shoes of the assignor. It means that an assignee of a contract right or a transferee of an instrument is subject to the same claims and defenses that would prevent collection by the assignor or transferor.

So, remember: deciding that a person is entitled to enforce a check does not mean much more than that she is a proper plaintiff who can sue. It does not mean that she will win a suit on the instrument. The defendant gets the chance to argue she did not sign the instrument and to assert defenses and claims that can defeat liability.

On the other hand, Article 3 creates a very important exception that protects a holder in due course of an instrument against certain claims and defenses. She takes free of most defenses to liability on the instrument that arose from an occurrence with a third party, and also takes free from a third party's claim to the instrument. Article 3 gives other favors to a holder in due course, but none so important as this immunity from claims and defenses. It is Article 3's most important property principle.

A later section of this chapter is dedicated to holders in due course. Before it is a section devoted to claims and defenses to contract liability. Right here is a discussion of instruments as property that begins by focusing on the most fundamental property right with respect to an instrument, the right to enforce it.

B. PERSONS ENTITLED TO ENFORCE

The contract liabilities of drawers and indorsers of checks and all other parties liable on instruments are alike in a most important respect: each of them is obligated to:

- "a person entitled to enforce the instrument * * *," or
- an indorser who pays the instrument, except that indorsers themselves are liable inter se only to subsequent indorsers.

3–412, 3–413(a), 3–414(b), 3–415(a). "*Person entitled to enforce*" means

- the holder of the instrument,
- a nonholder in possession of the instrument who has the rights of a holder, or
- a person not in possession of the instrument who is entitled to enforce the instrument pursuant to Section 3–309 or 3–418(d), which concern instruments that are lost, were stolen, or paid by mistake.

3–301. Any person who fits any of these categories is entitled to enforce the instrument "even though the person is not the owner of the instrument or is in wrongful possession of the instrument." Id.

The next discussion briefly explains each of the three categories of persons entitled to enforce instruments under 3–301. It is followed by an explanation of how indorsers enforce liability that other parties owe them, which appears problematic because 3–301 does not mention indorsers as persons entitled to enforce.

WARNING! It's common to hear less informed folk say that only the holder of a check or other instrument can enforce it. Wrong. Being a holder is one way of being a person entitled to enforce, not the only way. On the other hand, being a holder is among several requirements for becoming a holder in due course. Being a holder in due course is important when the issue is the range of defenses that can be successfully asserted against a person suing to enforce. So, although being a holder is not necessary to be a person entitled to enforce, being a holder becomes important later in the analysis when deciding the defenses the defendant can successfully raise. A person who is entitled to enforce because she is a holder may therefore further qualify for holder in due course status and therefore acquire immunity against defenses that stop any other person entitled to enforce.

FURTHER WARNING!! Being a person entitled to enforce the instrument means only that the person is entitled to sue, not that she is entitled to win the lawsuit. If the plaintiff is not a person entitled to enforce, the suit on the instrument stops. If she is a person entitled to enforce, the ball moves to the defendant's court where she can raise claims and defenses that block or reduce the plaintiff's recovery, except to the extent the plaintiff is a holder in due course and takes free of such claims or defenses.

1. Holder by Issuance

Person entitled to enforce an instrument includes (but is not limited to) a person who is a holder. A holder is a person in possession of an instrument that is "payable either to bearer or to an identified person that is the person in possession." 1–201(b)(21)(A). There are two ways to become a holder:

> A person can become holder of an instrument when the instrument is *issued* to that person, or the status of holder can arise as the result of an event that occurs [apart from and usually] after issuance. "*Negotiation*" is the term used in Article 3 to describe this post-issuance event.

3–201 comment 1 (insert and emphasis added).

"*Issue*" means "the first delivery of an instrument by the maker or drawer, whether to a holder or nonholder, for the purpose of giving rights on the instrument to any person." 3–105(a). Almost always, the first holder of an instrument is the person to whom it is issued.

Consider the typical case. Drawer writes a check payable to bearer or, more probably, to order. The drawer and the payee are also the immediate parties to an underlying transaction involving the provision (sale or use) of property (real or personal, including money) or services. The instrument represents the buyer's obligation to pay for the property or services. The buyer creates the instrument and liability by signing it; and, rather than keeping it, she surrenders possession of the instrument by deliberately giving it to the supplier who is the payee. By getting possession, the payee is now a person who can enforce the instrument against the drawer who is liable on the instrument for having signed it in her particular capacity.

This conduct of the drawer in giving possession of the instrument and rights to the payee is "issue." It is "the first delivery of an instrument by the maker or drawer, whether to a holder or nonholder, for the purpose of giving rights on the instrument to any person." 3–105(a). In this role a drawer is known as the "issuer." 3–105(c). The "delivery" that is required means "voluntary transfer of possession." 1–201(b)(15). By this "issue" the payee becomes a "holder", 1–201(b)(21)(A), and is therefore a person entitled to enforce the instrument. 3–301.

2. Holder by Negotiation

Becoming a holder can result from an event that occurs apart from and usually after issuance: **negotiation**. 3–201 comment 1. **Negotiation** means a transfer of possession, whether voluntary or involuntary, of an instrument by a person other than the issuer to a person *who thereby becomes its holder*. 3–201(a) (emphasis added). It most commonly explains how a person—any person—becomes a subsequent holder, either immediately or remotely, after the first holder who normally will have acquired the instrument and become a holder by issue to her. Only by negotiation can "the status of holder * * * arise * * * after issuance." 3–201 comment 1.

The concept of negotiation encompasses both a noun and a verb, an end and the means for accomplishing it. The purpose of 3–201(a) is only to label the process and explain the result of negotiation, which is that the transferee becomes a holder. The process itself—the conduct necessary for this result—is the verb form of negotiation and is explained in 3–201(b). It depends on how the instrument is payable:

- If an instrument is *payable to an identified person*, negotiation requires:
  - ✓ transfer of possession of the instrument, *and*
  - ✓ its *indorsement* by the holder.
- If an instrument is *payable to bearer*, it may be negotiated by transfer of possession alone.

3–201(b). To engage in this conduct is **to negotiate** the instrument. Doing so is **a negotiation** of the instrument, and the result of this negotiation is that the transferee of possession becomes a holder. Her situation thereupon matches the Article 1 definition of "holder." See 1–201(b)(21)(A).

a. The Common Requirement: "Transfer of Possession"

Whether the instrument is payable to bearer or an identified person, a "*transfer of possession*" is necessary. "Negotiation always requires a change in possession of the instrument because nobody can be a holder without possessing the instrument, either directly or through an agent." 3–201 comment 1. *It is very important to understand that "transfer of possession" for purposes of 3–201 is not the same as the transfer of an instrument [when "[a]n instrument is transferred"] for purposes of 3–203.* The latter requires and is limited to a voluntary transfer. The former includes an involuntary transfer and any other change of possession. Indeed, how possession is acquired is unimportant, both as to means and motive. It is a transfer of possession when a thief steals an instrument.[9] In sum, the clearer and more accurate meaning of negotiation is becoming a holder by *getting or taking possession in any manner*, even without a voluntary or involuntary transfer by the person who thereby loses possession.

b. Indorsements

Whether or not an indorsement is necessary to negotiate an instrument depends on how the instrument is payable. Indorsement is necessary only if the instrument is payable to an identified person. If it is payable to bearer, getting possession of the instrument is alone sufficient for the process of negotiation, 3–201(b); and whoever gets possession is a holder because of the negotiation. 3–201(a). *There is more here than meets the eye because how an instrument is presently payable can turn on how it was formerly payable.*

---

[9] A thief stealing a note is not a transfer of the instrument.

i. How an Instrument Becomes Payable to an Identified Person or Bearer and How It Is Negotiated

A) Originally Made Payable to Order or to Bearer

As originally written, an instrument is payable either to order or to bearer. See 3–104(a)(1). If the instrument is payable to bearer, as defined in 3–109(a), it is equally payable to bearer for purposes of 3–201(b) and negotiation. The instrument "may be negotiated by transfer of possession alone." 3–201(b). For this purpose, "transfer of possession" means any change of possession. Negotiation occurs when anybody gets possession in any way. Anybody in possession is a holder. Suppose Buyer issued a check payable to cash or otherwise to bearer. Thief stole the instrument before Seller indorsed. Thief is a holder.[10] Seller's indorsement was unnecessary for negotiation.

An instrument originally drawn or made payable to order is—by definition—payable to an identified person. 3–109(b). Negotiation of the instrument requires the payee's indorsement, which means her signature on the instrument. She or her authorized representative must sign it. Nobody else's signature

---

[10] Being a holder, however, means only that the person is entitled to enforce the instrument, which really only means is a person who can sue on the instrument. It does not mean that the person will win the lawsuit. There are defenses and claims to consider that can protect the defendant from having to pay the plaintiff. Again, being a person entitled to enforce is not the same as being a person entitled to recover.

is her signature; therefore, nobody else's signature is her indorsement; thus, nobody can become a holder without her signature. Suppose Buyer issued a check payable to Seller's order. Thief stole the instrument before Seller indorsed. Thief indorsed the instrument using Seller's name. Thief is not a holder. The result is the same if an unauthorized representative of Seller indorsed rather than Thief.

B) Thereafter—Blank or Special Indorsement

Whether an instrument originally was payable to order or to bearer, it is payable to an identified person if it is *specially indorsed.* A "*special indorsement*" is "an indorsement * * * made by the holder of an instrument, whether payable to an identified person or payable to bearer," that "identifies a person to whom it makes the instrument payable * * *." 3–205(a). It usually consists of a simple instruction to pay an identified person, such as "Pay Jane Smith" or "Pay Named Bank," that is followed by the holder's signature. It need not contain "order" language of 3–109(b), and can identify the person to pay in any manner that is permitted by 3–110, which contains rules for identifying the original payee.

A special indorsement changes an instrument from payable to bearer to payable to an identified person (the person whom the indorser named). The special indorsement would not be required for negotiation of a bearer instrument but would insure against enforcement by anyone except the identified person to whom the instrument is specially indorsed (or someone with her rights). Any further negotiation would require this person's indorsement. No one else could become a holder without it.

Suppose Buyer issued a bearer instrument to Seller. Negotiation would occur by anyone getting possession of the instrument. Anyone who got possession would become a holder entitled to enforce even without Seller's consent. To guard against this happening, Seller could specially indorse to herself or another identified person whom Seller intends to become a holder. Negotiation would require the indorsement of whomever she named. No one could become a holder without the person's consent.

An indorsement by a holder that is not special is a "*blank indorsement*," which means that the holder indorses without identifying a person to whom the instrument is payable. She just signs her name. A blank indorsement changes an instrument that is payable to the holder, as an identified person, to an instrument that is payable to bearer. 3–205(b). Thereafter, it "may be negotiated by transfer of possession alone until specially indorsed," id., just as if it had been issued originally as a bearer instrument.

Suppose Buyer issues a check payable to Seller's order, which is typical. Therefore, Seller's indorsement is required to negotiate the instrument. How the instrument is thereafter negotiated is determined by how Seller indorses when she transfers the instrument to her transferee. If Seller specially indorses to the transferee, the transferee's indorsement is required for negotiation. If Seller indorses in blank, negotiation occurs whenever anybody gets possession. Anyone in possession is a holder. To prevent this happening, if Seller indorsed in blank in negotiating the check to her transferee, the transferee could specially indorse the check herself or convert the blank indorsement to special merely by inserting "Pay" followed by her name directly above the blank indorsement.

ii. The Grand Importance of No Missing Indorsements

The foregoing discussion looks downstream (meaning forward from or after) the instrument's source. It explains and illustrates how negotiation occurs at each successive transfer. The view of the transferee is really upstream, however, when deciding what should be done to negotiate the instrument to her, or when deciding if negotiation occurred upon any earlier transfer. The focus is the situation of the instrument in the hands of the person from whom possession will be transferred, the present possessor. The question is not only if this person's indorsement is needed, but also if it is sufficient and if any other person's indorsement is necessary.

The present possessor's indorsement is not necessary for negotiation if the instrument is payable to bearer. 3–201(b). To be payable to bearer, however, an instrument must have the indorsement of any identified person to whom it was payable at any time, including an original payee and any special indorsee. The look upstream (meaning before and toward the check's source) is thus longer, beyond the person now in possession. If any such identified person has not indorsed, *by her own signature or a signature that binds her*, the instrument is not payable to bearer. It will not be payable to bearer unless every missing indorsement is added by the signature of the identified person whose indorsement is needed.

The present possessor's indorsement is necessary if the instrument is payable to her. 3–201(b). Her indorsement will not be sufficient, however, unless she is a holder. The precise rule of negotiation is that "if an instrument is payable to an *identified person*, negotiation requires transfer of possession of the instrument and its indorsement *by the holder*." Id. (emphasis added). For the present possessor to be a holder, she herself must have taken by negotiation unless the instrument was issued to her. By the same rule that governs her negotiation to someone else, the instrument could not have been negotiated to her, except by a holder. This inquiry continues upstream to the source. There must be an unbroken line of holders. If at any point the instrument was payable to a holder as an identified person, this holder's indorsement would be needed for anyone thereafter to become a holder. Without this indorsement, the present possessor cannot negotiate the instrument under 3–201(b) because she is not a holder, even if the instrument in form is payable to her. The substantive effect in such a case is that the instrument, really, is payable to the former holder whose indorsement is missing. It remains payable to her until she indorses. Thereafter, the instrument is payable to the first or next special indorsee who has not indorsed, or to bearer if all of the indorsees have indorsed.

This analysis should also inform the definition of "holder," which is a person in possession of an instrument payable to bearer or to her as an identified person. 1–201(b)(21)(A). An instrument is never really payable to a person in possession if, despite the form of the instrument, it is missing the indorsement of a former holder to whom, as an identified person herself, the instrument was payable. In substance, it remains payable to her rather than the person now in possession.

In the end, the whole process of negotiation can be encapsulated and summarized in two grand rules:

- An instrument cannot be negotiated that is missing the indorsement of any former or present holder to whom, as an identified person, the instrument was or is payable. Except for her, nobody is or can become a holder until she indorses.

- An instrument is negotiated whenever any person gets possession of an instrument that is indorsed by every former holder to whom, as identified persons, the instrument was payable. Anybody in possession is a holder.

In some exceptional circumstances, a person in possession can be a holder even though an indorsement is missing. In the case of notes the most important exception is *reacquisition*, which refers to the transfer of an instrument to a former holder. 3–207. If the instrument is payable to someone else because of indorsements that were added after she first became a holder, the former holder can cancel these indorsements so that the instrument once more is payable to her or to bearer. Id. She again becomes a holder and may negotiate the instrument even without the indorsement of the person to whom the instrument was payable when the former holder reacquired it.

c. Qualified Indorsements

Whether an indorsement is blank or special, it is in either case also *qualified* or *unqualified*. An indorsement is qualified that adds such words to the blank or special signature such as "without recourse." 3–415(b). The effect is to disclaim any liability on the instrument as an indorser. So, if the instrument is dishonored, the indorser is not liable to a person entitled to enforce the instrument or another indorser. However, qualifying an indorsement does not affect negotiation. If an indorsement is required for negotiation, a qualified indorsement works just as well as an unqualified indorsement.

Occasionally an instrument payable to order or to a special indorsee is delivered for value by the payee or the indorsee without her indorsement. When this occurs, the transferee's status may be summarized as follows: (1) The transferee is not a holder. (2) The transferee acquires only the rights of the transferor against prior parties. (3) Unless the transferor and transferee have agreed otherwise, "the transferee has a specifically enforceable right to the unqualified indorsement of the transferor." 3–203(c). It means that the transferee may obtain a decree of specific performance ordering the transferor, under pain of punishment for contempt of court, to indorse. Because this order is issued by a court of equity, the transferee is sometimes said to have equitable title prior to obtaining the indorsement. Actually, if her transferor owned the instrument, the transferee is the true owner even though she is not yet the holder. (4) When the transferor completes the negotiation by indorsing, only then does the transferee become the holder. "[N]egotiation of the instrument does not occur until the indorsement is made." Id.

d. Restrictive Indorsements

In addition to the qualities of qualified or unqualified and blank or special, every indorsement is also either restrictive or unrestrictive. 3–206. A restrictive indorsement is an indorsement that would limit the purpose to which the proceeds of an instrument are applied, so that a person is accountable who pays the instrument for any other use. A restrictive indorsement generally does not prevent further transfer or negotiation or affect an indorsee's right to enforce the instrument. 3–206(a–b). Moreover, neither the indorsement nor knowledge of it prevents or affects a person's becoming a holder in due course. The consequence of a restrictive indorsement occurs when the terms of an effective restriction are violated by someone who is bound by the indorsement. The violation can prevent the person becoming a holder in due course or result in her personal liability.

Typically, indorsements are blank, unqualified, and silently unrestrictive, containing no restriction of any kind on the use or purpose of the instrument or its proceeds or how they should be applied. Restrictions are uncommon but not rare. The most familiar restrictive indorsements, which may also be the only legally effective ones, are collection and trust indorsements, such as "For Deposit Only" or "Pay to T in trust for B." Between them, collection indorsements are more common.

e. Negotiation by Multiple Payees

An instrument payable to order may name several payees either in the alternative, as "A, B, or C," or together as "A, B and C." A special indorsement may do the same. Negotiability is unaffected, but there are special rules about how to negotiate such an instrument.

- If the instrument is payable to two or more payees in the alternative, it is payable to any one of them and it may be negotiated, discharged or enforced by any one of them who has possession of it. To negotiate such an instrument, the indorsement of only one of them is required.

- If the instrument is payable to several payees together, it may be negotiated, discharged, or enforced only by all of them acting together. To negotiate an instrument that names several payees together, it must be indorsed by all of them.

- If an instrument payable to two or more people is ambiguous as to whether it is payable to the persons alternatively, the instrument is payable to the persons alternatively.

3–110(d).

3. Nonholder in Possession with Holder's Rights

A nonholder is entitled to enforce an instrument in her possession if she "has the rights of a holder." 3–301(ii). A nonholder having a holder's rights occasionally happens by subrogation or succession, and most commonly when a holder *transfers the instrument* to a person who does not herself become (i.e., qualify as or meet the requirements of) a holder. For example, Payee gives a check payable to her order to another person to satisfy a debt or pay for property and fails to indorse. A transfer occurred but not negotiation. Payee was a holder. Payee's transferee, however, is not a holder. Nevertheless, as a result of the *transfer*, 3–203(a), the transferee acquires the right of the transferor, as a holder, to enforce the instrument. 3–203(b). The transferee therefore becomes a person entitled to enforce it within the meaning of 3–301, even though she is a nonholder. In sum, because a holder enjoys the right to enforce an instrument, so does her transferee even if the transferee is not herself a holder.

The same holds true for a remote transferee of a holder if the mediate conveyances between them were all transfers of the instrument, i.e., deliveries of the instrument intended to give each transferee the right to enforce the instrument. The right to enforce an instrument, which originates with any holder, will slide undiluted through an infinite number of transfers and can be asserted by the ultimate transferee as if she had taken the instrument directly from the holder. The transferee's only problem is proving that she claims through a holder and inherits the holder's right to enforce.

This derivative right of enforcement flows from the upside of a very basic principle of property law that title is derivative. The familiar down side is that a transferee gets only the interest in the property that belonged to her transferor and nothing more. All of the limits that applied to the transferor apply equally to the transferee. (A large exception is the holder-in-due-course doctrine which is not relevant at this point but terribly important later. See the related discussion later in this chapter.)

The up side of derivative title, which applies here, is the rule that whatever interest the transferor could and did convey, it fully passes to the transferee with any accompanying benefits. This upside is known as the "*shelter principle*." It means that whatever rights a transferor could have enjoyed, these rights belong to her transferee who can freely assert them even though she does not personally and directly qualify for the rights. Because the transferor could have exercised the rights had she kept them, her transferee can use them in the transferor's stead. In doing so, the transferee does not act for the transferor as agent for principal; rather, the transferee acts for her own account, instead or in place of the transferor who likewise could have enforced the rights. The purpose of the "shelter principle" is to insure the widest market for property interests and rights and thereby enlarge their value.

This shelter principle works with any property rights, not just a holder's right to enforce. Most significantly, it works equally well to give a transferee the protections of a holder in due course that her transferor enjoyed, even though the transferee does not qualify for the status herself. More is said later on this point. (See the related discussion later in this chapter.)

A **couple of caveats** are needed here. First, if a check or other instrument is transferred for value, the transferee enjoys a specifically enforceable right to the transferor's unqualified indorsement. 3–203(c). If the transferor does not comply, a court will order compliance. So, if the payee of a check gives the check to another person in payment of goods or something else, the transferee has a right to the payee's unqualified indorsement.

On the other hand, the transferee is not a holder until the indorsement is actually added. Until then, the transferee is a person entitled to enforce even though not a holder; but acquiring the holder status makes it possible for the transferee to acquire holder in due course status, which would give the transferee greater immunity against defenses in enforcing the check against the drawer if the check is dishonored.

The other caveat involves a check deposited with a bank for collection. Suppose drawer buys goods from seller and gives the seller a check for the price of the goods. The seller deposits the check in her bank, which usually is not the drawee bank. The seller's bank, known as the depositary bank, will act for the seller in presenting the check to the drawee bank for payment.

Suppose the seller forgets to indorse the check. In this case the depositary bank becomes a holder as soon as the bank receives the item for collection. 4–205(1). The status accrues automatically and even though seller has not and does not actually indorse the check. Again, this status is important because if the check is dishonored, it is possible that the depositary bank, as holder, also satisfies the other requirements for holder in due course status; and this status will give the depositary bank freedom from defenses not otherwise available if the bank is forced to sue the drawer of the check.

4. Nonholder Without Possession in Exceptional Cases

Ordinarily, to enforce an instrument, a nonholder must not only have the rights of a holder, she must have possession of the instrument itself. 3–301(ii). The same is true for a holder because her very status requires possession. It is an element of the definition of "holder." 1–201(b)(21)(A). In sum, possession is essential for almost every person's right to enforce an instrument. Only in two very narrow, exceptional cases is a person entitled to enforce an instrument not in her possession.

a. Lost, Destroyed, or Stolen Instruments

The easier exception to understand is the case in which the person would be entitled to enforce the instrument if she had possession of it, but the instrument was *lost, destroyed, or stolen*. Enforcement is possible in this case but only if these conditions are met:

- the person was in possession of the instrument and entitled to enforce it when loss of possession occurred (or acquired ownership from a person who was),
- the loss of possession was not the result of a transfer by the person or a lawful seizure,
- the person cannot reasonably obtain possession of the instrument because the instrument was destroyed, its whereabouts cannot be determined, or it is in the wrongful possession of an unknown person or a person that cannot be found or is not amenable to service of process, and
- the person seeking enforcement proves the terms of the instrument and the person's right to enforce the instrument.

3–309(a–b). There is room here for harmful mischief or costly mistake. The instrument could be found or set free and end up in the hands of a holder in due course. This person would be entitled to payment even though the instrument had already been enforced through 3–309. For this reason, 3–309, provides for insurance:

> The court may not enter judgment in favor of the person seeking enforcement unless it finds that the person required to pay the instrument is adequately protected against loss that might occur by reason of a claim by another person to enforce the instrument. Adequate protection may be provided by any reasonable means.

3–309(b).

A different statutory rule applies to cashier's, teller's, and certified checks. A person who claims to own such a check that is lost, destroyed or stolen can notify the bank of her claim; and, if a certain time period has passed and the check has not been presented for payment, she is entitled to payment from the bank without providing security. The bank is discharged of all liability with respect to the check. 3–312(b). More is said later about this and other special rules that apply to cashier's checks and the like. See Chapter 7 *infra*.

b. Instruments Paid by Mistake

In the other case in which a person can enforce an instrument not in her possession, a payor has paid the instrument by mistake and recovered the money. The person from whom payment is recovered should be free to collect from the right person; but the person who mistakenly paid the instrument probably got possession at that time and may be unable to return it in actionable form. In this case, the person from whom payment is recovered "has rights as a person entitled to enforce the * * * instrument." 3–418(d). Significantly, any discharge that resulted from the mistaken payment is effectively expunged because, upon recovery of the payment, the instrument is deemed dishonored. 3–418(d).

Suppose, for example, that Buyer gives Seller a check as prepayment for goods that Seller promised to deliver. Bank pays the check, but payment is a mistake because Buyer's account is empty. The Bank gets restitution from Seller. Seller can sue Buyer on the check, even if Bank inadvertently had returned the check to Buyer. Also, Buyer cannot defend on the basis of discharge by payment. When the Bank recovered the payment, the check was deemed dishonored.

5. Indorsers as Other People Who Can Enforce

The contract liability of parties to instruments runs not only to a "person entitled to enforce" the instrument, which 3–301 defines. It also runs to an indorser who pays the instrument. The reason is that an indorser is really a surety to any other party, except subsequent indorsers; and, as between a surety and the principal obligor, the latter should ultimately bear the responsibility of payment.

C. PROCEDURES OF ENFORCEMENT

1. Plaintiff's Prima Facie Case

A person's liability on an instrument is based on her having signed it. Therefore, to make a prima facie case in court to enforce an instrument, the plaintiff need only produce the instrument and prove that she, the plaintiff, is a person entitled to enforce it under 3–301. Without more, the plaintiff "is entitled to payment * * *." 3–308(b), but this abbreviated procedure may lengthen at both ends and in the middle.

2. Establishing That Signature Binds Defendant

Because liability is based on the defendant's signature, the plaintiff's entitlement to payment assumes that the signature on the instrument binds the defendant, which would *not* be true if:

- the defendant did not make the signature, nor was it made by a representative whose signature bound the defendant; or,
- the defendant made the signature but she was acting with authority for someone else for the purpose of binding the other person rather than herself.

Generally, however, proving that the signature binds the defendant is not part of the plaintiff's case. *The law rebuttably presumes that the signature is effective unless the defendant pointedly challenges it.* Here is the rule:

> In an action with respect to an instrument, the authenticity of, and authority to make, each signature on the instrument is admitted unless specifically denied in the pleadings.

3–308(a).

If the defendant properly denies the signature, "the burden of establishing validity is on the person claiming validity." Id. This means that the burden of persuasion, by a preponderance of the evidence, rests with the plaintiff to prove that the signature is authentic and authorized. 1–201(b)(8) ("persuading the trier of fact that the existence of the fact is more probable than its non-existence"). The plaintiff must carry this burden regardless of the reason the defendant denies the signature, even when the action is against an undisclosed principal. The plaintiff must prove that the instrument was signed for the defendant by an authorized representative whose signature bound the defendant.

On the other hand, generally "*the signature is presumed to be authentic and authorized,*" 3–308(a) (emphasis added). The effect is to put the burden of going forward with the evidence on the defendant. "[U]ntil some evidence is introduced which would support a finding that the signature is forged or unauthorized, the plaintiff is not required to prove that it is valid." 3–308 comment 1. If the defendant produces this evidence, the plaintiff is put to her proof that the signature is authentic and authorized.

3. Proving Plaintiff's Entitlement to Enforce

Even if the defendant's signature is admitted or proved, the plaintiff suing on an instrument cannot recover unless she "proves entitlement to enforce the instrument under Section 3–301." 3–308(b). This proof is always part of the prima facie case and is made from the instrument itself if the plaintiff is a holder. 3–301(i); 3–308 comment 2 ("mere production * * * proves entitlement"). Any other person in possession must prove by any admissible evidence that she claims through a holder by transfer, subrogation, succession or the like and thereby inherited the holder's right to enforce the instrument. 3–301(ii); 3–308 comment 2. In the rare case of a nonholder without possession, she must prove that at the time of losing possession, she had holder status or the rights of a holder (or acquired it from one who did). This requirement is explicit in the case of a lost, destroyed, or stolen instrument, 3–309(a)(i); it is necessarily implied in a 3–418(d) case to enforce an instrument that was mistakenly paid.

4. Producing the Instrument

The plaintiff must produce the instrument to make her case. Production is essential to judge authenticity and also to enable the defendant, in appropriate circumstances, to acquire possession of the instrument upon paying it. Otherwise, the defendant risks double payment of the instrument to a holder in due course.

Production of the instrument is excused in only two very narrow cases, when the instrument was lost, stolen, or destroyed or the instrument was paid by mistake. See 3–301(iii), 3–309, 3–418(d). In these cases, which are discussed earlier in this chapter, the plaintiff is a person entitled to enforce even without possession of the instrument. 3–301(iii).

5. Lost, Destroyed or Stolen Checks: 3–309

After issue to Payee, a check may become lost or destroyed or be stolen. There is now no writing to present for payment or dishonor. Accordingly, Payee is in limbo. It can enforce neither the check nor the underlying obligation. This dilemma is alleviated by 3–309(a).

a. Requirements for Enforcement

A payee or other person not in possession of a check is entitled to enforce it against Drawer or any other party if three requirements are met.

- First, Payee must have been "entitled to enforce the instrument when loss of possession occurred" (or must have acquired ownership from a person who was) 3–309(a)(1). A payee to whom a check was issued satisfies this requirement.

- Second, possession must not be lost because of a transfer by Payee or "a lawful seizure." 3–309(a)(2).

- Third, possession cannot be "reasonably" obtained "because the instrument was destroyed, its whereabouts cannot be determined, or it is in the wrongful possession of an unknown person or a person that cannot be found or is not amenable to service of process." 3–309(a)(3).

b. Proof and Adequate Protection

If the requirements of 3–309(a) are satisfied, Payee must still "prove the terms of the instrument and the person's right to enforce the instrument." 3–309(b). If that proof is made, the benefits of 3–308 apply "as if the person seeking enforcement had produced the instrument." 3–309(b).

Even so, this is not enough. There is still some risk that the check will turn up in the hands of a person entitled to enforce it. This risk might materialize if the check was issued to bearer or if Payee indorsed the check before it disappeared or if Payee misrepresented the facts of disappearance.

Under 3–309(b), a court "may not enter judgment in favor of the person seeking enforcement unless it finds that the person required to pay the instrument is adequately protected. . . ." Adequate protection may be provided "by any reasonable means." According to the comment, "reasonable means" should be geared to the degree of risk that a holder with the check will turn up. Thus, if the check was issued to the "order of Payee," it was not indorsed before loss and the court believes Payee's explanation, no security may be required at all. The greater the risk, the more likely a court will require Payee to post a surety bond in the full amount of the check.

6. Liability Over

Often a party who loses an action on a negotiable instrument has a right of recourse against some prior party, who in turn may have recourse against a party prior to her, and so on. When a right of recourse exists, it is possible to have the matter settled in several lawsuits. Usually, however, it is more efficient to settle the various issues and determine the various liabilities in a single lawsuit. For the purpose of supplementing existing state and federal statutes relating to procedures for interpleader and joinder of parties, and also to help provide for more efficient disposal of multi-party litigation, the rule is:

> In an action for breach of an obligation for which a third person is answerable over pursuant to this Article or Article 4, the defendant may give the third person notice of the litigation in a record, and the person notified may then give similar notice to any other person who is answerable over. If the notice states (i) that the person notified may come in and defend and (ii) that failure to do so bind the person notified in an action later brought by the person giving the notice as to any determination of fact common to the two litigations, the person notified is so bound unless after seasonable receipt of the notice the person notified does come in and defend.

3–119.

7. Statutes of Limitations

Section 3–118 includes six statutes of limitations for suits on instruments. Which statute applies depends on the nature of the instrument and when it is payable. For a typical check, an action to enforce the obligation of a party "must be commenced within three years after dishonor" by the drawee bank "or 10 years after the date of the" check. 3–118(c).

It is very important to understand that the applicable statute applies the same to any party's obligation on the instrument. Thus, for example, "indorsers who may become liable on an instrument after issue are subject to a period of limitations running from the same date as that of the maker or drawer." 3–118 comment 2.

Section 3–118 covers more than suits on instruments. Its subsection (g) "covers warranty and conversion cases and other actions to enforce obligations or rights arising under Article 3" that are extrinsic to instruments themselves. 3–118 comment 6. It does not answer all questions that arise with respect to statutes of limitations. Most significant, "the circumstances under which the running of a limitations period may be tolled is left to other law pursuant to Section 1–103." 3–118 comment 1.

8. DEFENSES TO LIABILITY

Ultimately, the value of an instrument is determined by whether or not the obligor must pay the instrument and, if so, whether or not she is financially able to do so. The latter issue is beyond this book and mostly beyond the law. The former issue is discussed here. It largely depends on whether or not a claim to the instrument or a defense to payment is proved and, if so, whether or not the plaintiff is subject or immune to the claim or defense. Usually, immunity depends on the plaintiff having the rights of a holder in due course, which means she takes free of most claims and defenses that arose before the instrument was negotiated to her. Accordingly, in a suit to enforce an instrument, the major burdens of proof are ordered and assigned this way:

- FIRST, if the validity of signatures is admitted or proved, a plaintiff producing the instrument is entitled to payment if the plaintiff proves that she is a person entitled to enforce the instrument. [See earlier in this chapter.]

- SECOND, the defendant nevertheless is not obligated to pay the instrument to the extent that she proves a defense or claim in recoupment for which the plaintiff is accountable. [See later in this chapter.]

- THIRD, the plaintiff nevertheless is entitled to payment to the extent that she proves the rights of a holder in due course which are not subject to the defense or claim. [See later in this chapter.]

See 3–308(b). It is true that even a holder in due course takes subject to some defenses, and that a mere holder is not subject to every defense and claim.

It is also true, however, that in the typical, common case, the obligor's defenses are good against a holder but not against a holder in due course. Usually, therefore, who wins a suit on a negotiable instrument depends on whether or not the plaintiff enjoys the rights of a holder in due course.

The suit always begins, however, at the beginning, with the plaintiff proving her right to enforce the instrument and sometimes having to establish the validity of the defendant's signature. This first step of the process is discussed earlier in this chapter. This section of the book focuses on the second step and outlines the full range of claims and defenses to an instrument that generally limit the right to enforce it. The outline begins with the "*real defenses*" collected in 3–305(a)(1). They are the relatively few, mostly narrow defenses that are good against any person entitled to enforce the instrument, including a holder in due course. The issue of holder in due course is mooted to the extent that the defendant proves a real defense.

Next discussed are the so-called "*ordinary*" or "*personal defenses*" and then *recoupment,* which generally refers to a related counterclaim for damages that is asserted defensively only. The personal defenses and recoupment are good against every person entitled to enforce an instrument, except a person having the rights of a holder in due course. A holder in due course takes free of personal defenses. Section 3–305(a) describes these defenses as follows:

(2) a defense of the obligor stated in another section of this Article or a defense of the obligor that would be available if the person entitled to enforce the instrument were enforcing a right to payment under a simple contract; and

(3) a claim in recoupment of the obligor against the original payee of the instrument if the claim arose from the transaction that gave rise to the instrument; but the claim of the obligor may be asserted against a transferee of the instrument only to reduce the amount owing on the instrument at the time the action is brought.

3–305(a)(2–3).

Different from any class of defenses to payment of an instrument are "*claims*" to an instrument, which are discussed later in this chapter after all of the defenses. These claims are property interests and possessory rights in instruments that follow them everywhere and into the hands of every person, except holders in due course. Just as holders in due course take free of personal defenses, they also take free of all prior claims to instruments. 3–306. A claim in recoupment does not fit here. It is a cause of action that acts as a defense to payment of the instrument and is not a property interest or right to the instrument.

If an ordinary defense is proved in a suit to enforce an instrument, or if the plaintiff is suing to replevy the instrument from the defendant because of a prior claim, the case reaches the issue of holder in due course and turns on this issue. Who wins usually is decided by whether or not the plaintiff has the rights of such a holder. How a person acquires these rights is the subject of later discussion in this chapter.

A. REAL DEFENSES

The principal advantage of being a holder in due course is that the person takes free of—cuts off—most of the defenses to payment that arose before the instrument was negotiated to her. These defenses are called *personal defenses*. They are good against everybody entitled to enforce an instrument, except a person with the rights of a holder in due course. She is immune to them. A holder in due course is not immune to *real defenses*. They always survive and, without exception, are good against everybody. Any person suing to enforce an instrument is subject to them. The Code does not use the terms "real" and "personal" as applied to defenses. Nevertheless, they are widely used by courts, lawyers, and law teachers as easy and familiar tools for organizing and distinguishing defenses on the basis of their potency against holders in due course.

The *real defenses* are discussed here. There are only a few of them. They are narrow and mostly depend on outside law. Article 3 collects them in 3–305(a)(1):

- infancy of the obligor to the extent that infancy is a defense to a simple contract;

- duress, lack of legal capacity, or illegality of the transaction which, under other law, nullifies the obligation of the obligor;
- fraud that induced the obligor to sign the instrument with neither knowledge nor reasonable opportunity to learn of its character or its essential terms; and
- discharge of the obligor in insolvency proceedings (i.e., bankruptcy).

1. Other Defenses Good Against Everybody

It is true that 3–305(a)(1) collects all of the defenses that are traditionally labeled as "real defenses" good against even a holder in due course. It is not true that they are the only reasons for not paying an instrument that are good against a holder in due course. There are other reasons for not paying that may be asserted even against a holder in due course. Here are the most important.

a. Forgery

A person is not liable on an instrument unless she signed it or an authorized representative signed for her. 3–401(a). This freedom from liability is effective against the world, including a holder in due course.

b. Alteration

No one can enforce an altered instrument beyond its original terms. 3–407(b–c). To the extent of the alteration, the obligor is immune to liability even when the person entitled to enforce the instrument is a holder in due course.

c. Discharge of Which There Is Notice

An Article 3 discharge of a party's liability on an instrument is a personal defense, 3–601(b); but even a holder in due course takes subject to a party's discharge of which the holder has notice when she takes the instrument. The notice does not have the greater effect of preventing due-course status, and the holder who takes in due course can enforce the instrument against other parties free of their personal defenses.

d. Subsequent Claims and Defenses

A holder in due course takes free of *prior* claims and defenses only, not any arising *when or after* she becomes a holder in due course. The need for good faith and other requirements for becoming a holder in due course minimize the likelihood of a defense arising from the transaction of negotiation to a holder in due course. Occasionally, however, a defense arises at that time. For example, as part of the transaction of transfer, the holder in due course may agree to cancel her transferor's obligation by striking out her signature; or unknown to the holder in due course, a transaction may be voidable on the ground of illegality; or the parties may be acting on the basis of a mutual material mistake.

Also, defenses may arise after she acquires an instrument. For example, an obligor might pay the holder in due course; the latter might renounce her rights in a separate writing without giving up the instrument; the transferor or a prior party might obtain a discharge in bankruptcy; or a secondary party might be discharged by the holder's failure to make a proper presentment or to give due notice of dishonor. Another possibility is the holder impairing collateral for the instrument and thereby creating a defense for an obligor. Regardless of the nature of the defense arising when she receives the instrument or later, a holder in due course is subject to the defense just as if she were not a holder in due course.

e. Claims and Defenses Chargeable to the Holder

A holder in due course is not immune to liability or other accountability for her own conduct that creates a defense or claim for relief. She is liable for her own contracts, accountable for her own actions under Article 3 that create defenses or claims, and is liable for the breach of any duty imposed on her by other law that gives the obligor an offsetting defense or counterclaim in a suit on the instrument. It makes no difference when this liability arose, either before or after the holder became a holder in due course; and it makes no difference that the liability would be a personal claim or defense not enforceable against her if a prior party were responsible for it. Taking an instrument in due course will not permit a holder to escape responsibility for her own conduct, or for the conduct of others, when the law charges the holder directly and not merely derivatively through the transfer of the instrument.

This vulnerability of a holder in due course is absolutely clear but the language establishing it is very murky. It is 3–305(b). The first part of this section straight forwardly says a holder in due course is subject to real defenses (described in 3–305(a)(1)) but not subject to—takes free of—personal defenses (described in 3–305(a)(2)) or recoupment claims (described in 3–305(a)(3)). Then 3–305(b) adds, with respect to personal defenses and recoupment, that the freedom extends only to personal defenses and claims of "recoupment" that the obligor-defendant has "against a person other than the holder." So, by implication, the holder in due course is subject to any personal defenses or claims in recoupment the obligor has against the holder in due course herself.

This language is basically meaningful only when the plaintiff-holder was involved in the underlying transaction that produced the instrument. In this event, the holder—even if she is a holder in due course—cannot by this status avoid liabilities that other law attaches to her because of or in connection with the underlying transaction. The language has no limiting effect on freedom of a holder in due course from defenses "that arose from an occurrence [between the defendant-obligor and] a third party." 3–305 comment 2.

Suppose, for example, that Buyer purchases goods from Seller and pays by check. Buyer inspects the goods and discovers that, unbeknownst to Seller, the goods are not as contractually warranted. Buyer therefore orders the drawee-bank to stop payment of the check. The drawee accordingly dishonors the check, which is returned to Seller. Seller sues Buyer on the check. Buyer's defense is breach of warranty, which is a good personal defense under 3–305(a)(2).

A payee can be a holder in due course, and it's possible on these facts that Seller is a holder in due course. Nevertheless, a holder in due course only takes free of the defendant-obligor's personal defenses "against a person other than the holder." She is subject to personal defenses of other law, such as breach of warranty, against the holder herself.

Suppose, however, the deal worked this way: Seller negotiated the check to Transferee, to whom the check was returned upon dishonor by the Buyer's bank. If the Transferee sues Buyer and is a holder in due course, she takes free of the Buyer's defense of breach of warranty.

B. ORDINARY OR PERSONAL DEFENSES

Ordinary or *personal defenses* are reasons of the law for reducing or eliminating an obligor's liability on an instrument except as against a holder in due course. The rule is:

> Except as otherwise provided in this section, the right to enforce the obligation of a party to pay an instrument is subject to * * * a defense of the obligor stated in another section of this Article or a defense of the obligor that would be available if the person entitled to enforce the instrument were enforcing a right to payment under a simple contract * * *.

3–305(a)(2). Except for a holder in due course, these defenses are good against every person entitled to enforce the instrument, including the original payee and any transferee. A holder in due course takes free of the personal defenses that are attributable to prior parties, which means that the defenses cannot be asserted against a holder in due course or someone claiming through her. 3–305(b). The personal defenses are found in Article 3 itself and also in the contract law that surrounds and governs the underlying transaction that produced the instrument or for which the instrument was taken.

1. Article 3 Defenses

The ordinary defenses created by Article 3 itself are spread throughout the statute, but they are conveniently listed in a comment to 3–305:

- nonissuance of the instrument, conditional issuance, and issuance for a special purpose (Section 3–105(b));
- failure to countersign a traveler's check (Section 3–106(c));
- modification of the obligation by a separate agreement (Section 3–117);
- payment that violates a restrictive indorsement (Section 3–206(f));
- instruments issued without consideration or for which promised performance has not been given (Section 3–303(b)),

- and breach of warranty when a draft is accepted (Section 3–417(b)).

3–305 comment 2. Most of these defenses are tiny and tied to a very specific situation or context discussed elsewhere. The most important defense on this list concerns the "consideration" for the instrument. Really, this defense is rooted in the contract law of the underlying transaction. Article 3 recognizes and regulates the defense but does not create it. A more appropriate place to discuss the consideration defense is later, under the heading of defenses based on contract law.

Article 3 provides special personal defenses for parties who are *sureties* on an instrument, either actually or functionally. 3–605. These parties include "*accommodation parties*" who are actual sureties. They signed the instrument for the deliberate purpose of backing or securing the obligation of another party to the instrument. Typical checks in typical cases don't involve actual sureties. However, the special defenses for accommodation parties generally apply to *ordinary indorsers* of checks and other instruments. Indorsers functionally secure payment by a drawee or another party to the instrument whom everybody intends is the ultimate payor. The truth is, however, that the suretyship defenses for indorsers of typical checks in typical cases are practically, usually unimportant.[11]

---

[11] The further truth is that, in practice, the 3–605 suretyship defenses aren't very important to sureties with respect to notes. Sureties are common in bank loans and the like when notes are signed. However, the sureties more often sign separate suretyship

2. Discharge—The Not-a-Defense Defense

The most important Article 3 defense is not on the list of defenses in Article 3. It is "discharge," which means that an obligor is released from liability on the instrument for reasons of Article 3 or contract law. Discharge is not thought of, technically, as a defense and therefore is not included in the ordinary defenses of 3–305(a)(2). See 3–302 comment 3. For the same reason, discharge is not discussed here but in a separate section earlier in this chapter that concerns the contract aspects of instruments. Nevertheless, "[d]ischarge is effective against anybody except a person having rights of a holder in due course who took the instrument without notice of the discharge." Id.; see also 3–601(b). It is, functionally, a defense. The only distinction is that notice of discharge does not prevent holder in due course status as does notice of a defense. 3–302(a)(2)(vi). Notice of discharge merely subjects the holder to the discharge despite her due-course status. 3–302(b). In sum, therefore, discharge is not a defense only for purposes of 3–302(a).

3. Defenses of Contract Law

In addition to the Article 3 defenses specifically stated in Article 3, the personal defenses to an instrument also include defenses "of the obligor that would be available if the person entitled to enforce the instrument were enforcing a right to payment

---

agreements, not the notes themselves. Moreover, whatever they sign, sureties often effectively waive any and all suretyship defenses otherwise available to them by law.

under a simple contract." 3–305(a)(2). These defenses derive from the underlying obligation and are based on the contract law that governs it. *This law includes the common law and any applicable statutory law*, such as UCC Article 2 when a sale of goods is involved.

a. Range of Defenses, Especially Including Problems of Consideration

The contract defenses cover a wide range. At one end are broad common-law defenses concerned with fairness in the very beginning of the contract when it was formed, such as fraud, misrepresentation, and mistake. At the other end is breach of contract which turns on precise, very narrow issues of contract interpretation and on events that often occurred at the end of the contractual relationship. There is everything in between that would be available to the obligor if contract law governed the enforceability of her promise to pay, including the age-old defense of no consideration. It is an Article 3 defense that the instrument was issued or taken without consideration, 3–303(b); but, for the most part, it is contract law that defines consideration and it is the underlying transaction that is the source of any consideration. Really, therefore, lack of consideration is a contract defense.

Consideration is not an element of the plaintiff's prima facie case in a suit on an instrument, as it is when a person sues for breach of common-law contract. Nevertheless, "[t]he drawer or maker of an instrument has a defense if the instrument is issued without consideration." 3–303(b). Moreover, the issuer has a defense to the extent that she was promised performance that has not been duly performed. Id. It is a different issue whether or not the holder of an instrument gave "value" to qualify as holder in due course. See 3–302(a)(2), 3–303(a). The lack of value for that purpose is not itself a defense to payment of an instrument. The issue, in terms of defense to payment, is whether or not the drawer or maker got "consideration" in exchange for issuing the instrument. If not, she has a defense.

Not only are the issues different, the key terms are defined differently. "Consideration" basically keeps its common-law meaning, 3–303(b), but Article 3 gives a meaning to "value" that is both broader and more narrow that common-law consideration. See 3–303(a). Value is broader because it includes a preexisting debt, 3–303(a)(3), and more narrow because a bare executory promise is not "value." Significantly, Article 3 enlarges the definition of "consideration" to include anything that is "value." Therefore, by statute, consideration—like value—includes preexisting debt. Because of the common-law meaning, consideration—unlike value—also includes an executory promise.

Nevertheless, if an obligor issues an instrument in exchange for consideration that is an executory promise, she gets a pro tanto defense to the extent that the promise is due and unperformed. 3–303(b). Correspondingly, for purposes of holder in due course, "value" includes an executory promise to the extent the promise has been performed, 3–303(a)(1), but this point is relevant here solely to complete the comparison between value and consideration.

To illustrate, suppose that R gave P a $500 check as a birthday gift. The drawee dishonored the check because R stopped payment. P will not recover on the check because R has the defense of lack of consideration. 3–303(b). It is possible, however, that P can prove a local substitute for consideration that supports recovery under the common law if not on the instrument.

Suppose R gave P the check as prepayment for goods that P promised, by contract, to deliver later. R stops payment. P sues. The defense of lack of consideration is not available to R. P's executory promise itself was consideration. On the other hand, R has a defense to the extent that P's promise is due and unperformed. R has no defense if the time for P's performance has not yet arrived, and R loses the defense altogether if a holder in due course takes the instrument.

Significantly, 3–303(b) does not extend the defense of no consideration to an indorser. A probable reason is the reality that indorsers rarely act gratuitously. Even an anomalous indorser or other surety, known as an "accommodation party," 3–419(a), typically gets consideration in the value that is given to the principal debtor. It is so common that by express provision, consideration is unnecessary to bind an accommodation party. 3–419(b). Practically, it is always there, so having to prove it is wasted effort.

b. *Caveat: Defense Must Be Chargeable to Plaintiff*

The contract defenses that the obligor can raise are the defenses that applicable law gives to her, not the defenses of someone else. 3–305(a)(2) ("of the obligor"). Another limitation is that the defenses must be chargeable to the plaintiff against whom they are asserted. In other words, the plaintiff must be subject to the defenses by other law or agreement. Suppose, for example, that A and B signed a note to Bank that evidenced a loan. Unbeknownst to Bank, A was induced to sign the note only because of B's fraud that amounted to a personal defense. A got nothing from the loan. If B paid the instrument and sued A for contribution, A would have a good defense against B. On the other hand, if Bank sued A on the note, B's fraud would not be a good defense against Bank. Whether Bank is a holder in due course is irrelevant. A's obligation runs directly to Bank. The Bank's rights against A because of this obligation are not subject to the tacky conduct of someone else that is not attributable to Bank.

The result is different if B's fraud resulted in A issuing a note payable to B that B transferred to Bank. In this case, if Bank sued A on the note, B's fraud would be a good defense for A, unless Bank was a holder in due course. The difference is that, in this case, Bank's rights derive from B and are therefore subject to any defenses good against B. As a holder in due course, however, Bank's rights would be greater and Bank would take free of fraud that amounted to only a personal defense.

Even if Bank is a holder in due course, the result is different in both cases if B's fraud or other tacky conduct amounts to a real defense. Real defenses are good against the world. It would make no difference that Bank took the instrument directly from A because to the extent that a real defense exists, the law effectively deems that the obligor never became liable to anyone on the instrument.

C. RECOUPMENT (DEFENSIVE COUNTERCLAIMS)

Strictly speaking, *recoupment* is not a defense but accomplishes as much. A defense is a reason why *liability* is reduced, eliminated or never arises because of the plaintiff's conduct in the transaction that gives rise to her cause of action. A *claim in recoupment* is similarly related to the plaintiff's cause but reduces or eliminates *damages* by way of offset. Basically, recoupment is a related cause of action that is asserted only so far as is possible and necessary to reduce the amount of liability, only to wipe out or cut down the plaintiff's demand. In this respect recoupment differs from a counterclaim which, when it exceeds the amount of liability, is asserted both to offset damages for liability and also to produce a net recovery against the plaintiff. In sum, recoupment is essentially a counterclaim that is asserted defensively only.

When a person lacks the rights of a holder in due course, her right to enforce the instrument is subject to "a claim in recoupment of the obligor against the original payee of the instrument if the claim arose from the transaction that gave rise to the instrument * * *." 3–305(a)(3). The claim, however, can be asserted against a transferee only for purposes of recoupment, "only to reduce the amount owing on the instrument at the time the action is brought." Id. In short, it cannot be asserted as a counterclaim. If the person enforcing the instrument is the original payee, this limitation does not apply. The claim can be asserted fully, as a counterclaim, to permit an affirmative, net recovery for the obligor.

Different from recoupment is *setoff*. It concerns *un*related debts and claims. The rule on setoff as applied to instruments is that a transferee, whether or not a holder in due course, is not subject to the obligor's setoffs against a *prior party*. Yet, in line with local procedure, the obligor should be allowed to assert any setoff she has against the transferee personally, just as it should be appropriate for her to setoff against the original payee if this person sued to enforce the instrument. The reason for protecting a transferee from a prior-party setoff is that "it is not reasonable to require the transferee to bear the risk that wholly unrelated claims may also be asserted [as well as claims arising from the transaction that produced the instrument]." 3–305 comment 3. This reason does not apply to setoff against the plaintiff herself, whether she is the original payee or a transferee and whether or not she is a holder in due course.

D. CLAIMS (PROPERTY INTERESTS)

Holdership is different from ownership. A person can own a property interest in an instrument even though somebody else holds the instrument and is the person entitled to enforce it. On the other hand, everybody except a holder in due course takes an instrument "subject to a claim of a property or possessory right in the instrument or its proceeds, including a claim to rescind a negotiation and to recover the instrument or its proceeds * * *." 3–306. Here, the term "*claim*" is broad. It includes:

> not only claims to ownership but also any other claim of a property or possessory right. It includes the claim to a lien or the claim of a person in rightful possession of an instrument who was wrongfully deprived of possession. Also included is a claim * * * for rescission of a negotiation of the instrument by the claimant.

3–306 comment. It does not include a claim in recoupment which is a counterclaim used as a defense to payment rather than a property right or interest.

An obligor can safely pay the holder of an instrument and be discharged from liability even though the obligor knows of a third person's claim to the instrument and even though the claim is valid. 3–602(c). The claimant's remedy is to sue to recover the instrument and prevent payment. In the meantime, the obligor is not required to pay the holder who can be forced to sue to enforce the instrument. The issue then is whether or not the obligor can defend against liability on the basis of the third-party claim. (This is sometimes referred to as the defense of *jus tertii*, meaning right of a third party.) The answer is no unless the third person "is joined in the action and personally asserts the claim against the person entitled to enforce the instrument." 3–305(c). The only exception is when the plaintiff lacks the rights of a holder in due course "and the obligor proves that the instrument is a lost or stolen instrument." Id.

In no event can the obligor avoid payment of an instrument, or can anyone else enforce a prior claim to it, if the instrument was taken by a holder in due course and is held by her or someone claiming through this person. "A person having rights of a holder in due course takes free of the claim to the instrument." 3–306.

9. HOLDER IN DUE COURSE

A. REQUIREMENTS OF DUE-COURSE STATUS

A holder in due course is Article 3's most favored person. It gives her advantages with respect to an instrument that no one else enjoys. These advantages are scattered throughout Article 3 and are discussed throughout this book. Most important, a holder in due course is immune to the personal defenses of prior parties, and takes free of all property claims to the instrument. See the immediately preceding section of this chapter. In this respect, holder in due course is an exception to the general rule of derivative title which provides that a transferee of property gets no greater rights than her transferor.

To earn the special protections of a holder in due course, the holder of an instrument must meet certain requirements. First and second, she must be the *holder* of an *instrument*. These basic requirements are discussed elsewhere. This section of the book focuses on the additional, peculiar requirements commonly known as the *due-course requirements*. They require the holder to take the instrument

- for value;
- without notice—
- that the instrument is overdue or has been dishonored or that there is an uncured default with respect to payment of another instrument issued as part of the same series,
- that the instrument contains an unauthorized signature or has been altered,
- of any claim to the instrument, and
- that any party has a defense or claim in recoupment described in subsection (a) of Section 3–305 of this title;
- without reason to question the authenticity of the instrument;
- in good faith; and
- apart from certain unusual circumstances.

3–302(a).

1. For Value

The Code contains two overlapping but clearly different definitions of "value." A general definition in Article 1 defines value broadly as including, among other things, "any consideration sufficient to support a simple contract." 1–204(4). Article 3 defines value much more narrowly, 3–303(a), and this definition controls the meaning of value for purposes of Article 3. Throughout this discussion, therefore, value is used only in the narrower sense of 3–303.

Fundamentally important is the distinction between "value" and "consideration." First, their major roles under Article 3 are quite different. The primary legal significance of value is as a requirement for holder in due course. 3–302(a)(2)(i). Value is an essential element in establishing this status. The primary legal significance of consideration is that a defect in consideration for the instrument (lack of, nonperformance, failure) is a defense to payment against a person who lacks the rights of a holder in due course. 3–303(b), 3–305(a)(2).

Second, the meanings of value and consideration are not the same, but to some extent the key to the meaning of value is consideration. Consideration means the same in Article 3 as in the law of simple contracts. 3–303(b). A reasonably workable definition is that consideration consists of doing or promising to do what one is not already legally bound to do, or refraining or promising to refrain from doing what one has a legal right to do, in return for a promise.

Value is defined by 3–303(a), which provides that an instrument is issued or transferred for value if:

- the instrument is issued or transferred for a promise of performance, to the extent the promise has been performed;
- the transferee acquires a security interest or other lien in the instrument other than a lien obtained by judicial proceeding;
- the instrument is issued or transferred as payment of, or as security for, an antecedent claim against any person, whether or not the claim is due;
- the instrument is issued or transferred in exchange for a negotiable instrument; or
- the instrument is issued or transferred in exchange for the incurring of an irrevocable obligation to a third party by the person taking the instrument.

Thus, value is both broader and more narrow than consideration: broader because it includes preexisting debt and more narrow because it excludes an executory promise.

2. Without Notice

A further requirement of holder in due course is taking the instrument "without notice"—

- that the instrument is overdue or has been dishonored or that there is an uncured default with respect to payment of another instrument issued as part of the same series,

- that the instrument contains an unauthorized signature or has been altered,
- of any claim to the instrument, or
- that any party has a defense or claim in recoupment described in 3–305(a).

3–302(a)(2). Notice of any of these facts should serve as a danger signal to a person who is contemplating taking an instrument for value. It should warn her that she may be buying a lawsuit and that she should not expect to occupy the favored position of holder in due course.

Of course, a person should be barred from being a holder in due course by *actual* knowledge of any of these facts. If she sees the danger signal but chooses to disregard it, she must take the consequences. But actual knowledge is not essential to "notice" of a fact, which is established by any of three alternative tests:

(1) he has actual knowledge of it; or

(2) he has received a notice or notification of it; or

(3) from all the facts or circumstances known to him at the time in question he has reason to know that it exists.

1–202(a).

3. Authenticity of the Instrument

Former law provided that a person has notice of a defense or claim if "the instrument is so incomplete, bears such visible evidence of forgery or alteration, or is otherwise so irregular as to call into question its validity, terms or ownership or to create an ambiguity as to the party to pay." 3–304(1)(a) (1989 Official Text). *The current Article 3 makes the condition of the instrument a wholly separate requirement of holder in due course*, requiring that "the instrument when issued or negotiated to the holder does not bear such apparent evidence of forgery or alteration or is not otherwise so irregular or incomplete as to call into question its authenticity." 3–302(a)(1).

The word " 'authenticity' is used to make clear that the irregularity or incompleteness must indicate that the instrument may not be what it purports to be." 3–302 comment 1. It makes no difference, at least under the new law, that the obligor's claim or defense is unrelated to the irregularity or incompleteness of the instrument. It also makes no difference, technically, that the taker is without notice of the irregularity or incompleteness; but the problem must be "apparent" and in this event the taker ordinarily would have reason to know of the problem and thus would have notice of it.

4. Good Faith

Even though a holder acquires an apparently perfect instrument for value and without prohibited notice, she does not qualify as a holder in due course unless she also takes the instrument in "*good faith.*" Because the requirement of good faith is so often confused with the requirement of taking without notice, it's worth emphasizing that these two requirements are separate. No degree of good faith makes it possible for one who fails to meet the notice requirement to qualify as a holder in due course, and good faith is not established by showing that a person received an instrument without notice. Of course, these two requirements are closely related so that the conclusion that a holder has failed to satisfy one of these requirements is often bolstered by evidence that she failed to meet the other; but doing so is overkill. Failing either requirement, however, is sufficient by itself to deny due-course status.

The Article 3 test of good faith is both subjective and objective. It means "honesty in fact *and the observance of reasonable commercial standards of fair dealing*," 3–103(a)(6) (emphasis added), which is "concerned with the fairness of conduct rather than the care with which an act is performed." 3–103 comment 4. History explains that when this objective test is added to the subjective, "a business man engaging in a commercial transaction is not entitled to claim the peculiar advantages which the law accords to the * * * holder in due course * * * on a bare showing of 'honesty in fact' when his actions fail to meet the generally accepted standards current in his business, trade, or profession." 3–302 comment 1 (1952 Official Text).

The most important issue of the component of the objective test of good faith is whether or not it imposes an obligation to investigate the circumstances of an instrument before purchasing it. Because accepted business practice will seldom require investigation and because the law strongly favors the free flow of negotiable instruments, it is likely that only the most compelling circumstances would trigger any duty to inquire that might be part of the new objective test of good faith. For one reason or another, therefore, neither the objective nor subjective component of good faith is likely to require much—if any—investigation.

5. Apart from Certain Unusual Circumstances

Even though she satisfies the usual requirements previously described, a person does not acquire the rights of a holder in due course of an instrument taken:

- by legal process or by purchase in an execution, bankruptcy, or creditor's sale or similar proceeding,
- by purchase as part of a bulk transaction not in the ordinary course of business of the transferor, or
- as a successor in interest to an estate or other organization.

3–302(c). In these situations the transferee merely is acquiring the rights of the prior holder and there is no substantial interest in facilitating commercial transactions, which is the underlying reason for giving holders in due course their special advantages.

B. PAYEE AS HOLDER IN DUE COURSE

The payee of an instrument, like any other holder, can be a holder in due course so long as she meets the usual requirements, "but use of the holder-in-due-course doctrine by the payee of an instrument is not the normal situation." 3–302 comment 4. The doctrine assumes that in the typical case, the holder in due course is not the payee but is an immediate or remote transferee of the payee. When the issuer and the payee are the only parties, "the holder-in-due-course doctrine is irrelevant in determining rights between Obligor and Obligee with respect to the instrument." Id. For example:

> If Buyer issues an instrument to Seller and Buyer has a defense against Seller, that defense can obviously be asserted. Buyer and Seller are the only people involved. The holder-in-due-course doctrine has no relevance. The doctrine applies only to cases in which more than two parties are involved.

3–305 comment 2. Similarly, the Buyer can assert a breach of warranty claim or other counterclaim against the Seller. "It is not relevant whether Seller is or is not a holder in due course * * * or whether Seller knew or had notice that Buyer had the * * * claim. It is obvious that holder-in-due-course doctrine cannot be used to allow Seller to cut off a * * * claim that Buyer has against Seller." 3–305 comment 3; see also 3–305(b) ("other than the holder").

About the only case in which it makes any difference that a payee is a holder in due course is that in which she does not deal directly with the drawer or issuer of another kind of instrument but instead obtains the instrument from a remitter who obtained it from the maker or drawer. In this case, if the payee qualifies as a holder in due course, she takes the instrument free of any defense or claim based on the remitter's wrongdoing; otherwise not. See 3–302 comment 4.

C. TAKING THROUGH A HOLDER IN DUE COURSE—THE SHELTER PRINCIPLE

A transferee of an instrument may have the rights of a holder in due course without necessarily having the status of a holder in due course. It is possible because of the *shelter principle* of 3–203(b), the "[t]ransfer of an instrument, whether or not the transfer is a negotiation, vests in the transferee any right of the transferor to enforce the instrument, including any right as a holder in due course * * *." By virtue of this broad principle (which applies to most other forms of property as well), even though a person in her own right does not satisfy the requirements for being a holder in due course, she is entitled to enjoy the benefits of that status that were enjoyed by any holder in due course prior to her in the chain of transfer of the instrument. The primary significance of the shelter principle, and the basis for its name, is the fact that it enables one who is not a holder in due course to share the shelter from claims and defenses to the extent enjoyed by a holder in due course through or from whom she acquired the instrument.

Giving the transferee who is not a holder in due course the rights of a prior transferor who was such a holder, has the effect of increasing the market for instruments held by holders in due course. But this rule does not apply to improve the position of a transferee who has been a party to any fraud or illegality affecting the instrument or who as a prior holder had notice of a claim or defense. Id. And, of course, one to whom a holder in due course transfers an instrument as security, acquires no greater interest in the instrument than the amount due on the obligation secured.

10. SHIFTING LOSS FOR CERTAIN RISKS— WARRANTY AND RESTITUTION

When someone sues on an instrument and loses, or someone pays an instrument to the wrong person or by mistake, there are two possible, limited theories for shifting the loss: warranty and restitution.

A person incurs contract liability on an instrument because she signs it. A person incurs warranty liability with respect to an instrument because she transfers the instrument and also because the instrument is presented for payment or acceptance. Warranty liability is a property concept. It is not dependent on promise and contract. Therefore, warranty liability attaches whether or not the warrantor indorsed the instrument. In case she indorsed, her contract liability is in addition to the warranty liability.

Warranty liability is personal liability that the law imposes on a person because of a breach of the warranties that Articles 3 and 4 separately impose with respect to the transfer and presentment of instruments. The purpose of transfer warranties, like warranties in the sale of goods or other property, is to insure the instrument's "title" and basic "quality." They assure or guarantee a right to enforce the instrument and against the existence of certain defenses and claims to the instrument that would dilute the instrument's value.

The main purpose of presentment warranties is to assure the person who pays the instrument that the person presenting the instrument for payment is entitled to the money. Presentment warranties are not insurance that payment was proper by the terms of the contract or other relationship that provides the underlying reason for the payment. There is no warranty against payment beyond these terms, by mistake. Avoiding mistake is within the personal control of the payor and, for reasons of finality, the law is slow to provide any remedy for mistake. On the other hand, the common law of restitution permits recovering mistaken payments in limited (very limited) circumstances. This law has always supplemented the statutory law of negotiable instruments, but Article 3 explicitly codifies a restitution recovery for some mistakes. Restitution from any source is always very limited, however, because the remedy generally cannot reach innocent persons who gave value or who detrimentally relied on the mistaken payment or acceptance.

In largest effect, warranties and restitution serve the same purpose. They are the law's principal means for distributing risks (and thereby losses) in dealing with checks and other instruments; and the distribution is complete because the risks that are not covered by warranties or restitution are necessarily assigned and left to the transferee, payor, or whoever else suffers the loss. What is not covered is therefore equally important to what is covered. Article 3 is the general source of warranty law for all instruments. Section 3–416 creates the transfer warranties and 3–417 the presentment warranties. Article 4 restates its own warranties, 4–207 for transfer and 4–208 for presentment, and also adds additional warranties. In the main, however, the Article 4 warranties are the same as the warranties of Article 3. Because warranties with respect to checks are most commonly applied in cases involving check collection and check fraud, further discussion about warranties and also restitution is mainly reserved for later chapters that are completely dedicated to check collection and check fraud. See Chapters 3 and 5 *infra*.

CHAPTER 3

CHECK COLLECTION

A check has little efficacy until presented to the drawee for payment. Presentment itself is required and defined by Article 3. Article 4, however, governs the largely banking process of getting a check presented and hopefully paid. This process is called **check collection** and is the focus of this chapter, particularly the **end result** of the process which is **either payment or dishonor of the check** by the **drawee** bank (which Article 4 calls the **payor bank,** 4–105(3)).

Let's review some basics. Suppose D buys a TV from P. D decides to pay the price by check. P takes the check. The issuance of the check by D to P, and P taking the check for the price, has several important consequences.

1. Since the check is taken by P for D's obligation to pay the price of the TV, this underlying obligation (which arises under Article 2) is suspended until the check is dishonored or paid. 3–310(b).

2. P becomes a "person entitled to enforce" the check with certain rights on the instrument. See 1–201(b)(21)(A) & 3–105(a). These rights include presenting the check to the drawee bank ("payor bank" in Article 4 terms) for payment and to sue to enforce the check against D if the payor bank dishonors it. 3–301.

3. If and when the payor bank **dishonors** the check, D, as the drawer, is obligated to pay the instrument "according to its terms." 3–414(b). Thus, P cannot enforce the underlying obligation or the check against D until dishonor of the check; but, upon dishonor, P can enforce either the check or the underlying obligation. 3–310(b)(3).

4. However, if the payor bank **pays** the check, D's obligations on the underlying obligation and on the check are discharged.

So, the big issue when a check goes through the check collection process, which this chapter describes, is whether the payor bank **dishonors** or **pays** the check. The particulars of the check collection process and associated liabilities depend on whether the check is presented directly to the payor bank over the counter for payment in cash or is deposited for collection either with the payor bank or another bank. This chapter is organized accordingly, with further attention to related issues of check collection.

1. PRESENTING THE CHECK FOR PAYMENT: PAYOR BANK AS SOLE BANK

Suppose you are a payee in possession of a check issued by a drawer in payment of an obligation. This is somewhat better than having the "check in the mail," but how do you get the money? The answer is that the check must be presented to the payor (drawee) bank, 3–501(a), and the payor bank must pay the "item." See 4–104(a)(9), which defines "item" to include "an * * * order [including a check] to pay money handled by a bank for collection or payment."

Presentment may be made directly by you to the payor bank or through the bank collection process. In this subsection, we will discuss payment and dishonor where (1) Payee presents the check to Payor Bank "over the counter" and demands cash and (2) Payee deposits the check in its account in the same bank where Drawer has an account.

A. PRESENTMENT OVER THE COUNTER FOR PAYMENT IN CASH

Section 3–501(a) defines presentment to include a "demand" made by a payee "to pay the instrument made to the drawee." In the case of a United States bank, presentment must be "at the place of payment," and can be made "by any commercially reasonable means." 3–501(b)(1). In some cases the payee will simply appear at a teller window of the payor bank, exhibit the check, and demand immediate payment in cash. This presentment is "over the counter" for cash. It is easy to imagine and explain but is relatively uncommon.

In an over-the-counter presentment, the check is dishonored if it is duly presented for payment and "not paid on the day of presentment." 3–502(b)(2). Be careful: there are two timing questions.

The first timing question is what starts the clock running. It is due presentment, which means presenting the check to the payor bank is the manner described by Article 3. See the related discussion in Chapter 2 *supra*.

The second timing question is when exactly the clock starts to run, which is a two-part question. Part one is that the clock doesn't start unless the demand for payment is a due or proper presentment. See Chapter 2 *supra*.

Part two is that presentment isn't effective until "received by the person to whom presentment is made." 3–501(b)(1). If, however, the payor has established a cut-off hour of "not earlier than 2:00 p.m." and presentment is made after that time, Payor Bank may treat presentment "as occurring on the next business day after the day of presentment." 3–501(b)(4) & 4–108.[1]

Assume a cut-off hour of 2:00 p.m. Payee presents the check at 1:59 p.m. on May 8. The presentment is effective and payor must pay or dishonor before the end of the day, see 4–104(a)(3), on May 8, though not by 2:00 p.m. If the check is presented at 2:01 p.m., however, the payor bank "may" treat the presentment as occurring on the next business day. If May 9 is a Saturday, the next business day is Monday, May 11. Monday, then, is the big day for decision, unless the payor elects to pay on May 8.

If the check that is presented for payment in cash over the counter is not so paid by the end of the

---

[1] For law school exam purposes this difference in a day becomes important when connected to the Article 3 rules about the timing of presentment and the effects of delay on the liabilities of secondary parties. See the related discussion in Chapter 2 *supra*.

appropriate day, the check is deemed dishonored. Not timely paying is dishonor. The statute requires nothing more. In a real-live typical case, however, the teller will probably quietly say "there's a problem" and push the check back across the counter. Very likely, the teller will also stamp the check indicating "refused" or the like. This stamp is acceptable proof of dishonor, 3–505, which becomes important in suing the drawer on the check. The drawer's liability is conditioned on dishonor, and suing the drawer on the check or the underlying transaction between them is the payee's only remedy.

There is here a finer point. Just suppose that before the cut-off hour on Tuesday, Payee presents a check for payment in cash over the counter. The nice teller takes the check and says, "I'll have to get back to you. Come back Thursday." (Assume for this problem that each day is a banking day.) Payee returns on Thursday and the teller reports that the bank could not pay the check and gives it back to Payee, properly stamped indicating nonpayment. Okay. You already know this conduct amounts to dishonor, and the drawer's Article 3 liability is triggered.

On these facts, however, there is something else: payor bank "accountability." If a check is presented and received by the payor bank for payment in cash over the counter, the bank itself is accountable for the amount of the item if the bank delays too long in paying or returning the item or sending notice of dishonor. 4–302(a). Accountability is statutory, Article 4 liability, not Article 3 liability on the instrument itself. Functionally, though, they are the same in the sense that Payee can recover from the bank.

In our case the bank must have acted no later than its "midnight deadline" or arguably sooner, depending on how 4–302(a)(1) is read and applied. "Midnight deadline" means "midnight on its next banking day following the banking day on which it [the bank] receives the relevant item. . . ." 4–104(a)(10).

By this rule the payor bank in our case should have returned the check no later than midnight on Wednesday or maybe sooner. On the basis of breaching this rule, the bank is accountable for the amount of the check and thus liable to Payee for this amount.

WARNING! This accountability does not mean payment. The check was not paid, which would have required the bank to pay on the day of presentment. Because the check was not paid then, the check was dishonored. Drawer is liable on the check, and payor bank is liable on the basis of the Article 4 accountability. Of course, Payee is entitled to a single recovery.

FURTHER WARNING!! Accountability under 4–302 is rare. Practically speaking, it never happens in real life when a check is deposited for collection rather than presented over the counter for cash, not even when a check is finally paid because the payor bank fails timely to dishonor. In such a case the payor bank is liable in the sense of making good on the payment but is not accountable under 4–302.

Most typically, of course, the payor bank pays the check by pushing cash across the counter within minutes of presentment. The delivery of the cash is, in Article 4, "final payment" under 4–215(a)(1), subject to limited, restitution recovery by Payor for payment by mistake set out in 3–418. The effect of final payment is that Payor Bank has satisfied its contractual obligation to Drawer (under the deposit agreement between them), and the obligation of Drawer on the check and on the underlying obligation are discharged. 3–602 & 3–310(a–b).

Payment does not occur, however, unless and until Payor Bank has "paid the item in cash" on the day of presentment. 4–215(a)(1). Cash is folding money and coins. Does cash also include a "cashier's check"? A cashier's check is the bank's own check drawn against itself. See Chapter 7 *infra*. The technical answer is probably no, but some courts have held that giving a cashier's check is final payment for various purposes throughout Article 4 because a cashier's check is commonly treated as a cash equivalent.

What if Payee asks the teller to deposit the money in the Payee's own account at Payor Bank? These facts are likely to convert the case from an "over the counter" presentment for cash to an "on us" deposit, which is governed by different rules.

B. "ON US" CHECKS: PAYOR BANK AS DEPOSITARY BANK

In some cases both Drawer and Payee of the check may have an account with the Payor Bank. Rather than demand cash over the counter, suppose that Payee deposits the check (called an "on us" item) in her account for collection. In this case, the Payor Bank is also the Depositary Bank, because it is the "first bank to take an item even though it is also the payor bank," 4–105(2).[2]

Suppose Payee deposits the check on May 1. What happens next? The key sections here are 4–301 and 4–215.

First, Payor Bank may or may not give Payee a provisional credit (settlement) to her account. The law does not require it. In almost all cases, however, a provisional settlement is given. If Payor Bank gives a provisional settlement, the credit can be revoked and the account charged back if and by Payor Bank dishonoring the check in a timely manner. 4–301(a).

Second, unlike a demand for payment over the counter, Payor Bank does not dishonor the check by failing to pay it on the day of deposit. Bank may dishonor up to its **midnight deadline**. 4–301(b). The important phrase, "midnight deadline," see 4–104(a)(10), means "midnight on its next banking day

---

[2] Note, however, Payor Bank is not also a collecting bank 4–105(5), which is not important here but is very important for purposes of rules discussed later. With respect to typical checks a payor bank is never a collecting bank. It is always a payor bank and sometimes a depositary bank, too, but never a collecting bank.

following the banking day on which it receives the relevant item or notice or from which the time for taking action commences to run, whichever is later." Thus, in our illustration, the midnight deadline is midnight on May 2, the banking day following deposit of the item.

Third, the dishonor occurs only if, by the midnight deadline, the Payor Bank "returns the item," "returns an image of the item" if the parties have so agreed, or "sends a record providing notice of dishonor or nonpayment if the item is unavailable for return." 4–301(a)(1–3). In the case of an "on us" item, return is accomplished by sending or delivering the dishonored check to the bank customer who deposited it. 4–301(d)(2).

Fourth, if Payor Bank returns the check by the midnight deadline, the check is dishonored, thus triggering the consequences that attend dishonor under Article 3.

Fifth, if Payor Bank fails for any reason, deliberate or not, to return the item before the midnight deadline, the check is deemed finally paid, 4–215(a)(3), whether payment of the check was wrongful or rightful as between Payor Bank and drawer. As a result:

- The provisional settlement or credit to Payee's account (which occurred when she deposited the check) hardens or becomes final, which means the credit belongs to Payee and the bank cannot lawfully take it back; and

- The consequences attending payment under Article 3 apply, which means the liabilities of parties to the instrument are discharged.

2. PRESENTING THE CHECK FOR PAYMENT: MULTIPLE BANKS

A. FORWARD COLLECTION PROCESS IN GENERAL

This section discusses the collection process where Depositary Bank and Payor Bank are truly, completely separate banks and where there may be at least one other bank between them in the collection process. This middle bank is called an intermediary, collecting bank. The discussion builds and elaborates on the discussion in the previous section. Here is an illustration.

Payee deposits a check in Depositary Bank in Moline, Illinois drawn on Payor Bank in Philadelphia. Payee's objective is the same as in an "over the counter" or "on us" transaction: To obtain payment from Payor Bank. The problem is that there are at least two banks involved and they are in different states. How does Payee get paid?

First, the check still must be presented to Payor Bank for payment. Even at a distance, this is not difficult to accomplish. Depositary Bank could send the check electronically or by express mail directly to Payor Bank, see 4–204(b)(1), or use other banks as agents to accomplish the same purpose. These banks in the middle are intermediary, collecting banks. For example, Depositary Bank may use the Federal

Reserve Banks of Chicago and Philadelphia for collection services. Either of these methods is permitted under Article 4, see 4–204, but the latter is more likely. Thus, there will probably be at least two more collecting banks involved in the process.

Second, presentment from a distance is not done "cold turkey." Usually, there is a pre-existing agreement between the banks that facilitates this process. More particularly, if there is no such agreement between Depositary Bank and Payor Bank (or no correspondent bank), Depositary Bank will use the Federal Reserve System. Thus, if Depositary Bank is a member bank or has access to the system, the check will be presented through the Federal Reserve System to the Payor Bank. The journey from Moline to Philadelphia through the Fed will be regulated by agreements among the banks, Federal Reserve circulars and Regulation J, which controls the collection of checks and other items by Federal Reserve Banks. The journey will also be expedited by the computer. Information is encoded on the check that routes the check to Payor Bank and states the amount of the item.

Third, Payee's check is but one of several billion checks which are being processed around the country at any given time. There is volume pressure on the system, both in number of checks to be processed and the amount of money represented. Moreover, on any given day, most Depositary Banks will be forwarding a large number of checks for collection and receiving a large number of checks drawn on them. Thus, there are bookkeeping problems at all points in the system.

Since deposited checks are provisionally credited to and checks drawn on are provisionally debited from Depositary Bank's own accounts with other banks or the Federal Reserve, a daily net balance must be determined. This balance helps determine whether Depositary Bank has sufficient reserves at day's end and, therefore, whether it must borrow funds to meet the daily reserve requirements.

In an effort to relieve some of this volume pressure, Congress in 2003 enacted the **Check Clearing for the 21st Century Act (Check 21).** 12 U.S.C. § 5001 et seq. That statute allowed a person to deposit, send for collection, or present a "**substitute check**" in place of the original paper check. A "substitute check" is simply a paper reproduction which contains an image of the front and back of the original check and bears a legend indicating that it is a legal copy. 12 U.S.C. § 5002(16). Banks in the collection chain were thus encouraged to speed up processing and reduce costs by forwarding electronic images of checks, which could then be turned back into paper (the substitute check) if necessary at some point further down the chain. The remarkable success of Check 21 is reflected by the latest available statistics. "Reserve Banks estimate that, by the end of 2013, more than 99.9 percent of all forward checks" and "99.0 percent of FedReturn checks . . . will be processed in electronic form."[3] The Federal Reserve Board is encouraging this trend by proposing alternative

---

[3] Availability of Funds and Collection of Checks: Proposed Rule, 79 FR 6674–01, 6675 (Feb. 4, 2014) [hereinafter Proposed Rule]

frameworks designed to discourage depositary banks from requiring the paper return of checks. Id.

Fourth, assuming that the various sorting and routing procedures have been successful, the presentment and bookkeeping issues are usually handled through some type of clearing arrangement.

Check 21 "plus the greater use of electronic payments, has led to a major reduction in paper check processing and dramatic changes in the way the Fed processes checks. * * * [T]he Federal Reserve has adapted its operations . . . by consolidating its check-processing operations into two sites: The Atlanta Fed handles electronic check processing and the Cleveland Fed, paper check processing."[4] During the clearing process, all of the checks drawn on Payor Bank are exchanged for all of the checks deposited in Payor Bank and being sent forward for collection. Drawer's check will be included, ready for internal processing by Payor Bank.

In sum, as the check moves forward, Payee, Depositary Bank and Collecting Banks are all given credits (settlements) in their accounts with each other in anticipation of payment. Under Article 4, these credits are provisional. If payment is made by not timely returning the check, the accounts of Drawer and Payor Bank are debited and the provisional credits become final under Article 4. If the check is dishonored by timely return of the check,

---

[4] *See Supporting the Nation's Payment Systems: Check Processing.* Federal Reserve Bank of Philadelphia, https://www.philadelphiafed.org/about-the-fed/who-we-are/payment-system.cfm (last visited Sept. 26, 2014).

there are no debits to the accounts of Drawer and Payor Bank and the provisional credits given to collecting banks can be charged back, ultimately to Payee's account.

Let's follow the check through the process from deposit to presentment and possible return to see the rights and liabilities that attach along the way. Keep in mind that the most important point in this trip is the fork in the road when the payor bank either honors or dishonors. Until this point every step is legally common with some permissible variations in process; after this point the legal consequences under Articles 3 and 4 are vastly different depending on whether the check is paid or dishonored.

B. DEPOSITING THE CHECK FOR COLLECTION

1. Indorsement and Transfer to Depositary Bank

To commence the collection process, Payee [also a "customer," 4–104(a)(5)] will normally sign and indorse the check for "deposit" or "collection" only and deliver it physically or electronically to Depositary Bank. This delivery is a transfer, not a presentment for payment.

This indorsement is restrictive, see 3–206(c), but it does not prevent Depositary Bank from being a holder or from transferring or negotiating the instrument. 3–206(a). In fact, upon delivery of the item to Depositary Bank for collection, the "depositary bank becomes a holder of the item at the time it receives the item for collection if the customer at the time of delivery was a holder of the item, whether or not the customer indorses the item * * *." 4–205(1).

2. Crediting the Customer's Account—Provisional Settlement Under Article 4

Depositary Bank will "settle" with Payee by crediting the amount of the item to the account of Payee, its customer. See 4–104(a)(11) for the definition of "settle." This credit to Customer's account is also a credit in Depositary Bank's overall reserve account balance at the end of the banking day.

Under Article 4, this settlement is "provisional" rather than final, "[u]nless a contrary intent clearly appears." 4–201(a). Similarly, any settlements made by Depositary Bank with other collecting banks and any other settlements made in the process of collection are also provisional. The settlement does not become final or "firm up" until final payment is made by Payor Bank. See 4–215(c). At that point, Customer/Payee may, subject to 4–214, withdraw from the account as a matter of right. 4–215(d). [We discuss the **Expedited Funds Availability Act** (EFAA) later in this chapter.]

Section 4–214(a) states when a collecting bank which has made a provisional settlement may revoke that settlement and "charge back the amount of any credit given for the item to its customer's account" and the time within which that action must be taken. We will examine 4–214 a little bit later. For now, remember that under Article 4, credits for items deposited for forward collection are provisional. Whether they become final depends upon whether Payor Bank makes final payment. If the check is dishonored, all provisional settlements are revoked as the various banks scramble to restore balances to their pre-deposit position.

3. Depositary Bank Becomes Collecting Bank and Agent for Collection

Depositary Bank now begins to function also as a collecting bank, see 4–105(5), and becomes "an agent or subagent of the owner of the item." 4–201(a). In this role Depositary/Collecting Bank now assumes the responsibilities Article 4 imposes on a collecting bank in the forward collection of a check.

Under a restrictive indorsement, however, Collecting Bank is guilty of the tort of conversion unless the "amount paid by the bank with respect to the instrument is received by the indorser or applied consistently with the indorsement." 3–206(c)(2). Moreover, a depositary bank "warrants to collecting banks, the payor bank * * * and the drawer that the amount of the item was paid to the customer or deposited to the customer's account." 4–205(2). Thus, Article 4 both imposes duties upon the agent in the forward collection process and holds the collecting bank accountable if collected funds are applied other than as directed by the customer.

C. DUTIES OF COLLECTING BANKS

1. What Is a Collecting Bank?

Under Article 4, "collecting bank" means a "bank handling an item for collection except the payor bank." 4–105(5). This broad definition, then, includes depositary, intermediary and presenting banks as defined in 4–105. It does not include the payor bank. In our case, Payee deposits the check with her bank, which is the depositary bank. This bank acts for Payee to present the check to Payor Bank but, in our case, does so by sending the check (or its electronic equivalent pursuant to Check 21, 11 U.S.C. § 5001 et seq.) through possibly several banks in the banking collection system. In this role Depositary Bank is a collecting bank, and every bank through which the check passes is also a transferee of the check and a collecting bank working for the Payee, but not the payor bank. The last transferee, collecting bank in the chain is the bank that actually presents the check to the payor bank; and this last collecting bank is therefore also known as the presenting bank. In performing this role the collecting/presenting bank does not transfer the check to the payor bank. Rather, it presents the check for payment.

2. Responsibilities of Collecting Bank

A key provision is 4–202(a)(1), which provides that a "collecting bank must exercise ordinary care in: (1) presenting an item or sending it for presentment." Section 4–202(b) then states that a collecting bank "exercises ordinary care under subsection (a) by taking proper action before its midnight deadline following receipt of an item, notice, or settlement." The collecting bank may take even more time if it is "reasonable" and the bank establishes timeliness. Thus, the collecting bank has a "safe harbor" against potential liability for failing to exercise ordinary care in sending an item for presentment.

Note that "midnight deadline" means midnight of the "next banking day following the banking day on which it receives the relevant item." 4–104(a)(10). Thus, each collecting bank up to presentment has two banking days to act before it fails to exercise ordinary care. *The failure to exercise ordinary care does not mean that the check is paid or that the collecting bank is accountable for the item.* A check can be paid only by a payor bank failing timely to return the check after presentment. Untimely action of a collecting bank means only that the bank is liable to Payee for the "amount of the item reduced by an amount that could not have been realized by the exercise of ordinary care." 4–103(e).

3. Methods of Sending and Presenting

The check deposited by Payee for collection contains the following information: (1) name and address of Payor Bank; (2) drawer's account number in Payor Bank, encoded at the bottom center of the check; and (3) routing numbers locating Payor Bank in the Federal Reserve System, encoded at the bottom left of the check. After deposit, Depositary Bank will encode the amount of the check at the bottom right of the check. These funny numbers at the bottom are part of the Magnetic Ink Character Recognition (MICR) system and play an important role in the collection process.

Section 4–204(a) provides that a collecting bank "shall send items by a reasonably prompt method, taking into consideration relevant instructions, the nature of the item, the number of those items on hand, the cost of collection involved, and the method generally used by it or others to present those items." The emphasis here is upon both predictability and flexibility. Thus, Collecting Bank is protected if it uses the Federal Reserve System, since this method is "generally used" and has the capacity to employ quicker and less costly methods of presentment.

U.C.C. 4–204(b)(1) states that a collecting bank "may send * * * an item directly to the payor bank" by direct mail, express, messenger or the like. Id. comment 2. Although this practice is generally approved, an item may not be sent directly to a nonbank payor unless "authorized by its transferor." 4–204(b)(2). The reason is that nonbank payors, in most cases, presumably have less responsibility than bank payors and thus increase the risk of conversion, nonpayment and the like.

To summarize by an illustration, suppose that Payee-Customer deposits a check for $5,000 drawn on a Philadelphia bank at 1:00 p.m. on Monday, May 11 in its account with Depositary Bank in Moline. Depositary Bank will encode the amount of the check, $5,000, and has until midnight on May 12 to take proper action. 4–202(b). Before that time, Depositary Bank may either send the check for presentment through the Federal Reserve System or present the item directly to Payor Bank. 4–202(a)(1) & 4–204. If the former method is selected, Depositary Bank assumes only the duties of a collecting bank in the process. If the latter method is selected, Depositary Bank is both a collecting and a presenting bank. It must exercise ordinary care in presenting the item, 4–202(a)(1) and must comply with provisions dealing with the place, method and time for presentment. See 3–501, which governs in the absence of contrary agreement.

4. Truncation

Since the enactment of Check 21, 11 U.S.C. § 5001 et seq., there is a much greater likelihood that Depositary Bank will truncate checks deposited for collection. Truncation basically means that data is captured from the paper check, and then an image of the check, or simply its electronic information, is forwarded and presented electronically to Payor Bank.[5] This means of sending items through the collection process was allowed in the past pursuant to pre-arrangement among banks based on an "agreement for electronic presentment," which can

---

[5] A fuller definition is "any number of arrangements in which the original paper checks are removed from the collection or return process before reaching either paying or depositary banks, respectively, or reaching their customer." Letter and accompanying section-by-section analysis from Hon. Alan Greenspan (Chairman, Board of Governors of the Federal Reserve System) to Hon. Paul S. Sarbanes (Chairman of the U.S. Senate Committee on Banking, Housing, and Urban Affairs), transmitting and explaining proposed Check Truncation Act (Dec.17, 2001).

result from actual agreement, clearing-house rule, or federal regulation. 4–110.

Check 21 however, encouraged check truncation even if a collecting or payor bank would not voluntarily agree to accept digital images. Some banks simply did not have the requisite technology to do so. Rather than force banks to accept digital images, therefore, Check 21 instead mandated that those banks accept "substitute checks"—paper reproductions of the original check. 12 U.S.C. § 5003. This meant that banks earlier in the collection chain could truncate and process checks electronically, then turn them back into paper substitutes for any bank incapable of processing electronic images.

The Federal Reserve Board has continued to strenuously push "the banking industry's ongoing transition to fully-electronic interbank check collection and return,"[6] asserting that electronic processing is quicker, less costly, and results in fewer errors.[7] In fact, since the "dedicated air and ground transportation systems for paper checks have largely been discontinued,"[8] the handling of paper checks has become even slower and more expensive.

Customers who used to demand their actual "cancelled" paper checks every month for purposes of reviewing their accounts and retaining evidence of payment have become comfortable with statements that merely include reproductions or summaries of

---

6 Proposed Rule, 79 FR 6674–01, 6675 (Feb. 4, 2014).

7 Id.

8 Id.

their transactions. Article 4 allows banks to send these customers images or other digital forms or records of cancelled checks. 4–406(a).

If the paper image provided by the bank meets the requirements for a "substitute check" set out in Check 21, the paper reproduction is deemed to be "the legal equivalent of the original check for all purposes." 12 U.S.C. § 5003(b). Check 21 further establishes warranty and indemnity rights which will be available against banks that create and transfer such substitute checks, 12 U.S.C. § 5004–5, and the Federal Reserve Board has proposed that those warranties be extended to electronic check information and images.[9]

D. SETTLEMENTS

1. Under Article 4

Section 4–104(a)(11) defines "settle" as paying "in cash, by clearing-house settlement, in a charge or credit or by remittance, or otherwise as agreed. A settlement may be either provisional or final." In the forward collection process, a bank to which a check is forwarded for collection or presented for payment is expected to settle with the forwarding or presenting bank. Under Article 4, at least, these settlements are usually provisional. They are conditioned upon final payment by Payor Bank under 4–215(a). Thus, provisional settlements "become final upon final payment of the item by the payor bank." See 4–215(c). If the check is dishonored, the provisional

---

[9] Id. at 6683–6685.

settlements are revoked and the various accounts charged back. See 4–214.

The medium and time of settlement by banks is regulated by agreement, including Federal Reserve regulations and circulars, clearing-house rules and the like and, in the absence of agreement or regulations, by 4–213. In our Moline-Philadelphia transaction, settlement will undoubtedly be by a credit to an account in a Federal Reserve Bank and will be effective when the credit is made. 4–213(a). Thus, if Depositary Bank in Moline forwards the check for collection to the Federal Reserve Bank in Chicago, the Federal Reserve Bank, as a collecting bank, will settle by crediting Depositary Bank's account in the Federal Reserve Bank for $5,000. Similarly, the Federal Reserve Bank in Philadelphia will credit the account of the Federal Reserve Bank in Chicago and the Payor Bank in Philadelphia will credit the account of the Federal Reserve Bank in Philadelphia and debit Drawer's account. This provisional house of credits and debits will stand or fall depending upon whether Payor Bank finally pays or returns the check.

2. Under Regulation CC

Federal law sometimes supplements Article 4 but rarely adds much that is important for typical cases and virtually never preempts anything important. Regulation CC, which implements the Expedited Funds Availability Act, mainly supplements Article 4 with respect to the process of returning checks a payor bank has dishonored. The regulation does speak some to the forward collection process and really confuses a student's study and understanding of the process.

What Regulation CC says that causes confusion is that settlements in the forward collection process are final, not provisional as Article 4 provides. Don't panic! In practice, nothing really changes in applying Article 4, which remains the principal source of law on check collection.

Article 4 makes the forward-collection settlements provisional as a means of balancing accounts and on the assumption that a dishonored check is returned ultimately to the depositary bank by reversing the path the check followed in getting to the payor bank. The customer who deposited the check and each collecting bank pushing the check forward gets a credit on the assumption that the check will be paid. In this event, all the credits harden in cascading order all the way back to the credit the customer received upon deposit. In the event the check is dishonored, the effect is brought home to the customer by returning the checks through the very same banks. Along the way each bank takes back the provisional settlement it gave for the check in the forward collection process. In the end, the reversal visits the customer. The banks have netted out. The customer nets out by suing and recovering on the check.

The problem with this approach is that returning a check along the exact same forward-collection route is not always the best or quickest route to the depositary bank. To allow for speedier—more expeditious returns—Regulation CC preemptively allows banks to return a dishonored check by any reasonable, expeditious route and means.

The problem, in turn, is that changing the route may leave out of balance an intermediary, collecting bank involved in the forward collection of the check. The bank settled for the item when it took the check and is left with this debit on its books if the bank is cut out of the return process. To solve this accounting problem, Regulation CC therefore provides that settlements going forward are final.

This federal labeling of forward-collection settlements as "final" does not mean, however, that the settlement a payor bank makes upon receiving a check from a presenting bank is "final payment" for purposes of Article 4. Final settlement under Regulation CC is not the equivalent of final payment under Article 4. The payor bank is free to dishonor the check by the midnight deadline of 4–301; and the payor bank recoups its presentment settlement by expeditiously returning the check directly to the depositary bank or indirectly through the presenting bank or some other intermediary bank, even though the bank was not involved in the forward collection of the check. Any bank to which the check is returned must credit the payor bank for the amount of the item.

E. WARRANTIES IN FORWARD COLLECTION

1. Transfer and Presentment Warranties

Customers and collecting banks make three types of warranties when they pass checks along in the collection process: "transfer" warranties under 4–207, "presentment" warranties under 4–208, and "encoding and retention" warranties under 4–209. Their function is to determine which parties bear what economic losses when certain things go wrong.

To illustrate the application of transfer and presentment warranties, suppose a check issued for $5,000 to Payee is altered by Payee to $15,000 and deposited in Depositary Bank. Depositary Bank sends the item to Collecting Bank which presents it for payment to Payor Bank and the item is finally paid. If payee has withdrawn the $15,000 and disappeared, who is responsible for the $10,000 loss beyond the original terms of the check? See 3–407.

The answer is Depositary Bank, the first solvent party after the thief. Although Payor Bank is liable to Drawer for paying an altered check, see 4–401(a), Payor Bank can shift that loss through warranty theory back to Depositary Bank. The reason is that a collecting bank which "transfers an item and receives a settlement * * * warrants to the transferee and to any subsequent collecting bank that * * * the item has not been altered." 4–207(a)(3). Similarly, a presenting bank which presents a check to and obtains payment from a payor bank warrants that the check "has not been altered." 4–208(a)(2). Payor Bank, therefore, can claim a breach of warranty by

Presenting Bank and recover "an amount equal to the amount paid plus expenses and loss of interest resulting from the breach." 4–208(d). Presenting Bank, in turn, can make the same claim against Depositary Bank under 4–207 and Depositary Bank can make the same claim against Payee, if that thief can be found.

More is said later about these warranties in Chapters 5 and 6 *infra*, which discuss check fraud.

2. Encoding Warranties

Section 4–209 deals with disputes where information is misencoded on the MICR line of the check. A "person who encodes information on or with respect to an item after issue warrants to any subsequent collecting bank and to the payor bank * * * that the information is correctly encoded." 4–209(a). Also, if the "customer of a depositary bank encodes, that bank also makes the warranty." Id. In either case, a person to whom the warranties were made and "who took the item in good faith may recover from the warrantor as damages for breach of warranty an amount equal to the loss suffered as a result of the breach, plus expenses and loss of interest incurred as a result of the breach." 4–209(c).

To illustrate, suppose, first, that the check was drawn for $5,000, Payee misencoded the amount of $15,000 on the MICR line and deposited the check in Depositary Bank. If Payor Bank pays, Customer may claim a recredit of $10,000, since only $5,000 was properly payable under 4–401(a). Payor Bank, however, can bypass any collecting banks and go directly against Depositary Bank for breach of an encoding warranty. Even though a customer encoded the information, Depositary Bank made a warranty. 4–209(a) (last sentence).

Suppose, second, that the check was drawn for $15,000, Depositary Bank misencoded $5,000 and Payor Bank paid $5,000. Here, Payor Bank is liable for the full amount of the check, since $15,000 was properly payable from Drawer's account. If Drawer's account contains $10,000 or more, Payor Bank can cover the loss by debiting that account for an additional $10,000 (beyond the $5000 already paid and debited). If Drawer's account contains less than $10,000, Payor Bank has a loss to the extent of the deficit and can sue Depositary Bank for that deficit under 4–209(c). See 4–209 comment 2.

F. ACTION REQUIRED OF PAYOR BANK UPON PRESENTMENT—DISHONOR BY TIMELY RETURN OR FINAL PAYMENT BY INACTION

The end of the collection chain is the collecting/presenting bank presenting Payee's check to Payor Bank for payment. The presenting bank may be the Depositary Bank having presented directly to Payor Bank; or, more likely, it is an intermediary/collecting bank through which Depositary Bank transferred the check for purposes of collection. In any event, the check gets duly presented.

Immediately or later the same banking day Payor Bank provisionally settles for the item, that is, the presenting bank gets credit for the check. This credit is not final payment, only provisional settlement.

Payor Bank has until its midnight deadline to dishonor the check. 4–301(a). Remember: when applied to any item received by a bank, the midnight deadline refers to midnight of the next banking day following the banking day of receipt. Dishonor occurs if by this time Payor Bank returns the item (or an image) or sends notice of dishonor or nonpayment if the item itself is not available for return. Article 4 requires returning the check to whichever bank presented it. 4–301(d)(1). Federal law preempts a tiny bit at this point by allowing Payor Bank to dishonor by returning the check to the Depositary Bank directly or indirectly by any other expeditious route. With a tiny exception discussed later, federal law preempts neither the time for a return, i.e., the midnight deadline, nor the consequences of acting within the time limit or missing it.

If the check is so timely returned and therefore dishonored, the effect is to trigger the consequences that attend dishonor under Article 3, mainly triggering the liabilities of the drawer and any indorser. If the check is not timely returned, the effects are final payment under Article 4; hardening of provisional settlements given by each bank throughout the collection process; and triggering of the Article 3 consequences of payment of an instrument, mainly discharge of liabilities.

Be careful! Payor Bank's internal decision to pay or dishonor is irrelevant. To illustrate, suppose a check drawn on Payor Bank is presented for payment by Collecting Bank at 1:00 a.m. on May 11. Payor Bank immediately, or after an initial computer run, makes a provisional settlement for the item before midnight on May 11. For whatever reason, Payor Bank returns the check to Collecting Bank before midnight on May 12. Final payment has not occurred. Rather, the check is dishonored.

On the other hand, if Payor Bank has made a provisional settlement on May 11 and does nothing on May 12, the item is finally paid when the midnight deadline expires. 4–301(a), 4–302(a) and 4–215(a)(3). The failure to make a timely dishonor *alone* is a final payment.

Suppose, however, that Payor Bank made a provisional settlement on May 11 and by 2:00 p.m. on May 12 completed the internal process of posting the check to Drawer's account. In short, Payor Bank completed all of its internal, operational steps, decided to pay the check and debited Drawer's account. Suppose, further, that at 3:00 p.m. Payor Bank for whatever reason decided to dishonor the check and returned the check before midnight. Payee of the check claims that final payment was made and that its provisional credit is final.

Under earlier law, a few cases held that final payment was made when the internal process of posting was completed and that an otherwise timely return before the midnight deadline was not effective. This approach required an inquiry into whether that process of posting had been completed. Presently, there is no reference to "process of posting" in 4–215. It is therefore clear that Payor Bank has until its midnight deadline to return the item regardless of any internal payment decisions. In short, final payment does not occur if the item is returned before midnight even though Payor Bank had, at one point, completed the process of posting and decided to pay it. This internal decision does not amount to final payment or limit Payor Bank's right of return by the midnight deadline under 4–301.

1. Excuse for Missing Midnight Deadline

Section 4–109(b) excuses delay by a collecting or payor bank "beyond time limits prescribed or permitted by this [Act] * * * if (i) the delay is caused by interruption of communication or computer facilities, suspension of payments by another bank, war, emergency conditions, failure of equipment, or other circumstances beyond the control of the bank and (ii) the bank exercises such diligence as the circumstances require."

Suppose Payor Bank missed its midnight deadline on checks it intended to dishonor because of a computer failure. Payor Bank can claim that the delay was caused by "failure of equipment," but the real question is whether Payor Bank exercised such "diligence as the circumstances require." Should Payor Bank have anticipated the circumstances and purchased a backup computer or made arrangements for alternative processing? If not, what efforts should be taken to minimize the delay after the equipment fails? These are familiar questions for which there are no pat answers.

Presumably, the fragility of complex computers and the likelihood of flood, storm, or maybe even terrorism dictate that a wide range of precautions be taken before excuse can be granted. The need for these precautions is foreseeable, and the occurrence of a foreseeable calamity is no basis for excuse under 4–109. Excuses the courts will accept are very rare.

2. Regulation CC—Supplemental Rules for Returning Checks

The primary aim of Regulation CC is to speed up the return process by providing for and requiring "expeditious return." Regulation CC accomplishes this goal by allowing a payor bank to return a dishonored check by sending it to the depositary bank directly or by other expeditious route. The federal rule prescribes various details and tests for making and measuring expeditious returns. In this respect, Regulation CC disputes and preempts the rule of Article 4 that the payor bank must dishonor by sending the check to the presenting bank or otherwise back through whatever channel the check followed in getting to the payor bank.

WARNING! Regulation CC does not preempt the basic midnight deadline rule of 4–301. A check that a payor bank fails to return by the midnight deadline is finally paid. Regulation CC does not disagree but changes only the process: requiring the use of expeditious ways and means of sending a timely returned check to the depositary bank.

FURTHER WARNING!! In an effort to encourage depositary banks to agree to receive returned checks electronically, the Federal Reserve Board has proposed two alternatives via amendments to Regulation CC. [Proposed Rule, 79 FR 6674 (Feb. 4, 2014). The premise is that electronic returns have already become expeditious, and that "requiring expeditious return of paper checks imposes substantial cost on banks returning checks." Id. at 6677. The proposals therefore alter a depositary bank's current rights to receive expeditious return or notice of nonpayment in regard to a paper check.

EVEN FURTHER WARNING!! A payor bank that violates Regulation CC by failing to return a dishonored check expeditiously does not thereby negate the dishonor under Article 4, as long as the rules of Article 4 are satisfied. The consequence of violating Regulation CC in this respect is liability for damages for actual losses under federal law, not a bungled dishonor and final payment under Article 4.

In a very small instance, however, Regulation CC preemptively changes the 4–301 midnight deadline rule. Suppose a check deposited in a bank in Hawaii is presented for payment, through various intermediary/collecting banks, to the drawee/payor bank in New Hampshire. Payor Bank decides to dishonor the check. Article 4 requires Payor Bank to return the check by sending it back through the banking channel the check followed to get to Payor Bank.

Regulation CC allows any practical route that is expeditious. So, Payor Bank could mail the check by overnight express to Depositary Bank as long as the check was actually sent, i.e., dispatched, by the 4–301 midnight deadline. Waiting to mail the check until the next morning would be too late. The check would be finally paid because the check was not returned, i.e., sent, before the midnight deadline. Final payment would result even if Depositary Bank would receive the late-mailed check sooner than if Payor Bank returned the check before midnight but through banking channels the check followed getting to New Hampshire.

Regulation CC provides:

> The deadline for return . . . under the U.C.C. [4–301] . . . is extended to the time of dispatch of such return . . . where a paying bank uses a means of delivery that would ordinarily result in receipt by the bank to which it is sent . . . [o]n or before the receiving bank's next banking day following the otherwise applicable deadline, . . . ; this deadline is extended further if a paying bank uses a highly expeditious means of transportation, even if this means of transportation would ordinarily result in delivery after the receiving bank's next . . . banking day. . . .

12 C.F.R. § 229.30(c) (which may also be modified by those newly proposed rules). This provision effectively says that missing the 4–301 midnight deadline is okay if Payor Bank returns the check using a highly expeditious means, which surely includes express, overnight mail that would deliver the dishonored check to Depositary Bank sooner than returning the check toward ordinary banking channels.

G. LARGE-DOLLAR NOTICE

Section 4–301 does not require a payor bank to notify anybody when the bank dishonors a check. The requirement is simply and only to return the check by the midnight deadline. Notice of the dishonor is a substitute only when the check itself is unavailable for return. (The dog ate it!)

Federal law adds something important here. Even when a payor bank makes a timely and otherwise proper return under 4–301, the bank is also bound to give quick, special notice if the item is for $2,500 or more. This special notice is required by a rule of Regulation CC commonly called the large-dollar notice requirement:

> If a paying bank determines not to pay a check in the amount of $2,500 or more, it shall provide notice of nonpayment such that the notice is received by the depositary bank by 4:00 p.m. (local time) on the second business day following the banking day on which the check was presented to the paying bank.

12 C.F.R. § 229.33(a).

WARNING! The large dollar notice would be altered if recently proposed amendments become final. [Proposed Rule, 79 FR 6674 (Feb. 4, 2014).] The consolidation of the regional check processing centers from 45 down to one has speeded up check return to such an extent that even small checks should be returned within the time frame set by the large-dollar notice, at least if electronically processed.

The notice carries no value, and is no substitute for returning the check in compliance with Regulation CC (the expeditious return rule) and U.C.C. 4–301 (the midnight deadline rule). To reiterate, this large-dollar notice requirement is currently in addition to the rule of Article 4 requiring a timely, proper 4–301 return in order to recover a settlement. Satisfying the large-dollar notice requirement does not satisfy 4–301. On the other hand, the large-dollar notice requirement is not part of 4–301, so that failing to meet the requirement does not bar a payor bank from recovering a settlement if 4–301 is met. The consequence of violating the large-dollar notice requirement is liability for damages under Regulation CC.

3. MORE ON FINAL PAYMENT BY PAYOR BANK

A. RELATIONSHIP BETWEEN FINAL PAYMENT AND ACCOUNTABILITY

Upon presentment of a check, Payor Bank's basic choice is to pay or dishonor the item. Usually, dishonor occurs because Payor Bank "makes timely return of the check or sends timely notice of dishonor or nonpayment under Section 4–301 or 4–302." 3–502(b)(1). Dishonor also occurs when Payor Bank becomes "accountable for the amount of the check under Section 4–302" but does not pay it. 3–502(b)(1). Under what circumstances is Payor Bank accountable for the amount of a "demand item" (check) that has not been finally paid?

WARNING! This issue is truly "inside baseball," which makes it a perfect candidate for (1) discussion and examination in law school and (2) debate among law professors. So, make sure you know your own teacher's answer.

Payor Bank is "accountable" for a check "whether properly payable or not, if the bank, in any case in which it is not also the depositary bank, retains the item beyond midnight of the banking day of receipt without settling for it or, whether or not it is also the depositary bank, does not pay or return the item or send notice of dishonor until after its midnight deadline. . . ." 4–302(a).

The key to understanding this statute is seeing that neither of its provisions applies whenever Payor Bank has paid the instrument. Accountability under 4–302 assumes no final payment. As a result, when Payor Bank has finally paid a check by failing timely to return it before the midnight deadline under 4–301, accountability under 4–302 is not possible.

Now, it's entirely possible that a payor bank that has failed timely to return a check and so finally paid it will revoke a settlement given for the item, even though the settlement is now final and legally irrevocable. It's not lawful, and the bank is liable for the tort of conversion. Nevertheless, the bank isn't "accountable" within the meaning of 4–302.

Accountability is really limited to the rare case in which an on us item is deposited with the payor bank, or a presenting bank presents for payment, and the payor bank does not provisionally settle for the item.

In this event, unless the bank acts within the prescribed time limits to dishonor or pay, the bank is then accountable and liable for the item under 4–302. This liability is needed because the bank cannot take the check and do nothing, and the self-effecting remedy of making a settlement final is not available because no settlement was made when the check was presented.

A clear example is where the check is presented to a payor bank that is not also the depositary bank. This means that the check is presented by Presenting Bank rather than a Payee-Customer and Payor Bank is expected to settle for it. If the check is presented on May 11, Payor Bank fails to settle by midnight on May 11, but Payor Bank sends a timely notice of dishonor before its midnight deadline on May 12, Payor Bank is accountable for the item. Section 4–302(a)(1) provides that Payor Bank is accountable for the item because it retained the item "beyond midnight of the banking day of receipt without settling for it." Note, however, that Payor Bank's accountability for the item (presumably to Presenting Bank) does not constitute final payment. See 4–215(a). Final payment requires that Payor Bank first make a timely provisional settlement and then fail to dishonor before its midnight deadline.

The same result would follow if the check were presented to Payor Bank which is also the depositary bank on May 11, no settlement was made before midnight on May 11, but Payor Bank sent a notice of dishonor on May 13. Here, Payor Bank in an "on us" transaction is not required to settle by midnight of the day of receipt. It is accountable for the item because it delayed the notice of dishonor until "after its midnight deadline" on May 12. 4–302(a)(1). The delay, however, does not amount to final payment under 4–215(a), because Payor Bank neither paid cash nor settled for the item.

Bottom line: in the case of a typical check in the typical case, 4–302(a) never applies and Payor Bank is never accountable under 4–302 because, in practice, payor banks always timely, provisionally settle for checks deposited by their customers or presented for payment by presenting banks, and they usually settle with credit to an account of the customer or bank. So, with respect to checks payor banks finally pay by failing to return them by the midnight deadline, the consequence is that the settlements become final and legally cannot be revoked. If the payor bank nevertheless revokes a final settlement, the action is unlawful and the bank is liable for stealing. The basis of liability, however, is not 4–302 accountability.

Told you it was inside baseball.

B. RESTITUTION FOR MISTAKEN PAYMENT DESPITE FINAL PAYMENT

How "final" is final payment under 4–215? The answer is that "final" means "final" under Article 4 and Regulation CC, but that 3–418 provides a limited exception for Payor Bank when payment is made by mistake. There is a statutory right to recover in cases of stop orders and forged checks. 3–418(a). In all other cases, recovery for mistaken payments is determined "by the law governing mistake and restitution." 3–418(b).

The remedy of restitution was mentioned in the last chapter and is discussed in the cases of stop payment orders in Chapter 4 and forged checks in Chapter 5, *infra*.

For now, one simple example will suffice. Suppose Payor Bank finally paid Payee's check by failing to dishonor before its midnight deadline. See 4–215(a)(3). The next day it discovered that there were insufficient funds in Drawer's account. Payment was due to a careless mistake.

Read 3–418 in its entirety. Note that 3–418(a) does not apply here, since payment was not on the mistaken belief that payment had not been stopped or the signature of the drawer was not forged. The mistake involved the amount of funds in the drawer's account. Section 3–418(b), however, does apply since the check was paid "by mistake and the case is not covered by subsection (a)." Unlike 3–418(a), 3–418(b) does not explicitly provide that Payor Bank can recover "the amount of the draft from the person to whom or for whose benefit payment was made." Rather, mistaken Payor Bank may "to the extent permitted by the law governing mistake and restitution * * * recover the payment from the person to whom or for whose benefit payment was made." Thus, Payor Bank must take a trip through 1–103 to other state law to determine whether there is any right to recover. Furthermore, that right may, under 3–418(b), be limited if Payor Bank failed to exercise ordinary care.

In all cases, however, the right to recover is limited by 3–418(c): A person who "took the instrument in good faith and for value or who in good faith changed position in reliance on the payment" will not be liable. The amount of the check can probably be recovered from a payee who did not take the check in good faith and for value or did not in good faith change position in reliance on the payment. In a direct recovery from the payee, the effect is that the "instrument is deemed not to have been paid or accepted and is treated as dishonored, and the person from whom payment is recovered has rights as a person entitled to enforce the dishonored instrument." 3–418(d).

Here's one final note. Even though Payor Bank cannot recover the amount of the check from the payee, it might have a claim against a collecting bank for breach of warranty. See 3–418(c), last sentence. That claim will not work in this case, because no one in the forward collection process ever warrants that Drawer's account will contain sufficient funds. This is a risk which Payor Bank assumes. See 4–207 & 4–208.

4. DISHONORED CHECKS

A. RIGHTS AND REMEDIES OF THE DEPOSITARY BANK

Okay. You're tired of reading about final payment of a check. What happens when the opposite happens: the check is dishonored. You already know the consequences under Article 3 (or can read about them in Chapter 2, *supra*): dishonor triggers the Article 3 liabilities of the drawer and any indorser on the instrument and also resurrects liability on any underlying obligation for which the instrument was taken.

Article 4 adds a few wrinkles when the check was deposited as an "on us" item or presented for payment by the depositary or other presenting bank. In both of these cases the most important Article 4 wrinkles concern the rights of the depositary bank.

The depositary bank will have given a provisional credit to the person who deposited the check. This person is a "customer" whether or not she maintains her own account at the bank. In real life, however, she usually has an account there because banks usually won't take checks for deposit or collection from people without accounts.[10]

In the case of an "on us" item, the bank will have dishonored by sending the dishonored check physically or electronically back to its customer who deposited it. In the case of a check presented by the depositary bank directly or indirectly through a presenting bank, the payor bank will have sent the check directly or indirectly to the depositary bank. Also, any settlement the depositary bank received for the item in the forward-collection process will have been lost. So, to this point the depositary bank is out

---

[10] The story is different if a customer without an account walks into a bank and presents for payment in cash over the counter a check drawn against the bank. The bank cannot simply refuse service without consequence. For one thing, this refusal would amount to dishonor of the check, which might well violate the bank's deposit agreement with the drawer.

of balance: it credited the account of the customer who deposited the check but has itself finally received nothing. What to do?

The answer, of course, is to take back the credit given the customer when the check was deposited, which Article 4 allows. Here's the rule in simplified, dissected parts:

1. If a depositary bank has made provisional settlement with its customer for a check that the customer deposited for collection, **and**
2. the check is dishonored and therefore not finally paid, **and**
3. the bank itself therefore fails to receive a final settlement for the check, then the bank may:
    a. revoke the settlement it gave to its customer,
    b. charge back the amount of any credit given for the item to the customer's account, **or**
    c. obtain refund from its customer, **so long as the bank**
4. returns the item or notice of the facts to its customer by midnight of the next banking bank following the banking day on which the bank learned the facts (i.e., another midnight deadline rule) or within a longer reasonable time after the bank learns the facts.

4–214(a) & (b). In addition, the bank retains any common-right right of setoff against the customer's account, which largely, functionally mirrors the 4–214 right of charge back.

Note that this 4–214 charge back is not limited to the specific funds somehow attributable to the dishonored check. Charge back applies against any funds in the account.

The customer then recoups by suing parties liable on the check or suing on the underlying transaction for which the check was taken. These actions are available under Article 3 and discussed in the previous chapter.

What if the account is not sufficient to cover a charge back? The customer may have deposited the check, later deposited other funds, but wiped out the account before the check was later dishonored and returned by the payor bank. Or, the depositary bank that was not also the payor bank may have "cashed" the check for its customer who left the bank with the money in hand.[11]

In this event the depositary bank "enjoys" several options. First, the bank can sue its customer on a couple of theories. The customer is liable on the basis of 4–214, which allows the depositary bank to "obtain refund from its customer." Second, the customer probably indorsed the check when she deposited it.

---

[11] Cashing the check in this case is not final payment resulting from presenting the check for payment in cash over the counter, which only happens when the bank to which the check is presented is the payor bank. As stated in the text, the depositary bank is not the payor bank; and giving a customer cash in such a case is, in itself, a provisional settlement that the depositary bank can recoup under 4–214.

The check has been dishonored. The bank is a holder and thus a person entitled to enforce the instrument. Therefore, the bank can sue the customer as indorser of the check.

Any other indorser on the check is also liable to the bank, and the bank can pick any of them to sue. Of course, the drawer is liable, too. In suing anybody liable on the check, the bank may enjoy the freedom from claims and defenses that Article 3 gives a holder in due course.

Let's suppose that the customer's account is empty and, in fact, the customer is generally insolvent. So, going after the customer on any theory makes no sense. Depositary Bank therefore sues the drawer on the check. Drawer, however, has a defense based on the underlying transactions between drawer and customer for which the check was issued and taken.

Depositary Bank is subject to this defense unless the bank is a holder in due course. In the typical case, when deciding if the bank enjoys this status, the question is whether or not the bank gave value within the meaning of the requirements for due-course status. The value requirement is fully defined under Article 3. See 3–303(a). For this case, Article 4 adds some complementary pieces. See 4–211; 4–210. Here's how they work together in this case.

1. Under Article 3, value includes acquiring a security interest or other lien in the instrument. 3–303(a)(2).

2. Article 4 agrees: "[f]or purposes of determining its status as a holder in due

course, a bank has given value to the extent it has a security interest in an item. . . ." 4–211.

3. Then, 4–210 explains when a collecting bank [which includes Depositary Bank in our case] has a security interest in an item, which includes: "in case of an item deposited in an account, to the extent to which credit given for the item has been withdrawn or applied." 4–210(a)(1).

This fits our case perfectly. Depositary Bank gave its customer a provisional credit for the check when the customer deposited it. This credit, along with everything else in the account, has been withdrawn by the customer. Thus, Depositary Bank has a security interest in the check, has given value for the item, and is a holder in due course (assuming, as is usually true, all the other requirements have been satisfied). In the end, therefore, Depositary Bank is immune from the drawer's personal defenses and wins in the bank's suit on the check against the drawer.

Suppose the customer's account is not empty. It is filled with money sufficient to cover a charge back. Can the bank decide to prefer its customer, not pursue her on any theory, and go straight after another indorser or the drawer? Yes. The problem for the bank is establishing holder in due course status if the drawer has personal defenses to her liability on the check. Again the issue is value.

The problem goes away without adding more law if the bank can prove that, even though the account is now full, the customer withdrew "the" credit given for the check on which the drawer is liable. The bank would make this case using appropriate, common-law principles of tracing or the like.

Suppose "the" credit is still there. In defining when a bank has a security interest in an item, and thereby defining value, 4–210 adds: "in case of an item for which it [the bank] has given credit available for withdrawal as of right, to the extent of the credit given, *whether or not* the credit is drawn upon or there is a right of charge-back." 4–210(a)(2) (emphasis added). The bank confronts two problems in relying on this rule. The first problem is proving that the customer, though she has not actually withdrawn the credit, could have done so, i.e., she had a right to withdraw it. This issue is decided, in turn, by other rules providing when such a right exists, which are described in the next chapter. It is important to understand, here and there, that in the typical case and absent an unusual agreement, no such right attaches as soon as a check is deposited in a customer's account. There is a waiting period.

The second problem for the bank flows from this delay in the accrual of the right to withdraw. Even if the right eventually attached so that the bank is deemed to have given value for the credit, the bank will not be a holder in due course if it acquired disqualifying notice before the right attached and the value was thus given. Remember: giving value is only one of the requirements for holder in due course status. The bank must satisfy all of the other Article

3 requirements in order to win due-course status and thereby take free of the drawer's personal defenses.

B. RIGHTS AND REMEDIES OF THE CUSTOMER

1. When the Check Is Dishonored

In the situation where the depositary bank rightfully exercises the rights and remedies of 4–214, the customer who deposited the check and is the victim of these remedies has no recourse against the depositary or the payor bank. She must look to her rights and remedies that are triggered by the dishonor of the check. Mainly, she can sue parties liable to her on the check and on the underlying transaction. See Chapter 2 *supra*. These remedies assume, however, that the check really was dishonored. If the check was bounced but not truly dishonored, the customer can't sue on the instrument or the underlying transaction. Her remedies are entirely something else. See below.

2. When the Check Is Bounced Despite Final Payment

A payor bank that misses the 4–301 midnight deadline loses the right to dishonor and return the check. The check is finally paid. The bank nevertheless retains the ability to treat the check as dishonored; send it back through collection channels; and recoup the settlement the payor bank gave upon presentment. This conduct is unlawful under Article 4 but it happens.

The check will bounce back to the depositary bank which is unlikely to notice the payor bank's tackiness and will likely treat the check as if the check had been dishonored. Therefore, in the ordinary course of things the depositary bank will charge back the check against the account of the customer who deposited it or pursue the other rights and remedies that 4–214 provides.

The problem for the depositary bank is that charge back and the other 4–214 rights and remedies are conditioned on the check having been dishonored. Therefore, the depositary bank cannot sue anybody on the check. The liabilities of the drawer and any indorser were discharged by the payor bank's final payment of the check.

Also, because all the 4–214 rights and remedies are conditioned on dishonor, charging back the check against the customer's account is illegal. The customer can force the depositary bank to re-credit her account; and the depositary bank in turn can recover from the payor bank. Probably, the customer could skip the depositary bank and recover directly from the payor bank, but the direct action is practically unnecessary and too costly.

Additionally, the wrongful charge back may have reduced the customer's account so as to cause dishonor of the customer's own checks drawn against her account that would have been paid but for the charge back. In this event the depositary bank—now cast in this role as the customer's payor bank with respect to checks the customer has drawn—will be liable for wrongful dishonor, which is a serious wrong with wide damages discussed in the next chapter.

CHAPTER 4

CHECKING ACCOUNTS

The previous chapter on check collection mainly considers the rights and liabilities of banks with respect to payees and other persons entitled to enforce checks. This chapter focuses on the rights and liabilities of a payor bank to its customer who owns the account against which the checks are drawn. Checking accounts, like check collection, are mainly governed by Article 4.

The general question is what are the bank's rights, duties, and liabilities to the customer when the bank either dishonors or pays a check drawn against the customer's account. A more specific context for this question is the very large subset of cases involving various kinds of check fraud. These cases and the associated legal issues are so common and important they deserve separate treatment, which is further explained in Chapters 5 and 6 *infra*.

1. BASIC RELATIONSHIP BETWEEN CUSTOMER AND BANK

A. DEFINED MAINLY BY DEPOSIT AGREEMENT

Whenever a person opens a checking or other account (4–104(a)(1)) at a bank, certain rules govern the rights and duties of the person, known as the "customer" (4–104(a)(5)) and the bank, known as the payor bank. A fundamental source of these rules is a "deposit agreement" between the parties, and thus the basic relationship is contractual and governed by contract law unless displaced by statute.

Depending upon the type of checking or other account that is created, this agreement normally provides information about the account and states the terms and conditions of the relationship, including the circumstances under which the payor bank is required to pay checks drawn against the account. For example, the agreement may require a minimum balance to avoid service charges, give Customer an option to elect overdraft protection, detail procedures for stop payment orders, provide a schedule of charges for certain services, and disclose when funds deposited are available for withdrawal. Most important, the agreement will specify who is authorized to draw checks against the account. Typically, deposit agreements are standard forms prepared by Payor Bank and offered on a take-it-or-leave-it basis.

The contractual relationship between the customer and bank and their agreement include, by default, the rules of Article 4 that apply to deposits. Be forewarned, however, that many of these rules, which are discussed below, may be varied by the parties' deposit agreement, except for the duties to act in good faith and to exercise ordinary care. See 4–103(a).

B. "PROPERLY PAYABLE" DEFINES MAIN DUTIES

The most important question with respect to a bank's handling of a customer's checking account is when the bank must or may pay checks drawn against the account and thereafter charge the customer's account for them. The answer is when the item is "properly payable," i.e., when it is (1) "authorized by the customer" and (2) "is in accordance with any agreement between the customer and bank." 4–401(a). Remember: when a check is presented to and paid by the payor bank, the payment is made with the bank's own funds or other credit. To the extent that the check is properly payable, however, the bank is acting for the drawer-customer and is allowed to recoup the payment by charging the customer's account.

A check is "authorized by the customer" when it is drawn by Customer and issued to a named payee or her order and presented for payment by that payee or other person entitled to enforce the check (directly or through a collecting bank). In this event, and if the check is otherwise in accordance with the deposit agreement, the bank must pay the check and can charge the customer's account. If the bank dishonors the check on these facts, the bank acts wrongfully and is liable for **wrongful dishonor**.

A check is not authorized if either the Customer's (drawer's) signature or the payee's indorsements are unauthorized (forged), see 1–201(b)(41), or the instrument is altered. See 3–407. Similarly, a check is not authorized for payment if, among other things, there is a valid stop payment order or the account has been closed. See 4–403. In this event, the check is not properly payable. The bank should dishonor the check; and, even if the bank pays the check, the bank cannot charge the customer's account for the amount of the check. The payment comes out of the bank's own funds; and, except in certain limited situations, the bank must cover the loss itself and cannot look to the customer's account or other property.

An authorized check can be dishonored by the bank if the check is otherwise inconsistent with the deposit agreement. This occurs most often when there are insufficient funds in the customer's account to cover the check and the deposit agreement does not require the bank to pay overdrafts. This is a classic case of "rightful" dishonor.

2. WRONGFUL DISHONOR IN GENERAL

A. WHEN IS A DISHONOR WRONGFUL?

Payor Bank's dishonor is "wrongful" if it "dishonors an item that is properly payable." 4–402(a). The most common example of "wrongful dishonor" is dishonor caused by Payor Bank's mistaken determination that the customer's account had insufficient funds to cover the check or that the account had been closed. In this case the check was, in fact, properly payable, and the bank's dishonor breached the deposit contract which, on these facts, required the bank to pay the check, not dishonor it.

1. Funds Availability

Now here's an important question: what credits in the drawer-customer's account does the payor bank count when determining if the funds in the account are sufficient to cover a check? Suppose, for example, that at the start of the day on Monday, the customer had a firm balance of $200. Later in the day she deposited cash or a check from her employer for $300. The next day a check for $450 she herself wrote against her account is presented for payment. In deciding if there are sufficient funds, do you count the cash or check deposited the day before?

If the bank is required to count the employer's check, the bank must pay the $450 check the customer wrote and acts wrongfully by dishonoring it. If the bank is not required to count the employer's check, the bank can freely dishonor the check, except in the unusual case of a special agreement with the customer that requires the bank to pay overdrafts. This question translates in legal terms to the issue: when are credits deposited to an account "available" so that the customer can withdraw the funds and, also, so that the credits must be counted for determining sufficiency of the account to cover checks the customer has drawn against the account.

Regulation CC is the principal and pre-emptive law governing this issue known as "funds availability." The regulation prescribes the availability of funds by a complicated schedule that turns on the nature of the deposit. Deposits that carry a low risk of fraud must be made available sooner than ordinary checks. The schedule assumes that the time a depositary bank can hold credit for ordinary checks should roughly correspond to the time ordinarily required to collect the items. Availability that is earlier than the time usually needed for collection increases the risk of fraud because of the greater chance that the funds will become available and will be withdrawn before notice of dishonor.

Outlined here is a shortened, very summary version of the availability schedule that shows only its biggest, most general points. Be aware that the schedule distinguishes between business and banking days. "*Business day*" means a calendar day other than a Saturday, Sunday, or certain stated dates that are holidays observed by the Federal Reserve. 12 C.F.R. § 229.2(g). "*Banking day*" means the part of any business day on which an office of a bank is open to the public for carrying on substantially all of its banking functions. 12 C.F.R. § 229.2(f).

a. Low-Risk Deposits—Next-Day Availability

The following kinds of deposits must be available for withdrawal at the start of business on the next business day following the banking day of receipt:

- Cash,
- Electronic payments (including wire transfers and Automated Clearing House (ACH) credit transfers),
- Certain government checks,
- Bank checks (such as cashier's, certified, and teller's checks),
- "On us" items, and
- $200 of all other checks deposited on the same banking day (which will be periodically

adjusted for inflation) 12 U.S.C.A. § 4002(a)(2)(D); 4006(f).[1]

b. Local Checks—Second-Day Availability

Until recently, the Federal Reserve Board adopted different time frames for availability depending upon whether a check was drawn on a local bank (a "local" check), or on a bank in a different check processing region (a "nonlocal" check). As a result of electronic processing, however, the 45 check processing centers that existed in 2003 were consolidated into two sites —"the Atlanta Fed handles electronic check processing and the Cleveland Fed, paper check processing."[2] Thereafter, there were no longer any nonlocal checks. The Board has proposed amendments to Regulation CC to reflect that reality [Proposed Rule, 76 F.R. 16862 (March 25 (2011)], which would eliminate all reference in Regulation CC to nonlocal checks. Meanwhile, all checks are subject to the rules currently mandated for "local checks."

Local checks must be available for withdrawal at the start of business on the **second business day** following the banking day when the funds were deposited. 12 C.F.R. § 229.12(b)(1). For example, a local check deposited on Monday must be available for withdrawal on Wednesday.

---

[1] These changes are not yet reflected in the corresponding regulations. See 12 C.F.R. § 229.10(c)(1)(vii)(A).

[2] *See Supporting the Nation's Payment System: Check Processing,* Federal Reserve Bank of Philadelphia, https://www.philadelphiafed.org/about-the-fed/who-we-are/payment-system.cfm (last visited Sept. 26, 2014).

2. Time for Determining Funds Sufficiency

Suppose a check for $1,000 is presented on Monday. On Tuesday at 10:00 a.m., Payor Bank determines—in line with the funds availability rules of Regulation CC—that Customer's account contains only $999 and decides to dishonor. At 11:00 a.m., Customer deposits $1 in cash, which is provisionally credited to its account. The account balance, however, is not checked again and Payor Bank dishonors the check before the midnight deadline. Is this a wrongful dishonor?

The answer is no. To paraphrase, 4–402(c) states that Payor Bank can determine the status of Customer's account "at any time between the time the item is received by the payor bank and the time that the payor bank returns the item or gives notice in lieu of return, and no more than one determination need be made." The "one" determination was made at 10:00 a.m. on Tuesday. If, however, Payor Bank had again checked the balance at 3:00 p.m. to reevaluate the situation, "the account balance at that time is determinative of whether a dishonor for insufficiency of available funds is wrongful." Id. The decision to check again, however, is "at the election of the payor bank." Thus, even though Payor Bank elected not to pay the overdraft, see 4–402(a), and not to check again, the dishonor is still rightful.

Remember, a deposit in cash "made in person to an employee of the depositary bank" is not available for withdrawal until the "business day after the banking day on which the cash is deposited." 12 C.F.R. § 229.10(a)(1). Even if Payor Bank checked again at

3:00 p.m. on Tuesday, the $1 cash deposit would not be available as a matter of right until Wednesday. Obviously, Payor Bank could permit Customer to withdraw, but is not required to do so. Section 4–402(c), on re-determination by Payor Bank, speaks of "available funds." Technically, the $1 cash deposit is not available unless a provisional credit is given, and a dishonor for insufficient funds, therefore, would be right.

3. Order of Paying Checks Presented at the Same Time

Suppose that the funds in the customer's account have been calculated accurately. The account contains $1,000 in available funds. At the same time, however, two checks for $600 each are presented for payment. The bank cannot rightly dishonor both checks. By what rule does the bank decide which check to pay and which check to dishonor? In the simple case where the checks are ordinary checks without any special priority by other law, the answer is very simple: "items may be . . . paid . . . or charged to the indicated account of its customer in any order" the bank chooses, 4–303(b), though surely a degree of good faith is required. For more complicated cases of special priority, see the discussion later in this chapter.

4. Overdrafts

Overdraft refers to a check that exceeds the funds available in the customer's account when the check is presented for payment. It is sometimes called an NSF check, which means "not sufficient funds." In the typical case, the bank is free to dishonor the check because the typical deposit agreement does not require the bank to pay NSF checks.

Even in this typical case, the bank may pay an NSF check. It may pay, but is not required to. Why would the bank pay? The usual answer is to accommodate its customer. If the bank does pay an NSF check, the bank can charge the amount of the check to the customer's account. 4–401(a). The check is deemed properly payable despite the insufficiency of funds in the account.

Great! What good is the right to charge the account, which is insufficient to cover the item? Well, maybe the account will fill with new funds, which then cover the overdraft. If not, the customer is personally liable to the bank for the amount of the unpaid overdraft.

Suppose the account is a "joint" account, meaning that any of two or more people can draw checks against the account. Is everyone with access to the account liable for overdrafts drawn by any one of them? The rule is: "[a] customer is not liable for the amount of an overdraft if the customer neither signed the item nor benefited from the proceeds of the item." 4–401(b).

Sometimes the bank agrees with a customer in the deposit agreement or otherwise that the bank will pay—is required to pay—overdrafts. The arrangement is a kind of credit line. In this case, dishonoring an overdraft that is within the terms of the agreement is wrongful dishonor.

B. REMEDIES FOR WRONGFUL DISHONOR

1. Liability to Whom

A payor bank's liability for wrongful dishonor runs to "its customer." 4–402(b). " 'Customer' means a person having an account with a bank or from whom a bank has agreed to collect items, including a bank that maintains an account at another bank." 4–104(a)(5). The payee or transferee of the check is not a customer for purposes of 4–402, even though she maintains her own account at the bank. She is not wronged by the bank's rightful or wrongful dishonor of checks drawn against somebody else's account and so cannot recover under 4–402. The remedy of the person entitled to enforce the check, which was dishonored, is to sue on the check or underlying transaction.

Who is the payor bank's "customer" in the case of an account in the name of a partnership or corporation? Following the restrictive definition of customer, most courts have held that an individual who signed a check on behalf of a partnership or corporation cannot herself recover for wrongful dishonor of the item even though the individual maintains a separate personal account with the payor bank.

2. Liability for Damages

A wrongful dishonor is a breach of the bank's contract with its customer. Since the account of Customer is *not* debited, the damages for breach are consequential rather than direct. Customer is not demanding that its account be re-credited by Payor Bank. Rather, Customer may seek damages for the impact, both economic (Customer may lose business) and physical (Customer may suffer mental anguish), of the wrongful dishonor on Customer and its relationships with others.

Section 4–402(b) provides the measure of damages for wrongful dishonor. Payor Bank is liable for "damages proximately caused by the wrongful dishonor of an item." But liability is "limited to actual damages proved" and whether consequential damages "are proximately caused by the wrongful dishonor is a question of fact to be determined in each case." Actual damages, however, "may include damages for an arrest or prosecution of the customer or other consequential damages."

3. WRONGFUL PAYMENT IN THE ABSENCE OF FRAUD OR FORGERY

A. IN GENERAL

Wrongful payment means that the payor bank has paid a check that is not properly payable under the deposit agreement with the customer against whose account the check was drawn. The payment, though wrongful against the customer, is fully effective under Article 4 to make final any settlements and to discharge liabilities under Article 3. The bank, however, is not entitled to charge the customer's account for the amount of the item. To do so is wrongful against the customer, who is entitled to have her account re-credited and in appropriate circumstances to recover other damages the wrongful payment caused.

Payment of a check may be unauthorized by Customer and thus wrongful in a number of circumstances. Cases of fraud and forgery will be discussed in Chapter 5 *infra*. This Section identifies and discusses several other potential limitations on Payor Bank's power to pay: (1) stop payment orders, 4–303 & 4–403; (2) account closed, 4–403(a), (3) postdated, 4–401(c), or stale, 4–404, checks; and (4) death or incompetence of the customer. 4–405.

In these situations, Customer or its representative will claim that payment was wrongful and seek to have its account recredited for the amount of the check. In addition, Customer may have consequential damages if the wrongful payment results in a wrongful dishonor of subsequent items. See 4–403(c).

Payor Bank's liability, however, will generally depend upon whether Payor or its representative has communicated the information imposing a limitation and whether Payor Bank has a "reasonable opportunity to act on it." See 4–403(a). Furthermore, Payor Bank may have no or reduced liability if, despite a wrongful payment, Customer would have been liable to the payee or a holder in due course in any event. In short, 4–407 subrogates Payor Bank to the rights against Customer of (1) any holder in due course, 4–407(1), or (2) the "payee or any other holder of the item against the drawer or maker either on the item or under the transaction out of which the item arose." 4–407(2).

B. STOP PAYMENT ORDERS: 4–403

1. Elements and Duration

Section 4–403(a) states what is required of Customer, in the absence of a varying agreement, to stop payment of a check drawn on the account. The duration of the effectiveness of the stop order is controlled by 4–403(b).

a. Who May Stop Payment

The "customer or any person authorized to draw on the account" may stop payment. 4–403(a). If the signature of "more than one person is required to draw on an account, any of these persons may stop payment." Id. The payee of a check, therefore, may not stop payment. Id. comment 2.

b. Form and Content of Order

The stop payment order to the bank may be written or oral and must describe the item "with reasonable certainty." 4–403(a) & comment 6. The deposit agreement, however, may require the order to be written or electronic, although most banks will honor an initial oral order and require written or electronic confirmation. The deposit agreement will also specify what information identifies the stopped item with "reasonable certainty." Thus, Customer may be required to furnish the check number, the amount, the date of the check and the name of the payee.

c. *Time and Manner of Order: Priority Under 4–303(a)*

The order must be made "at a time and in a manner that affords the bank a reasonable opportunity to act on it before any action by the bank with respect to the item described in Section 4–303." 4–403(a). Section 4–303 establishes priority between the item presented by Payee and other events affecting the Payor Bank's right or duty to pay the item. Some of the events specified in 4–303(a) include notice to Payor Bank of Customer's insolvency, a judicial lien imposed on Customer's account or a setoff by Payor Bank against Customer's account. If these events are timely, i.e., Payor Bank has a reasonable time to act upon them before final payment, they freeze or reduce Customer's account for the benefit of Customer's creditors and "terminate, suspend, or modify the bank's right or duty to pay an item." 4–303(a). In short, the payee is out of luck.

In this case, the race is between Customer's stop order and Payor Bank's final payment of payee's check. To illustrate, suppose Customer issues a check for $1,000 to Payee in payment for an oriental rug on Monday, October 5. On Tuesday, October 6, Payee deposits the check in Depositary Bank and Customer discovers that the rug is not merchantable. On Wednesday, October 7, the check is presented for payment to Payor Bank in the morning and Customer issues a proper oral stop order to Payor Bank in the afternoon. If Payor Bank does not dishonor the check by midnight, Thursday, October 8, there will be final payment. Does the oral stop order give Payor Bank "a reasonable opportunity" to act on it before any events occur under 4–303?

The answer is no if the October 7 stop order is "received * * * and a reasonable time for the bank to act thereon expires * * * *after* the earliest of the following: * * * (4) the bank becomes accountable for the amount of the item under Section 4–302."[3] 4–303(a) (emphasis added). In our illustration, if Payor Bank pays the check on October 8, it must establish that a "reasonable time" to process the stop order expired on October 9 after the check had been paid. This is highly unlikely on these facts. A closer case—one where Customer could lose—is where the stop order is received in the late afternoon of October 8.[4]

Note, however, that Payor Bank can always act fast to favor its customer so long as it dishonors before the midnight deadline. Under revised Article 4, both final payment under 4–215 and priorities under 4–303 are determined without reference to Payor Bank's internal decision process. Thus, even if Payor Bank decides on October 8 at 3:00 p.m. to pay

---

[3] Note that 4–303(b) establishes a priority system for competing checks that arrive on the same day. Unless limited by 4–303(a), they may be "accepted, paid, certified, or charged to the indicated account of its customer in any order."

[4] This likelihood is increased if Payor Bank has fixed a cutoff hour for receipt of stop orders under 4–303(a)(5) and the stop order is made after that time.

the check and posts it to and files it in Customer's account, it may still honor a 4:00 p.m. oral stop order by reversing that decision and dishonoring the check before its midnight deadline.

d. Duration

An original, written stop order is effective for six months and "may be renewed for additional six-month periods by a record given to the bank within a period during which the stop-payment order is effective." 4–403(b).

A stop order, however, "lapses after 14 calendar days if the original order was oral and was not confirmed in a record within that period." Id. Section 4–403(b), therefore, permits an oral stop order, but conditions its duration upon a written or electronic confirmation. 3–103(a)(14). Most banks accept stop orders over the telephone and promptly send a written or electronic confirmation form for execution within the 14 day period. This is true even though the deposit agreement may require the original stop order to be in writing. Perhaps this practice is motivated by a desire to preserve customer relations and doubts about whether such agreements are against public policy. See 4–403 comment 1, stating a strong policy in favor of stop orders. Clearly, a deposit agreement exculpating Payor Bank's responsibility for exercising ordinary care in handling a stop order would be unenforceable. 4–103(a).

2. Bank and Certified Checks

Despite some prior disagreement in the cases and among the commentators, it is now clear that a customer who purchases a cashier's or teller's check or obtains the certification of a check drawn by it cannot stop payment under 4–403. See 4–403 comment 4. See Chapter 7 *infra*.

3. Damages, 4–403(c)

Suppose Customer has $10,000 in a checking account with Payor Bank. On Monday, October 5, Customer issues a check for $5,000 to Payee #1 to pay for a used car. On Tuesday, October 6, Customer decides that he does not like the car and issues an effective stop payment order to Payor Bank. On the same day, Customer issues a check for $7,500 to Payee #2 to pay for another used car. Payor Bank, due to negligence, pays the $5,000 check over the stop order and subsequently dishonors the $7,500 check for insufficient funds. What relief is available to Customer?

Without more, Customer is entitled to have its account re-credited in the amount of $5,000. There was a "wrongful" payment. In addition, Customer is entitled to any damages established under 4–403(c) for the wrongful dishonor of the check issued to Payee #2. 4–403(c). Clearly, the $7,500 check would have been honored if Payor Bank had not improperly paid the $5,000 over the stop payment order. Customer, however, has the "burden of establishing the fact and amount of loss resulting from the payment of an item contrary to a stop-payment order." 4–403(c).

4. Payor Bank's Subrogation Rights, 4–407

Section 4–407 provides Payor Bank with a defense to Customer's suit for "wrongful" dishonor damages, including payment over a stop order. To "prevent unjust enrichment and only to the extent necessary to prevent loss to the bank by reason of its payment of the item," Payor Bank is given limited, statutory subrogation rights. Id.

To illustrate, suppose in our example above that Payee #1 negotiated the $5,000 check to a holder in due course and it was paid on due presentment. If that payment was "wrongful," Payor bank is subrogated to the "rights * * * of any holder in due course on the item against the drawer." 4–407(1). Those rights are strong and would prevail over Customer unless there was a "real" defense. On the other hand, if there is no holder in due course, Payor Bank is subrogated to the rights of "the payee or any other holder of the item against the drawer * * * either on the item or under the transaction out of which the item arose." 4–407(2). These rights are weaker and are subject to a wider range of possible defenses arising from the underlying transaction.

Although the statute is somewhat ambiguous, the order of procedure should unfold as follows. First, Customer should prove the damages caused by the wrongful payment under 4–403(c) without regard to the underlying transaction. Put differently, Customer need not prove the presence of a defense against any holder at this stage of the procedure. Second, Payor Bank should, as a defense, assert that it is subrogated to the right of the payee or a holder in due course to enforce the check against Customer. If Payor Bank fails to make the claim, Customer wins. Third, if Payor Bank asserts its subrogation rights, the burden shifts to Customer to establish that those rights were subject to valid defenses and that, in fact, Customer had no obligation to pay. If defenses are established, Payor Bank's subrogation defense is defeated and a judgment should enter for Customer.

Of course, Payor Bank could re-credit Customer's account in the amount of $5,000 and settle for any other damages caused. In this case, Payor Bank is subrogated to the rights of "the drawer * * * against the payee or any other holder of the item with respect to the transaction out of which the item arose." 4–407(3). Thus, if Customer, as a buyer, had a defense against Payee #1, the seller, and could reject the goods and cancel the contract, Payor Bank could assert those defenses and recover the $5,000 purchase price from the payee. See 2–711(1).

C. ORDER CLOSING ACCOUNT

An order by Customer closing a bank account is treated like a stop payment order for purposes of "wrongful" honor disputes, whether the question is effectiveness, duration, damages or subrogation. See 4–403 & 4–407. Thus, the stop payment analysis, above, applies to orders closing the account.

The deposit agreement, however, may give Payor Bank discretion to pay checks drawn on a closed account for a stated period after closure. Under such an agreement, a payment after closure is not wrongful. Such a policy, however, must be part of the agreement or, at the very least, communicated to Customer. A unilateral, internal bank policy will not be effective.

D. UNTIMELY CHECKS

1. Post-Dated Checks

A check is post-dated when the date in the upper right hand corner is later than the date of issue. In theory, the date of the check limits Payor Bank's power to pay. Thus, payment before that date would be wrongful.

Under 4–401(c), however, this theory is conditioned. Customer, to establish liability, must have "given notice to the bank of the postdating describing the check with reasonable certainty." Further, the notice, its effectiveness and the time Payor Bank may have to act on it are governed by 4–403 on stop payments. In short, 4–401(c) requires a post-dating notice that is treated, for all intents and purposes, like a stop payment order. The sensible reason for this treatment is that the date of a check, unlike its amount, will not be encoded in the MICR line and, under current practice at least, will not be kicked out during computer processing if it is later than the date of presentment.

If the post-dating notice is effective and the item is wrongfully honored, the bank is "liable for damages for the loss resulting from its act," including "damages for dishonor of subsequent items under Section 4–402." 4–401(c).

2. Stale Checks

A check is "stale" when it is presented "more than six months after its date." 4–404. The six months period is derived from "banking and commercial practice." Id. comment.

Under 4–404, a bank "is under no obligation to a customer having a checking account to pay" a stale check, "but it may charge its customer's account for a payment made thereafter in good faith." A certified check is excluded from this principle, since it is the "primary obligation of the certifying bank." See 4–404 comment.

What does this mean? First, Payor Bank can dishonor a stale check without liability. There is "no obligation" to pay. Second, Payor Bank, if it pays a stale check, must pay in good faith. Normally, Payor Bank will consult with Customer before paying. It may, however, honestly and reasonably believe that Customer wants payment to be made without a consultation. In that case, the payment is protected.

E. DEATH OR INCOMPETENCE OF CUSTOMER

Section 4–405 deals with situations where Customer draws a check and then dies before it is presented for payment, or Customer who draws a check is adjudicated an incompetent. The bottom line is that Payor Bank's authority to pay is not revoked "until the bank knows of the fact of death or of an adjudication of incompetence and has reasonable opportunity to act on it." 4–405(a). According to comment 1, the "justice and necessity of the rule are obvious" since Payor Bank, given the tremendous volume of checks, is in no position to "verify the continued life and competency of drawers." The burden of notice, therefore, is placed on the representatives of the decedent or incompetent.

Even with knowledge of death (but not incompetence), Payor Bank has a limited power to pay. The "bank may for 10 days after the date of death pay or certify checks drawn on or before that date unless ordered to stop payment by a person claiming an interest in the account." 4–405(b). The reason is to permit "holders of checks drawn and issued shortly before death to cash them without the necessity of filing a claim in probate." Id. comment 2. There is a broad category of persons who can claim an interest in the account [surviving relatives, executors, creditors] and all they must do is give a direction to stop payment. The conditions of a stop payment order under 4–403 are not imposed on a "death" stop order. See 4–405 comment 3.

F. PAYOR BANK'S REMEDIES UPON WRONGFUL PAYMENT

What are Payor Bank's remedies, if any, if it has wrongfully paid a check and has re-credited Customer's account? As noted above, Payor Bank is subrogated to Customer's rights "against the payee or any other holder of the item with respect to the transaction out of which the item arose." 4–407(3). Is there anything else?

1. Warranties

a. Encoding Warranties

As discussed in Chapter 3 *supra*, Payor Bank may obtain relief if the wrongful honor was caused by an encoding error. The person encoding information, usually the amount of the check, warrants to Payor Bank that the "information is correctly encoded." 4–209(a). If Payor Bank "took the item in good faith," it may recover "as damages for breach of warranty an amount equal to the loss suffered as a result of the breach, plus expenses and loss of interest incurred as a result of the breach." 4–209(c).

b. Presentment Warranties

Unfortunately for Payor Bank, warranties made by Presenting Bank do not cover the cases discussed in this chapter. See 4–208(a). Assuming that there is no fraud or forgery, Payor Bank assumes the risk (under warranty theory, at least) of its own errors in payment. Thus, if Payor Bank pays over a valid stop payment order or mistakenly pays when there are insufficient funds in Customer's account, these losses, if any, cannot be reallocated to presenting banks through warranty theory.

2. Restitution for Mistaken Payments: 3–418

A wrongful payment is still final payment. But if the payment was mistaken, Payor Bank may have a restitution claim against a person who took the instrument for value but not in good faith or a person who took in good faith but has not "changed position in reliance on the payment." 3–418(c). Review the related discussion in Chapter 3 *supra*.

Under 3–418(a), Payor Bank has a statutory claim for the amount of the draft if it was paid on the "mistaken belief that (i) payment of the draft had not been stopped pursuant to Section 4–403." This assumes, of course, that the defendant is not protected under 3–418(c).

Other claims for mistaken payment depend upon other law governing mistake and restitution. 3–418(b). Since this other law may be poorly defined or may vary from state to state, its benefit to Payor Bank is marginal at best.

4. PRIORITY DISPUTES INVOLVING THE ACCOUNT

A. THE "FOUR LEGALS"

The problem here is a check is properly presented for payment. The account is sufficient to pay the check. At about the same time, however, while the bank is processing the item, something happens. The bank:

- Receives legal notice affecting the check, mainly a writ or the like seizing the account on behalf of a judicial lien creditor;
- Learns that the customer who owns the account has filed bankruptcy;
- Gets an order from the customer-drawer to stop payment of the check; or

- Decides to exercise the bank's common-law right of setoff against the account to satisfy some mutual debt the customer owes the bank.

These events are known as the "**four legals**." The issue, in a broad sense, is priority: at what point does the "legal" event come too late to end the bank's duty to pay its customer's properly-payable items.

Suppose, for example, Payee's check is presented by Collecting Bank to Payor Bank for collection on May 11. A provisional settlement is made by midnight on May 11 and by 2:00 p.m. on May 12 the internal process of posting the check is completed, which basically means the Payor Bank determined to pay the check. At 2:30 p.m., however, suppose that one or more of the four following events occurred:

(1) Payor Bank learned that Drawer had defaulted on an unsecured note held by Payor Bank. Payor Bank immediately **set off** the amount of the note from Drawer's account. Since the setoff depleted funds in Drawer's account, Payor Bank reversed its decision to pay the check and returned it before midnight on May 12.

(2) At 2:30 p.m., Payor Bank received a timely **stop payment order** from Drawer, see 4–403(a), and complied with it by returning and therefore dishonoring the check before midnight on May 12.

(3) At 2:30 p.m., Payor Bank received notice that Drawer had filed **bankruptcy**. Recognizing

the Drawer's account was now property of the bankruptcy estate, Payor Bank timely returned and dishonored the check.

(4) At 2:30 p.m., Payor Bank was served with legal process imposing a **garnishment** lien on Drawer's bank account. Payor Bank timely returned and dishonored the check.

In all cases, the question is the same: who should have priority to the check or its proceeds. Is it the Payee or those whose claims disrupted the collection process, whether the bank itself, the drawer, the trustee in bankruptcy, or the lien creditor? More precisely, the question is whether the "four legals" came too late to upset the bank's decision to pay the check. The answer in all these cases is decided under 4–303.

B. PRIORITIES UNDER 4–303

Any of the four legal events "comes too late to terminate, suspend, or modify the bank's right or duty to pay an item or to charge its customer's account" if the event occurs "after the earliest" of five stated circumstances:

(1) the bank accepts or certifies the item;

(2) the bank pays the item in cash;

(3) the bank settles for the item without having a right to revoke the settlement under statute, clearing-house rule or agreement;

(4) the bank becomes accountable for the amount of the item under 4–302 dealing with

the payor bank's responsibility for late return of items; or

(5) with respect to checks, a cut-off hour no earlier than one hour after the opening of the next banking day after the banking day on which the bank received the check and no later than the close of that next banking day or, if no cut-off hour is fixed, the close of the next business day after the banking day on which the bank received the check.

4–303(a).

Read carefully the first four of the stated circumstances. Note, on our facts, that Payor Bank has not (1) accepted or certified the item, (2) paid the item in cash, (3) settled for the item without having a right to revoke the settlement, or (4) become accountable under 4–302(a). Thus, on our facts, each of the four events is timely, has priority with respect to the item, and is effective. In short, because the legal event was timely and Payor Bank dishonored before its midnight deadline, Payee has no claim against any bank and must sue Drawer on the instrument. Note that it makes no difference under 4–303 and in the outcome that Payor Bank had completed its internal process of posting before any of the four events occurs. See 4–303 comment 4.

The fifth circumstance in determining priority under 4–303 deals with bank "cutoff" hours. 4–303(a)(5). Under 4–108(a), a bank may "fix an afternoon hour of 2 p.m. or later as a cutoff hour for the handling of money and items and the making of entries on its books." An item received after the cutoff hour or after the close of the banking day "may be treated as being received at the opening of the next banking day." 4–108(b). Therefore, "[i]f a bank receives an item after its regular cutoff hour on Monday and an attachment is levied on Tuesday, the attachment is prior to the item if the bank had not before that hour taken the action described in [4–303(a)(1–2)]." 4–303 comment 4. So, the cutoff hour can extend the time for the effectiveness of a legal event.

The cut-off hour is also important in deciding priority, under 4–303, with respect to items received the preceding day and can work to limit the time for the effectiveness of a legal event. With respect to priority, 4–303(a)(5) provides that any of the four legal events is too late if the event happens after "a cutoff hour no earlier than one hour after the opening of the next banking day after the banking day on which the bank received the check and no later than the close of that banking day or, if no cutoff hour is fixed, the close of the next banking day after the banking day on which the bank received the check." Thus, with our facts, if Payor Bank had a fixed cutoff hour on May 12 occurring between one hour after opening on May 12 and before 2:30 p.m. on that day, which is when the legal event happened, the event would be too late. If no cutoff hour is fixed, the events are timely because they happen before the "close of the next banking day [May 12] after the banking day on which the bank received the check [May 11]." Id.

In sum, 4–303 attempts to resolve priority problems in a manner consistent with the principles of final payment and accountability in 4–215 and 4–302. Unless there is an earlier final payment or action is taken after a fixed cutoff hour, the relevant time for action is Payor Bank's midnight deadline.

CHAPTER 5

CHECK FRAUD—ALLOCATING RISK AND LOSS BETWEEN PAYOR BANK AND CUSTOMER

Check fraud mainly refers to wrongfully altering checks or making signatures on them that are unauthorized or otherwise ineffective. Who bears the loss in case of check fraud as between the payor bank and the customer whose account is charged with the tainted item? The usual answer is that the loss falls on the payor bank, unless the bank can establish a defense provided by Article 3 or 4 or extra-Code law. This chapter explains the basis of the payor bank's liability to its customer for the major kinds of check fraud, and also outlines the bank's major defenses against its customer in each case. The next chapter moves beyond the bilateral relationship between the payor bank and its customer to consider if and how, in check fraud cases, the loss should properly be shifted to a third person. The assumption here and in the next chapter is that collecting the loss from the wrongdoer, who in every case is ultimately responsible, is practically impossible because she is financially or otherwise unavailable.

1. BASIS OF PAYOR BANK'S LIABILITY TO ITS CHECKING-ACCOUNT CUSTOMER

In every instance of check fraud the fundamental basis of a payor bank's liability to its customer—where the item has been charged to the customer's account—is the rule that only properly payable items can be charged against a customer's account. See 4–401(a). Checks that have been materially altered, or that carry an ineffective signature, are not properly payable.

A. INEFFECTIVE DRAWER'S SIGNATURE

The deposit contract between a payor bank and its customer determines who can draw against the customer's account by specifying whose signature is necessary on checks that are chargeable against the customer's account. Therefore, a check drawn against the account of an individual customer that is signed by someone other than the customer, and without authority from her, is not properly payable and is not chargeable to the customer's account, inasmuch as any "unauthorized signature [on an instrument] is ineffective" as the signature of the person whose name is signed. 3–403(a). Similarly, a check is not properly payable that is drawn on the account of a corporate customer by someone other than the person or persons authorized to draw against the account. Also, in the case where a deposit contract requires multiple signatures on checks drawn against the account, a check not signed by all of the required signatories is unauthorized, 3–403(b), and is not properly payable.

B. INEFFECTIVE INDORSEMENT

1. What Is the Wrong to the Drawer?

A check that bears a forged or otherwise unauthorized or ineffective indorsement cannot rightfully be charged against the drawer-customer's account because the check was not paid consistently with the drawer's (or subsequent holder's) order and was not properly presented to the payor bank. (Presentment is a demand for payment made by or on behalf of the person entitled to enforce the instrument, usually a holder. 3–501(a). A transferee of a check with an ineffective indorsement cannot be a holder. See Chapter 2 *supra*.) In short, a check with any forged indorsement, or an indorsement that is otherwise ineffective, is not properly payable because it was not properly presented and paid. Because the check is not properly payable, it cannot rightfully be charged against the customer's account.

For example, suppose B drew a check to S in payment for goods. An employee of S indorsed the check and cashed it at the payor bank. This employee had no responsibilities with respect to S's checks, acted without any authority from S to indorse for S, and used her own name. The bank then charged the amount of the check against B's account. B can force bank to re-credit her account. The result is the same if the employee used S's name or indorsed in both her name and S's.

2. Where Is the Loss to the Drawer?

An important side issue here is why, in either example, *B* would complain against the payor bank for charging the item to her account. S's loss is obvious. Where is B's loss? It turns out that because of the employee's lack of authority to indorse for S, payment by the drawee was improper because payment was not made to a person entitled to enforce the instrument. As a result, B was not discharged on the instrument, see 3–602(c) (discharge requires payment to a person entitled to enforce à la 3–301); so she was not discharged on the underlying obligation. 3–310(b). B thus remains liable to the payee. If this liability to the payee is enforced, B effectively will "pay" twice, inasmuch as her account has already been debited for the amount of the check. There is the loss to B. (The fuller truth, however, is that S usually enjoys additional actions against other people and often shifts the loss to them instead of B. These other actions are considered in the next chapter.)

C. ALTERATION

A check is properly payable only on the terms ordered by the drawer. So an altered check, i.e., a check on which the terms have been wrongfully changed by the payee or someone else, is not properly payable. In the usual case of alteration, the wrongdoer raises the amount of the check. In this case, the check is not properly payable to the extent of the alteration. The payor bank can charge the customer's account according to the original tenor of the item (i.e., in the amount ordered by the customer), 4–401(d)(1), but the difference between the original and raised amounts of the check cannot be charged against the account.

For example, B drew a $50 check to S who cleverly and fraudulently raised the amount to $500, and cashed it, for $500, at payor bank. The bank then charged B's account for $500. B can force the bank to re-credit her account for $450.

D. WRONGFULLY COMPLETED CHECKS

For some purposes, a check that is completed other than as authorized is treated as an altered instrument. See 3–115 & 3–407. This is not true in deciding who, as between a payor bank and its customer, bears the loss from a wrongfully completed check. The rule is: A bank which in good faith makes payment to a holder may charge the indicated account of its customer according to the tenor of the check as actually completed, not just in the amount or as otherwise authorized by the customer. 4–401(d)(2). It makes no difference that the bank knows that the item was completed by someone other than the customer so long as the bank was unaware that the *completion* itself was improper. Id.

Here are two examples:

1. B drew a check to S, leaving the amount blank. S was authorized to complete the check in an amount not exceeding $50. S filled in the amount of $500 and cashed the item at payor bank. The bank can charge B's account to the full extent of $500.

2. B drew a $500 check, leaving blank the name of the payee. B then gave the check to T and directed T to use the check to purchase certain goods for B, filling in the name of the seller. T filled in her own name and cashed the check

at payor bank. The bank can charge the check to B's account.

2. PAYOR BANK'S DEFENSES

The UCC and other law provide an array of defenses for a payor bank or another defendant in a check fraud case as against a customer or other person who complains of a loss. The most important of these defenses are considered below as they might be applied when determining, as between the payor bank and its customer, who bears the loss for check fraud. Most of these defenses are applicable whether the complaint involves an allegedly ineffective signature or an alteration, but the emphasis here is on problem signatures because, in real life, the usual complaint in the vast majority of check fraud cases is lack of authority, forgery or an otherwise ineffective signature rather than alteration.

A. AUTHORITY

1. The Effect of the Defense—It Undercuts Wrong

When a customer demands the re-crediting of her account for the amount of an item that carried an allegedly ineffective signature, or that has been altered, the payor bank's most basic defense is that the alteration or signature was authorized by a proper person. Authority eliminates the wrong that is the foundation of the complaint.

2. Rules About Agents Authorized to Sign for Their Principals

The rules on signatures by agents are very important in establishing the defense of authority with respect to signatures. In practice, problem signatures usually are not made by strangers. Problem signatures commonly are made by wrongdoers who were associated with the person whose signature was necessary. They could have been authorized to sign for her. The rules are discussed earlier in Chapter 2 *supra*.

So, when a bank is sued by a customer who argues that she did not sign a check charged to her account, the bank's first defense always is that the person who did sign was authorized to sign for the customer. It is very important to remember that the necessary authority can be implied and is not limited to express authority. If such authority is established, the deposit agreement between bank and customer has not been breached. Sure, the agreement may require that only checks signed by the customer are properly payable; but, because of the actual signer's authority, the law deems that the customer did sign the check.

B. RATIFICATION

1. Signature Becomes Effective as That of Represented Person

A customer cannot recover against a payor bank on the basis that her signature or an indorsement was forged if the person whose name was signed ratifies the signature. "An unauthorized signature may be ratified for all purposes of this Article." 3–403(a). The effect is that "[t]he unauthorized signature becomes valid so far as its effect as a signature is concerned." 3–403 comment 3. Ratification is retroactive and may be found in conduct as well as in express statements.

Here is how it works: Suppose the deposit contract between D Corp. and Bank provides that Bank can and will pay checks drawn on the account by the president or comptroller of D Corp. Without authority, an employee of D Corp. draws a check on the account using the president's name. The check is used to purchase widgets. The Bank pays the check and debits the account of D Corp. Upon discovering the fraud, D Corp. fires the employee and confiscates the widgets for the use of D Corp. By retaining the benefits received in the transaction with knowledge of the unauthorized signature, D Corp. thereby ratifies the employee's signature. The signature is thus effective even though the employee was not an authorized agent of D Corp. So the check is deemed to have been properly payable and D Corp. cannot complain that the check was charged to the corporate account.

2. Effect on Signer's Liability

When a person makes an unauthorized signature of somebody else, the signer herself can be liable even though the represented person is not liable because of the lack of authority. See 3–403(a). If the represented person ratifies the signature, she thereby adopts it as her own and the actual signer may thereby be relieved of liability. Nevertheless:

> [The ratification] does not of itself relieve the signer of liability to the person whose name is signed. It does not in any way affect the criminal law.

3–403 comment 3.

C. PRECLUSION BY ESTOPPEL

Former law expressly provided that an unauthorized signature could operate as the signature of the represented person when, because of the peculiar circumstances, the person was "precluded from denying it." 3–404(1) (1989 Official Text). It recognized "the possibility of an estoppel against the person whose name is signed, as where he expressly or tacitly represents to an innocent purchaser that the signature is genuine * * *." 3–404 comment 4 (1989 Official Text). Even in the absence of this express provision in the new law, preclusion by estoppel remains possible because of 1–103(b), which allows principles of common law and equity to supplement the Code.

D. 3–406—NEGLIGENCE

The defense of 3–406 covers preclusion because of certain negligence:

> A person whose failure to exercise ordinary care *substantially contributes* to an alteration of an instrument or to the making of a forged signature on an instrument is precluded from asserting the alteration or the forgery against a

person who, in good faith, pays the instrument or takes it for value or for collection.

3–406(a) (emphasis added).

1. The "Substantially Contributes" Requirement

Not just any negligence effects preclusion under 3–406. The negligence must actually "contribute" to the forgery or alteration. That is, it must afford an opportunity of which advantage is in fact taken. Moreover, the contribution must be *substantial.* The test is less stringent than direct and proximate cause. It is an easier test requiring only that the negligence was a substantial contributing factor in bringing about the alteration or forgery. 3–406 comment 2. "The Code has thus abandoned the language of the older cases (negligence which 'directly and proximately affects the conduct of the bank in passing the forgery') and shortened the chain of causation which the defendant bank must establish. * * * In the instant case, the trial court could readily have concluded that plaintiff's business affairs were conducted in so negligent a fashion as to have 'substantially contributed' to the * * * forgeries, within the meaning of § 3–406." *Thompson Maple Products, Inc. v. Citizens Nat. Bank of Corry*, 234 A.2d 32, 34–35 (Pa.Super. 1967).

2. The Effect of Payor's Culpability

The defense of 3–406 may partially fail if the payor bank or other person asserting the preclusion also acted unreasonably in dealing with the instrument. A concept of comparative negligence applies.

> [I]f the person asserting the preclusion fails to exercise ordinary care in paying or taking the instrument and that failure substantially contributes to loss, the loss is allocated between the person precluded and the person asserting the preclusion according to the extent to which the failure of each to exercise ordinary care contributed to the loss.

3–406(b). " 'Ordinary care' in the case of a person engaged in business means observance of reasonable commercial standards, prevailing in the area in which the person is located, with respect to the business in which the person is engaged." 3–103(a)(9). Significantly, "[i]n the case of a bank that takes an instrument for processing for collection or payment by automated means, reasonable commercial standards do not require the bank to examine the instrument if the failure to examine does not violate the bank's prescribed procedures and the bank's procedures do not vary unreasonably from general banking usage not disapproved by this Article or Article 4." Id.

E. 4–406(c–d) (BREACH OF CONDITIONAL DUTY TO DISCOVER AND REPORT CHECK FRAUD)

Typically, a bank sends its checking-account customer a statement of account that shows payment of items from the customer's account, either by mail or electronically. In so doing the bank returns or makes available to the customer either the items themselves or information sufficient to allow the customer reasonably to identify the items. Article 4 does not directly require this accounting; but if the bank provides such a statement, Article 4 imposes a duty on the customer to examine the items or information with "reasonable promptness * * * *to determine* whether any payment was not authorized because of an alteration of an item or because a purported signature by or on behalf of the customer was not authorized. If, based on the statement or items provided, the customer should reasonably have discovered the unauthorized payment, the customer must promptly *notify* the bank of the relevant facts." 4–406(c) (emphasis added).

1. When Duty on Customer Is Triggered

The duty on the customer is not imposed unless the bank either (1) returns or makes available the checks paid or (2) provides information sufficient to allow the customer to identify them. 4–406(a). Which course the bank follows is a matter of bank-customer agreement; but if their agreement requires the bank only to provide identifying information, the duty on the customer requires adequate information—"sufficient to allow the customer reasonably to identify the items paid." 4–406(a). Images of the items will do but are not required. It is sufficient that the bank describes the checks by item numbers, amount, and dates of payment. 4–406 comment 1. It is not necessary for the bank to identify the payee of each item and the item's date. The customer should be able to determine these two pieces of information from her own records based on the number of the check, its amount and date of payment supplied by the bank.

2. Effect of Customer's Breach of the Duty

The effect of a customer's breach of the 4–406(c) duty is described by 4–406(d). Basically, if the bank proves that it suffered a loss because the customer failed to discover or report an unauthorized payment, the customer is precluded from asserting the alteration or the customer's unauthorized signature against the bank. See 4–406(d)(1).

Whether or not the bank can prove a loss, the customer is precluded from asserting her unauthorized signature or an alteration by the same wrongdoer on any item paid in good faith by the bank "if the payment was made before the bank received notice from the customer of the unauthorized signature or alteration and after the customer had been afforded a reasonable period of time, not exceeding 30 days, in which to examine the item or statement of account and notify the bank." 4–406(d)(2). This language covers the case of a string of forgeries or alterations by the same wrongdoer. The bank need not establish that it suffered a loss because, in this kind of case, the law presumes loss.

3. No Coverage of Forged Indorsements

The 4–406(d) preclusion is limited to alterations and forgeries and unauthorized signatures of the customer—the person who has the account and whose name should have been signed as drawer. The preclusion of (d) therefore never applies to forged indorsements. Typically, the checking account customer has no way of verifying indorsements.

4. Missing Drawer's Signature

Under former law the courts were divided on whether or not the duty and preclusion of 4–406 applies in the case where multiple signatures on a check are required by the deposit contract, but the bank pays checks missing one or more of the required signatures. The decisive question is whether or not, in such a case, there is an "unauthorized signature." Article 3 now clearly ends this dispute because the statute expressly provides that "[i]f the signature of more than one person is required to constitute the authorized signature of an organization, the signature of the organization is unauthorized if one of the required signatures is lacking." 3–403(b). This rule will apply even when two natural persons jointly hold an account in their individual capacities because "organization" is a broad term. It means any person "other than an individual," 1–201(b)(25), which presumably includes (as previous law explicitly provided) a corporation, government or governmental subdivision or agency, business trust, estate, trust, partnership or association, two or more persons having a joint or common interest, or any other legal or commercial entity.

5. Bank's Comparative Negligence Dilutes the 4–406(d) Defense

Even if the customer was negligent so that the preclusion of 4–406(d) applies against her, the bank nevertheless shares the loss if the customer proves that the bank failed to exercise ordinary care in paying the item and that the failure substantially contributed to the loss. 4–406(e). In this event loss is allocated between the customer and the bank according to the extent to which the customer's negligence in not finding or reporting the wrong and the bank's negligence in paying the item contributed to the loss.

6. Bank's Lack of Good Faith Forfeits the Defense

If the customer proves that the bank did not pay the item in good faith, the bank completely forfeits the 4–406(d) preclusion defense despite negligence by the customer. 4–406(e).

F. 4–406(F) (ONE-YEAR OUTSIDE LIMIT ON CUSTOMER'S COMPLAINTS ABOUT CUSTOMER'S UNAUTHORIZED SIGNATURE OR ALTERATION)

Application of the 4–406(d) preclusion rule, which is discussed immediately above, depends upon determinations as to ordinary care of the customer and the bank. In contrast, 4–406(f) places an *absolute* limit on the right of a customer to make a claim for payment of altered or unauthorized checks *without regard to care or lack of care of either the customer or* *the bank.* In any event, "a customer who does not within one year after the statement or items are made available to the customer * * * discover and report the customer's unauthorized signature on or any alteration on the item is precluded from asserting against the [payor] bank the unauthorized signature or alteration." 4–406(f). On the other hand, subsection (f) is like 4–406(d) in that neither preclusion defense applies to indorsements. "Section 4–406 imposes no duties on the drawer to look for unauthorized indorsements." 4–406 comment 5. Customers' complaints about ineffective indorsements are covered, however, by the general three-year statute of limitations that applies to any action to enforce any obligation, duty, or right arising under Article 4. See 4–111.

G. SPECIAL RULES FOR UNAUTHORIZED INDORSEMENTS IN CERTAIN CIRCUMSTANCES

Section 3–404 and 3–405 provide three different rules whereby indorsements of payees are deemed effective in law even though, in fact, they are unauthorized. These rules cover circumstances where, for overriding policy reasons, the loss is generally better left with the drawer-customer—she cannot shift her loss to the payor bank—because, in the covered cases, the customer is in the best position to protect against it. Generally, the rules operate in the same way. When an indorsement involves fraud that a rule covers, an indorsement by *any person* in the name of the identified payee is deemed effective as the payee's indorsement in favor of the person who pays or people who take the instrument for value or collection.

Section 3–404 applies in certain cases involving impostors and nominal or fictitious payees, and section 3–405 involves fraudulent indorsements by employees on instruments for which their employment gives them some responsibility. Although the main purpose of the statutes is to insulate payor banks from customers' complaints of losses in certain instances of unauthorized indorsements, neither 3–404 nor 3–405 is limited to this purpose, this situation, or to checks. Each statute is generally applicable to any instrument and in any situation that meets its peculiar requirements.

1. When Payees Are Impersonated or Imagined: Impostor Rule—3–404(a)

a. The Fraud

In the *impostor case*, a drawer is induced to issue an instrument because a thief impersonates someone else whom the drawer intends and names as payee. The thief indorses in the name of the payee and induces a third person to take or pay the instrument. Finally, the thief departs with her loot, and the law must determine which of the two innocent and defrauded parties must bear the cost of the wrong. The drawer often complains against her bank for paying the item, arguing that the indorsement was ineffective because the check was payable to the person whom the drawer intended rather than to the thief. Therefore, the item was not properly payable and not chargeable against the customer's account.

b. Pre-Code Law

Before the Code, the outcome of these cases usually depended on what the court found to be the dominant intent of the defrauded party. If she dealt face to face with the impostor, her dominant intent was usually found to be to deliver the instrument to the impostor. Consequently, the impostor was treated as holder, and the party who gave the instrument to the impostor bore the loss rather than the person who purchased the instrument or paid the impostor. If the parties dealt by mail or telegram, it usually was reasoned that the defrauded party intended to deliver the instrument to the person the impostor pretended to be. Consequently, the impostor did not become the holder and so the loss was borne by the person who purchased the instrument or paid the impostor.

c. The Code Rule When Payee Impersonated

The dominant intent test was criticized as a fiction because in the eyes of the deceived drawer or maker, the payee named and the defrauder are the same person so that there is only one intention, or if there are two, they are so intertwined as to be inseparable. The Code therefore rejects the test of dominant intent and refuses expressly to distinguish between imposture face to face and by correspondence. It states this wider *impostor rule* of 3–404(a):

> If an impostor, by use of the mails or otherwise, induces the issuer of an instrument to issue the instrument to the impostor, or to a person acting in concert with the impostor, by impersonating the payee of the instrument or a person authorized to act for the payee, an indorsement of the instrument by any person in the name of the payee is effective as the indorsement of the payee in favor of a person who, in good faith, pays the instrument or takes it for value or for collection.

Under the Code, regardless of how the imposture is carried out, when the impostor or her confederate or anyone else indorses the instrument, it is as if the real payee of an ordinary order instrument indorsed it. If the indorsement is in blank, the instrument immediately becomes payable to bearer so that the impostor or anyone else in possession of it becomes the holder and the proper person to negotiate it or to receive payment. If the instrument is indorsed specially, by anyone, and delivered to the special indorsee, the latter becomes the holder; and if she otherwise qualifies, she becomes a holder in due course who is entitled to enforce the instrument—free from defenses—against the defrauded maker or drawer. If a drawee pays the holder, whether she be the impostor or anyone else, the drawee is entitled to charge the drawer's account because a payment to the holder is in accordance with the drawer's order. The net result is that the ultimate loss is normally borne by the defrauded maker or drawer rather than by the transferee from the defrauder or by the drawee who pays the impostor or a transferee.

d. Impersonation of an Agent of the Named Payee

In a variant case, the defrauder, instead of misrepresenting herself to be another, misrepresents herself to be the agent of another, and thereby induces a maker or drawer to issue the negotiable instrument made payable to her alleged principal. The impostor rule of former law did not apply in this case, and effective negotiation of the instrument was not possible unless the alleged principal, herself, indorsed the instrument. The impostor rule of 3–404(a) changes this result. It is wider and expressly applies when an impostor impersonates "the payee of the instrument *or a person authorized to act for the payee.*" 3–404(a). An indorsement in the payee's name by the supposed "agent" or anyone else is effective. The defrauded maker or drawer again bears the loss.

2. Rule of the Nominal or Fictitious Payee—3–404(b)

a. The Fraud

The *nominal or fictitious payee* is an entirely different kind of fraud but is handled similarly by 3–404. Suppose that X gives Y general authority to issue checks drawn on B Bank to pay X's creditors and employees. Intending to cheat X, and enrich herself, Y draws a check for $3,000 on B Bank payable to the order of F, and signs X's name as drawer. F is neither a creditor nor an employee, and Y intends F to have no interest in the check. Y indorses the check in the name of F naming herself as special indorsee. Y promptly cashes the check at B Bank and retains the proceeds. B Bank charges X's account for the $3,000. When X learns of Y's duplicity, X demands that the bank re-credit her account for $3,000. When B Bank refuses, X sues B Bank. Both X and B Bank agree that X was liable on the check and that B Bank had a right to charge X's account if, but only if, the check was properly payable, which requires that Y was a holder. See 4–401(a). X contends that Y was not a holder because the check was payable to the order of F, who was therefore the only appropriate party to indorse. Because the instrument was never indorsed by F, Y could not become holder. Logically, there is much to be said for X's position.

b. The Code's Rule Favors the Bank

As a matter of policy, the Code favors B Bank. It does so by this rule:

> If (i) a person whose intent determines to whom an instrument is payable * * * does not intend the person identified as payee to have any interest in the instrument, or (ii) the person identified as payee of an instrument is a fictitious person, the following rules apply until the instrument is negotiated by special indorsement:
>
> (1) Any person in possession of the instrument is its holder.

> (2) An indorsement by any person in the name of the payee stated in the instrument is effective as the indorsement of the payee in favor of a person who, in good faith, pays the instrument or takes it for value or for collection.

3–404(b). In terms of this rule, Y's intent determined to whom the check was payable because Y was the person who signed the check, even though Y was signing on behalf of X. 3–110(a). At the time of issuing the check, Y did not intend F to have any interest in the check. Therefore, because of 3–404(b)(1), Y was a holder before the special indorsement. Also, the indorsement of Y (or her confederate or anyone else), in the name of F, the named payee, had the same effect as if F, the named payee, had indorsed. Consequently, after the special indorsement to herself, Y was a holder because she was still in possession of an instrument that ran to her. When a person draws a negotiable draft or check she orders the drawee to pay the holder. Therefore, when the bank in good faith paid Y who was a holder, the bank was obeying X's order and so was entitled to charge X's account.

The result is the same even with these variations in the problem:

- F was an actual creditor of X. The key is that Y did not intend F to have an interest in the check.
- F was nonexistent, made-up, and fictitious. Ditto.

- Checks of X must be signed by two persons, Y and Z. They both sign the check to F. As far as Z knows, the check is intended to pay a legitimate debt owed F. Y intends to keep the check for himself.

c. *Where Stealing Instrument Is Afterthought*

Section 3–404(b) would not apply if F, the payee, were a real person and Y did not decide to steal the check until after issuing it. If the payee is fictitious, it is irrelevant when Y makes the decision to steal the instrument.

d. *Where Actual Drawer Is Not Involved*

The rule of 3–404(b) also would not apply if Y had not actually signed the check as, or for, the drawer of the instrument. Suppose that, instead of actually drawing the check, Y merely prepared it for X's signature and that X signed it thinking that F was a creditor. Or suppose that instead of preparing the check, Y merely prepared a list or report on which F's name falsely appeared as creditor. In these situations, 3–404(b) does not apply because Y is not the person whose intent determined to whom the check is payable. It was X. The person to whom an instrument is payable is determined by the intent of the "person, whether or not authorized, signing as, or in the name or behalf of, the issuer of the instrument." 3–110(a). In effect, when the payee is a real person, 3–404(b) only applies if the actual "drawer or maker does not intend the payee to have any interest in the instrument." 3–404 comment 2.

It is a different case, however, if the payee is fictitious. In this event, 3–404(b) applies regardless of the intent of the actual drawer or maker.

It is also a different case, even if the payee is a real person, if X's signature is made by a check-writing machine or other automated means that Y uses to issue the check payable to F. In this event, the payee is determined by the intent of the person supplying the name of the payee. 3–110(b). On these facts, this person is Y. It would seem, therefore, that 3–404(b) applies. 3–404 comment 2 (Case #4). Section 3–405 may also apply if Y is an employee.

e. Where Drawer's Signature Is Unauthorized

Note that 3–404 works only on indorsements. Unauthorized drawer's signatures are not deemed effective by either 3–404(a) or (b). If in any of these examples the signature of X, the drawer, is ineffective, X is not liable to anyone on the check (but Y may be liable). The check, therefore, is not properly payable with respect to X's account and cannot be charged against this account by the drawee-bank whether or not 3–404 applies. Suppose, for example, that Y has no authority to act for X in any regard. Y drew a check on X's account using X's name. To hide the fraud, Y drew it payable to F, a person with whom X regularly does business. Y did not intend F to have an interest in the instrument. The drawee paid it. The check, however, is not properly payable because X did not draw it. Section 3–404 does not solve this problem. The bank cannot charge X's account.

3. Common Requirements of the Two Rules of 3–404

Although 3–404(a) and (b) are different rules that address different kinds of fraud, they share certain elements and are alike in certain respects.

a. Signature of Someone as Payee Is Required

The rules of 3–404(a) and (b) share an uncertainty. It is not clear whether an instrument that is payable to a fictitious payee or to an impersonated payee is payable to order or to bearer. Arguments can be made for either and neither. Perhaps it is best to recognize that such an instrument is anomalous and that although it is governed by some well-established principles in the law of commercial paper, it is treated in a way that cannot be reconciled with some other equally well recognized principles. The Code starts with a desire to help the good faith purchaser or drawee who pays. It might have done this simply by declaring such paper to be payable to bearer so as not to require any indorsement, as is essentially done by 4–205 with respect to instruments deposited for collection. But had the Code done so, it would have abandoned the appearance of a regular chain of indorsements and it did not wish to go this far. So it required that someone at least appear to sign on behalf of the person named as payee before anyone could become a holder of it.

b. Signature Must Be "In the Name of the Payee"

A similarity between 3–404(a) and (b) is that the only bogus indorsement that either rule makes effective is an indorsement "in the name of the payee." Under former law, some cases required the indorsement to be in exactly the same name as the named payee. These cases are rejected. Under 3–404(a) or (b), an indorsement is effective if in a name "substantially similar" to the name of the payee. 3–404(c). Moreover, an indorsement that is wildly different, or no indorsement at all, is effective if the instrument is deposited in a depositary bank to an account in a name substantially similar to that of the payee. Id. This allowance is based on the rule that checks may be deposited for collection without indorsement. See 4–205(1).

c. *Whom the Rules Protect*

Another similarity between 3–404(a) and (b) is that they both protect not only a person who pays an instrument in circumstances to which the rules apply. Both rules also protect a person who takes an instrument for value or for collection. For example, using the 3–404(b) problem to illustrate, suppose that instead of Y herself presenting the check and getting payment from the drawee bank, she promptly indorsed in F's name and cashed or deposited the check at C Bank. This bank presented the item for payment but B Bank, the drawee, dishonored. C Bank is a holder because of 3–404(b). It can sue Y as indorser and, more importantly, X as drawer. Moreover, if C Bank is a holder in due course, it can take free of X's defenses and claims, including any defense based on Y's tackiness.

d. Effect of Comparative Fault

Subsections 3–404(a) and (b) are also alike in that both rules equally take into account the negligence of the person who pays or takes the instrument for value or collection. They do so by this qualification to both rules:

> With respect to an instrument to which subsection (a) or (b) applies, if a person paying the instrument or taking it for value or for collection fails to exercise ordinary care in paying or taking the instrument and that failure substantially contributes to loss resulting from payment of the instrument, the person bearing the loss may recover from the person failing to exercise ordinary care to the extent the failure to exercise ordinary care contributed to the loss.

3–404(d). Such negligence can be even more potent. Suppose that in the example immediately above, C Bank was negligent in not detecting the wrongdoing when Y deposited or cashed the check there. In this event, even if C Bank was a holder in due course, X could discount its liability by the value of C Bank's negligence. Yet, becoming a holder in due course requires taking the instrument in good faith, which "means honesty in fact *and the observance of reasonable commercial standards of fair dealing*." 3–103(a)(6) (emphasis added). Arguably, then, C Bank's negligence prevents it from being a holder in due course so that X would have a complete defense to liability. The result is probably the same either way.

On the other hand, establishing that C Bank was negligent is not a slam dunk. Look at this definition of "*ordinary care*," which certainly applies to 3–404 and maybe also applies to the meaning of good faith:

> "Ordinary care" in the case of a person engaged in business means observance of reasonable commercial standards, prevailing in the area in which the person is located, with respect to the business in which the person is engaged. In the case of a bank that takes an instrument for processing for collection or payment by automated means, *reasonable commercial standards do not require the bank to examine the instrument if* the failure to examine does not violate the bank's prescribed procedures and the bank's procedures do not vary unreasonably from general banking usage not disapproved by this Article or Article 4.

3–103(a)(9) (emphasis added). The outcome in C Bank's case may depend on whether it dealt with Y through an individual who normally would be required to examine the instrument and check identification, or by some other means less likely to trigger such a duty.

e. Same Basic Policy Behind the Rules

Finally, 3–404(a) and (b) are most fundamentally alike because the same basic policy supports both of them. It puts the risk of these kinds of fraud on the drawer or maker because (1) she is in a better position to avoid the risks and (2) the costs of protecting against them is more appropriately borne by her rather than by the completely innocent payor or purchaser of the instrument. Adjustments are made in particular cases where negligence of the payor or purchaser dilutes her innocence, where she had the last chance to prevent the loss and bungled the job. In the end, it is a kind of comparative fault.

H. 3–405—WHEN EMPLOYEES STEAL CHECKS FOR WHICH THEY ARE RESPONSIBLE

Section 3–405 focuses on employee fraud. It was added in 1990 and is among the two or three most important innovations of the 1990 changes in Article 3. Formerly, employers often could shift and avoid losses caused by employee fraud if the fraud did not fit the relatively narrow rules of 3–404 covering impostors, nominal or fictitious payees and did not involve employer negligence that would trigger 3–406. The drafters of the 1990 Article 3 reconsidered how fairly to distribute losses caused by employee fraud. The balance they reached is different from former law, and less favorable to employers. It is expressed in the policy and language of 3–405 that employers should be originally responsible for a wider range of employee fraud when, and solely because, the fraud is committed by an employee who was entrusted with responsibilities with respect to instruments. The basic reason is that employee fraud is really an employment matter and is better dealt with as such.

Although 3–405 applies to any kind of instrument, the normal case for applying 3–405 will involve checks, and will usually be between the employer, as drawer or payee, and a collecting bank that cashed the checks or a drawee bank that paid them. The issue is always who bears the loss between the employer and the bank. The loser always has a right to recover over from the wrongdoer; but, almost always, the wrongdoer is financially unavailable.

Section 3–404, which is discussed earlier, overlaps with 3–405. Some cases fit both sections. As to these cases, 3–405 may eclipse 3–404 because the elements of the former may be easier to prove. The eclipse is not total, however, because 3–404 is not limited to employee fraud. On the other hand, the kinds of fraud that 3–404 covers are usually committed by employees, so that 3–404 will not work nearly as hard as its statutory predecessors or be as important in Article 3's scheme for distributing fraud losses. Section 3–405 will be worked to death because, although it is limited to employee fraud, it alone covers a wider range of fraudulent conduct than all of the former rules of check fraud combined, and also because most check fraud is committed by employees.

Section 3–405 is big but the core rule of 3–405 is small and easy to understand. It is the first sentence of subsection (b):

> [I]f an employer entrusted an employee with responsibility with respect to the instrument and the employee or a person acting in concert with the employee makes a fraudulent indorsement of the instrument, the indorsement is effective as the indorsement of the person to

whom the instrument is payable if it is made in the name of that person.

3–405(b). In some respects this rule is similar to the rules of 3–404. For both 3–404 and 3–405(b):

- The same standard determines if the indorsement is in the same name as the payee, "substantially similar."
- The indorsement is effective only in favor of a person who, in good faith, pays an instrument or takes it for value or for collection.
- Finally, the effectiveness is discounted by such a person's negligence in paying or taking the instrument.

These matters, however, are details. In the main, 3–405 is very different and much broader than 3–404, covering cases of employee fraud that would fit 3–404 and more. Most significantly, 3–405 covers the simple case in which an employee with certain responsibility does nothing more than steal checks that are issued *by* her employer for accounts payable, or checks that are issued *to* her employer for accounts receivable.

1. Employer as Drawer

Suppose that X gives Y, an employee, the job of verifying, electronically recording, and sending checks that X draws to pay accounts she owes other people. Y plays no role in deciding to whom these checks are payable. In fact, she plays no other role whatsoever with respect to the checks. One day, Y stole several checks and forged the payees' indorsements. The instruments were paid. Ordinarily, because of the ineffective indorsements of the payees, the checks are not properly payable; and the drawee bank cannot charge them to X's account. Because of 3–405, however, the indorsements are effective since X entrusted Y with responsibilities with respect to the checks. Because the indorsements are effective, the checks are properly payable and thus chargeable to X's account. The loss stays with X. She cannot shift it to anyone other than Y, who is financially unavailable. Of course, the result is the same if Y's duties include deciding to whom the checks are payable, as by determining and reporting accounts payable.

2. Employer as Payee

Suppose that the stolen checks were received by X before they were stolen, that is, the tacky person grabbed them after X got them. Instead of drawer, X was payee. Y could easily take the checks because her job also involved processing payments on accounts receivable. Y forged X's indorsement and the checks were cashed by D Bank, a depositary bank, and paid by the drawee. Ordinarily, X could shift the loss to either bank by way of a conversion action based on her forged indorsements. Because of 3–405, however, the indorsements by Y are effective. There is no basis for conversion against anyone. The loss once again stays with X.

Both of these examples are beyond 3–404. In the absence of 3–405, the employer very likely could shift the losses to the banks, which frequently happened under former law. The loss now stays with the employer.

3. Comparative Fault

Like 3–404 and 3–406, 3–405 also accounts for comparative fault. "If the person paying the instrument or taking it for value or for collection fails to exercise ordinary care * * * and that failure substantially contributes to loss resulting from the fraud, the person bearing the loss may recover from the person failing to exercise ordinary care to the extent the failure to exercise ordinary care contributed to the loss." 3–405(b) (second sentence).

Here is an example: A computer that controls Employer's check-writing machine was programmed to cause a very large check to be issued to a well-known national corporation, such as General Motors, Inc. (GM), to which Employer owed money. Employee fraudulently changed the address of GM in the computer data bank to Employee's post office box. Employee was an accounts payable clerk whose duties included entering information into the computer.

The check was subsequently produced by the check-writing machine and mailed to the Employee's box. She got the check, indorsed it in the name of GM, and deposited the check to an account in Depositary Bank which Employee had opened in GM's name. The Bank had opened the account without requiring

Employee to produce any resolution of the corporation's board or other evidence of authorization of Employee to act for GM. In due course, the check is presented for payment; Depositary Bank receives payment; and Employee is allowed to withdraw the credit by wire transfer to a foreign bank.

Employer remains obligated to General Motors, and cannot recover from the drawee bank because the indorsement was effective and thus the item was properly payable. Employer can recover from Depositary Bank, however, to the extent the finder of fact concludes (as it should) that Depositary Bank was negligent and that its negligence contributed to Employer's loss.

CHAPTER 6

SHIFTING CHECK FRAUD LOSSES

Chapter 5 ends by explaining who usually bears the losses from check fraud (alteration or unauthorized signature) as between a payor bank and its checking account customer. The losses often fall on the bank. This chapter begins by considering whether or not losses borne by the payor bank can be shifted to someone else involved in the collection of the tainted items. The remainder of this chapter considers other combinations of plaintiffs and defendants in check fraud suits (especially those involving forged indorsements) that permit the more direct and efficient shifting of losses to the persons who ultimately should bear them.

1. PAYOR BANK VERSUS PEOPLE UPSTREAM IN THE COLLECTION CHAIN—PRIMARILY, PRESENTMENT WARRANTIES

A check that has been altered, or that carries an unauthorized signature of the drawer or an indorser, is not properly payable and cannot rightfully be charged to the account against which it was drawn. Thus, if the payor bank pays the check, the payment cannot be recouped from the account. So, as against its checking account customer, the bank must bear the check fraud loss. Usually, the only way the payor bank can shift the loss to someone else is by a claim for breach of warranty based on 4–208. It establishes implied warranties that benefit payor banks which pay or accept items:

> If an unaccepted draft is presented to the drawee for payment or acceptance and the drawee pays or accepts the draft, (i) the person obtaining payment or acceptance, at the time of presentment, and (ii) a previous transferor of the draft, at the time of transfer, warrant to the drawee that pays or accepts the draft in good faith that:
>
> > (1) the warrantor is, or was, at the time the warrantor transferred the draft, a person entitled to enforce the draft or authorized to obtain payment or acceptance of the draft on behalf of a person entitled to enforce the draft;
> >
> > (2) the draft has not been altered; and
> >
> > (3) the warrantor has no knowledge that the signature of the purported drawer of the draft is unauthorized; and
> >
> > (4) with respect to any remotely-created consumer item, that the person on whose account the item is drawn authorized the issuance of the item in the amount for which the item is drawn.

4–208(a). As is apparent, these presentment warranties do not cover every kind of check fraud. Thus, the payor bank cannot unload every kind of check fraud loss.

A. WHO MAKES PRESENTMENT WARRANTIES TO THE PAYOR BANK UNDER 4–208

The warranties that run in favor of a payor bank are made by the person who obtains payment and also by every previous transferor. The warranties arise automatically, that is, the warranties are implied by law and are not conditioned on the warrantor expressly making them or even being aware that warranties are made as part of the collection process.

The warranties are triggered whenever a check is presented and paid, but the person obtaining payment is not the only warrantor. Also making the presentment warranties to the bank is every previous transferor of the check. This means that a payor bank is not limited, in a breach of warranty action on a check, to suing the person who presented the item and obtained payment. The payor bank can recover from any collecting bank or other person in the collection chain or from any prior transferor if a 4–208 warranty was breached at the time of this person's transfer. A previous transferor would not be responsible for breach of the warranty against alteration if the check was altered after she transferred it.

B. SCOPE OF PRESENTMENT WARRANTY PROTECTION UNDER 4–208

With respect to checks paid by payor banks, 4–208(a) implies four presentment warranties. The first three warranties are most important in typical cases:

1. Alteration

Section 4–208(a)(2) very clearly provides a warranty that "the draft has not been altered." Article 4 does not define "altered." Presumably, the definition in Article 3 applies. If so, for purposes of this warranty an alteration is "(i) an unauthorized change in an instrument that purports to modify in any respect the obligation of a party or (ii) an unauthorized addition of words or numbers or other change to an incomplete instrument relating to the obligation of a party." 3–407(a).

2. Unauthorized or Missing Indorsement

In so many words 4–208(a) creates a warranty against unauthorized (including missing) indorsements. The words are a warranty that "the warrantor is * * * a person entitled to enforce the draft" or is authorized by such a person. 4–208(a)(1). To be such a person ordinarily implies that the check or other item contains all necessary indorsements, and that the indorsements are genuine or otherwise effective. So, if the indorsement of a payee or special indorsee is missing or is signed without her authority, the 4–208(a)(1) warranty is breached, *even though the warrantor is completely unaware of any problem with the indorsement.* The warrantor's knowledge or lack of knowledge is totally irrelevant.

B drew a check on her account at PB Bank, and gave it to S in payment for goods. T stole the check from S and cashed it at DB Bank, after forging S's indorsement. DB Bank forwarded the item for collection through an intermediary bank, IB Bank.

IB presented the check for payment to PB Bank which paid the item and charged it to B's account. Upon learning of the theft, S demanded the price of the goods sold to B. B paid S in cash and then demanded that PB Bank re-credit her account for the amount of the check because the check was not properly payable. PB Bank did so. Now PB Bank can sue, for breach of warranty of presentment, any of the following: IB Bank, DB Bank, or T.

3. Unauthorized Drawer's Signature

There is only a limited warranty with regard to the drawer's signature. It is that the warrantor "has *no knowledge* that the signature of the purported drawer of the draft is unauthorized." 4–208(a)(3) (emphasis added).

Forging B's name, T drew a check against B's checking account at PB Bank. T used this check to pay for goods purchased from S. S deposited the check in her account at DB Bank, which forwarded the item for collection through IB Bank, which presented the check to PB Bank for payment. PB Bank paid the check and charged it to B's account. When the forgery was discovered, PB Bank recredited B's account because the check was not properly payable. PB Bank is probably stuck with the loss, however, because T, the wrongdoer, was the only person who breached the limited presentment warranty regarding an unauthorized drawer's signature.

C. DAMAGES

1. Kinds

The damages for breach of a presentment warranty include:

- Compensatory damages equaling the amount paid by the drawee less the amount the drawee received or is entitled to receive from the drawer because of payment.
- Incidental damages for expenses and loss of interest resulting from the breach.

4–208(b).

2. Disclaimer

The presentment warranties or, presumably, damages for breaching them can be limited or entirely disclaimed except with respect to checks. 4–208(e).

D. MAJOR DEFENSES IN WARRANTY ACTION

1. Payor Bank's Lack of Good Faith

No one is liable to a payor bank for breach of warranty with respect to a check the bank paid if, in paying the item, the payor bank acted without good faith. The presentment warranties of 4–208 are made only to a payor which *in good faith* pays or accepts the item. On the other hand, the drawee's negligence—failure to exercise ordinary care in making payment—is irrelevant. 4–208(b).

2. Laches

In asserting breach of warranty, a payor bank must notify the warrantor within 30 days after acquiring "reason to know of the breach and the identity of the warrantor." 4–208(e). Otherwise, "the warrantor is discharged to the extent of any loss caused by the delay in giving notice of the claim." Id.

3. Failure to Assert Defenses Against Customer

Remember that Articles 3 and 4 provide a payor bank with various defenses in check fraud cases. (See Chapter 5 *supra*.) In certain situations, ineffective indorsements are deemed valid; and for various reasons a drawer is precluded from complaining about an unauthorized indorsement or alteration. See 3–404, 3–405, 3–406 & 4–406. A payor bank should not be allowed to ignore these defenses, accept the check fraud loss from its customer, and then pass the loss to someone upstream in the collection process by way of a warranty or other action. To allow such shifting of the loss would undermine the purposes and policies behind the Code defenses or upset the balancing of liabilities that the whole scheme of defenses is designed to achieve. For this reason, Article 4 encourages a payor bank to assert its defenses against a customer by giving warrantors this derivative protection:

> If a drawee asserts a claim for breach of warranty under subsection (a) [4–208(a)] based on an unauthorized indorsement of the draft or an alteration of the draft, the warrantor may defend by proving that the indorsement is

> effective under Section 3–404 or 3–405 or the drawer is precluded under Section 3–406 or 4–406 from asserting against the drawee the unauthorized indorsement or alteration.

4–208(c).

B drew a check to S who fraudulently raised the amount of the item. S cashed the item at DB Bank which presented the item for payment to the drawee, PB Bank. The check, as altered, was paid and charged to B's account. B did not discover the alteration until 14 months after receiving from PB the canceled item and a statement of account covering it. B demanded that PB recredit her account, arguing that the check was not properly payable beyond the original tenor of the item. Although B's claim against PB was barred by 4–406(f), PB re-credited B's account for the amount of the alteration and, in the process, waived the 4–406 defense against B's claim. PB then sued DB Bank for breach of the 4–208(a) presentment warranty against alteration. DB wins. Because PB waived its 4–406 defense to B's claim, 4–208 and 4–406 preclude PB from asserting any claim against DB based on the alteration.

4. Forged Signature Not Unauthorized

When a payor bank's breach of warranty claim is based on an unauthorized signature, it is a good defense that the signature was actually authorized (expressly or impliedly) by the person whose name was signed, or was otherwise effective under agency law or other extra-Code law. This defense is asserted by the warrantor in its own right and directly against the payor bank, and is not premised on the payor bank having failed to raise the defense against the bank's customer. The defense, if proved, undermines completely the very foundation of the payor bank's claim.

B drew a check to S on an account at PB Bank. Signing S's name, T indorsed the check and cashed it at DB Bank. PB Bank paid the check and charged it to B's account. When B complained that the check was not properly payable because it lacked S's indorsement, PB Bank recredited B's account and sued DB Bank for breach of the 4–208(a)(1) warranty. DB Bank wins if it can establish that T had authority to indorse the check on S's behalf, just as DB would win (because of 4–208(c)) if the case were covered by 3–404 or 3–405 so that any person's indorsement in S's name was deemed effective.

E. RECOVERY OVER (PASSING THE BUCK) THROUGH 4–207 TRANSFER WARRANTIES

A person who is liable to a payor bank for breaching a 4–208 presentment warranty can often pass the loss to someone else further upstream in the collection process on the basis of the transfer warranties implied by 4–207, which provides:

> A customer or collecting bank that transfers an item and receives a settlement or other consideration warrants to the transferee and to any subsequent collecting bank that:

(1) the warrantor is a person entitled to enforce the item;

(2) all signatures on the item are authentic and authorized;

(3) the item has not been altered;

(4) the item is not subject to a defense or claim in recoupment (Section 3–305(a)) of any party that can be asserted against the warrantor;

(5) the warrantor has no knowledge of any insolvency proceeding commenced with respect to the maker or acceptor or, in the case of an unaccepted draft, the drawer; and

(6) with respect to any remotely-created consumer item, that the person on whose account the item is drawn authorized the issuance of the item in the amount for which the item is drawn.

4–207(a). In addition, each customer and collecting bank that transfers an item and receives a settlement or other consideration is obligated to pay the item if the item is dishonored. 4–207(b).

As you can see, the 4–207 transfer warranties cover the same kinds of fraud and more that are covered by the presentment warranties of 4–208. So, in any case where a presentment warranty is breached, there is a corresponding transfer warranty. The transfer warranties thus ordinarily insure that any check fraud loss unloaded by a payor bank can be passed upstream to the very beginning of the collection chain, thereby protecting every collecting bank through which the check passed. This is possible because the transfer warranties are made, in seriatim order, by *each* customer and collecting bank who transfers an item and receives a settlement or other consideration for it, and they run in favor of the customer's or collecting bank's "transferee and to *any subsequent collecting bank.*" 4–207(a) (emphasis added). A transferee not protected by 4–207 may find protection among the similar warranties of 3–416 which covers transfers of instruments outside of the check collection process.

Suppose B drew a check on her account at PB Bank, and gave it to S in payment for goods. T stole the check from S and cashed it at DB Bank, after forging S's indorsement. DB Bank forwarded the item for collection through an intermediary bank, IB Bank. IB presented the check for payment to PB Bank which paid the item and charged it to B's account. Upon learning of the theft, S demanded the price of the goods sold to B. B paid S in cash, and then demanded that PB Bank recredit her account for the amount of the check because the check was not properly payable. PB Bank did so. Now PB Bank can sue, for breach of the presentment warranty of 4–208(a)(1), any of the following: IB Bank, DB Bank, or T. Suppose that PB Bank sues IB Bank. IB Bank, in turn, can sue DB Bank or T for breach of the corresponding transfer warranty. See 4–207(a)(1). If IB Bank sues DB Bank, the latter bank can rely on the same transfer warranty to recover from T.

Upon scanning the 4–207 transfer warranties, you will notice that the list includes a warranty that "all signatures on the item are authentic and authorized," 4–207(a)(2), which is not limited by a requirement that the warrantor know of the problem. You might conclude that this warranty would permit a payor bank to shift a loss resulting from a forged drawer's signature where prior parties were unaware of the forgery. You are wrong! Remember: The 4–207 transfer warranties do not run in favor of payors. The only warranties to payors are the presentment warranties of 4–208, which are less inclusive than the transfer warranties.

F. PAYOR BANK'S RESTITUTION ACTION TO SHIFT LOSSES NOT COVERED BY PAYMENT WARRANTIES

1. The Claims for Restitution

You surely will notice that certain check fraud and other kinds of losses that a payor bank can suffer are not covered by the 4–208 payment warranties. Most noticeable are losses resulting from checks bearing unauthorized drawers' signatures when the lack of authority is unknown to prior parties, payments over valid stop orders, and losses resulting from overdrafts (a/k/a NSF checks) that cannot be collected from customers because the customers are insolvent or otherwise unable or unavailable to satisfy the overdrafts.

Payor banks sometimes argue mistake and rely on restitution law or some other common-law theory to recoup these losses from persons who obtained payment of such items or who otherwise received the proceeds of them. Section 3–418 sanctions the common-law restitution claim in 3–418(b) and, to some extent, codifies restitutionary liability in 3–418(a) which covers the two most common cases of mistaken payment: payment of forged checks and checks on which the drawer has stopped payment. If the case does not fit within (a), however, the bank is then free under (b) to resort to the common law which, rather than 3–418, will determine liability:

> (a) Except as provided in subsection (c), if the drawee of a draft pays or accepts the draft and the drawee acted on the mistaken belief that (i) payment of the draft had not been stopped pursuant to Section 4–403 or (ii) the signature of the drawer of the draft was authorized, the drawee may recover the amount of the draft from the person to whom or for whose benefit payment was made or, in the case of acceptance, may revoke the acceptance. Rights of the drawee under this subsection are not affected by failure of the drawee to exercise ordinary care in paying or accepting the draft.
>
> (b) Except as provided in subsection (c), if an instrument has been paid or accepted by mistake and the case is not covered by subsection (a), the person paying or accepting may, to the extent permitted by the law governing mistake and restitution, (i) recover the payment from the person to whom or for

> whose benefit payment was made or (ii) in the case of acceptance, may revoke the acceptance.

3–418(a–b).

2. The Defense to Restitution

At the same time, 3–418 creates a huge defense to both common law and statutory restitution:

> The remedies provided by subsection (a) or (b) may not be asserted against a person who took the instrument in good faith and for value or who in good faith changed position in reliance on the payment or acceptance. * * *

3–418(c). It is a defense to any action by any payor to recover payment or escape acceptance made on any instrument without regard to the nature of the error the payor made as to the state of the drawer's account. So the defense is available whether the loss to the payor was caused by a forged drawer's signature; an overdraft; payment over a stop order; or any other circumstance giving reason for the payor bank's complaint. Behind 3–418(c) is the argument for finality of payment, and this argument applies whatever the payor's reason for avoiding payment or acceptance. Also behind 3–418(c) is the additional reason that the drawee is responsible for knowing the state of the account before acceptance or payment.

There are two limitations on the 3–418(c) defense:

- First, the defense is only available to a holder in due course (or other good faith purchaser) or a person who in good faith changed her position in reliance on the payment. As against anyone else, the equities favor allowing the payor to recover payments mistakenly made. (Practically speaking, however, in most cases any solvent party who benefited from payment will have taken the check in good faith and for value so that the defense is available to her.)

- Second, 3–418(c) is no defense for anyone to a payor's recovery for breach of a presentment warranty or to recovery of a bank settlement under 4–301. In these cases other concerns override the policies behind 3–418(c).

2. PAYEE VERSUS DEPOSITARY-COLLECTING BANK

A. SETTING UP AND JUSTIFYING THE DIRECT ACTION IN THE TYPICAL CHECK FRAUD CASE

The most common kind of check fraud involves forged indorsements. In the typical case, a thief steals checks payable to someone else, forges the payee's indorsements, and deposits the checks at a bank where the thief maintains an account. The thief may have opened the account in the name of the payee, posing as a representative of the payee who is authorized to deal with the account; or the thief may have opened the account in some other name, even her own name. The stolen checks are eventually paid by the payor bank. The thief's account thus swells, and the drawers' accounts correspondingly shrink.

Obviously, the payee is the person who initially suffers loss from this fraudulent scheme. We know, however, that the payee can shift the loss to the drawers of the stolen checks. Because the checks carried forged indorsements, the checks were not paid to a holder. Therefore, the drawers of the checks were not discharged on the instruments or on their underlying obligations to the payee. The drawers thus remain liable to the payee.

Upon satisfying their obligations to the payee, the drawers thereby assume the check fraud loss, inasmuch as their checking accounts have already been reduced by the amounts of the stolen checks. The drawers have, in effect, paid twice. The drawers, however, can pass the loss to the payor banks. The stolen checks paid by the banks were not properly payable and could not rightfully be charged to the drawers' accounts. Therefore, their accounts must be re-credited.

The check fraud loss passes to the payor banks when they recredit the drawers' accounts. Of course, the payor banks can shift the loss back up the collection chain by relying on the presentment warranty that the warrantor was entitled to enforce the checks. 4–208(a)(1). The collecting banks that obtained payment of the checks, and each prior customer and collecting bank, made this warranty to the payor banks. They effectively warranted that the checks carried all necessary indorsements, and that the indorsements were authorized. Sooner or later, the loss will come to rest on the first collecting bank, i.e., the depositary bank, which is the bank where the thief deposited or cashed the stolen checks. In theory, this bank can recoup from the thief who herself breached the 4–207(a)(1) transfer warranty of right to enforce. By this time, however, the thief is long gone, physically or financially.

So the loss rests ultimately with the depositary-collecting bank in line with the policy of putting the loss on the person in the best position to protect against it. Yet, implementing this policy involves a very long, circuitous route of claims and recoveries over: payee v. drawers; drawers v. payor banks; payor banks v. depositary bank or intermediary banks; intermediary banks v. depositary bank. It would be much more efficient if the payee sued the depositary bank directly. After all, in this case the payee is the real victim of the check fraud, and the depositary bank is the entity that, in the end, is ultimately responsible.

B. THEORY OF THE DIRECT ACTION—CONVERSION

The holder of a check is the owner of it and the only rightful recipient of its proceeds unless she, or someone acting by her authority, directs otherwise. Therefore, when a check is stolen from a payee, her indorsement forged and the proceeds of the instrument are misappropriated, the thief is guilty of converting the payee's property and is liable to the payee for common-law conversion; and so is every transferee involved in the misappropriation even though the transferee acted innocently and without knowledge of the payee's superior rights. As a result, the bank at which the thief cashes the stolen check, or deposits it, is liable for conversion to the payee. Article 3 recognizes and codifies this conversion liability by providing:

> An instrument is * * * converted if it is taken by transfer, other than a negotiation, from a person not entitled to enforce the instrument or a bank makes or obtains payment with respect to the instrument for a person not entitled to enforce the instrument or receive payment.

3–420(a). "This covers cases in which a depositary or payor bank takes an instrument bearing a forged indorsement." 3–420 comment 1.

C. DAMAGES FOR CONVERSION

"[T]he measure of liability is presumed to be the amount payable on the instrument, but recovery may not exceed the amount of the plaintiff's interest in the instrument." 3–420(b).

Here is an example: T steals a check from Payee, forges Payee's indorsement, and cashes the check at DB Bank. The check is presented for payment and charged to the drawer's account at PB Bank. Payee sues DB Bank. In the absence of a defense, DB Bank is liable for the amount of the check. In case an instrument that pays interest is converted, the damages are presumed to include the loss of interest.

Suppose the same facts except that the check is payable jointly to two payees who are a building contractor and a supplier of building material. The check is delivered to the contractor who forges the supplier's indorsement. "The supplier should not, without qualification, be able to recover the entire amount of the check from the bank that converted the check. Depending upon the contract between the contractor and the supplier, the amount of the check may be due entirely to the contractor, in which case there should be no recovery, entirely to the supplier, in which case recovery should be for the entire amount, or part may be due to one and the rest to the other, in which case recovery should be limited to the amount due to the supplier." 3–420 comment 2.

D. NO DEFENSE OF GOOD FAITH TO THE DIRECT ACTION

1. Former Law

Under former law the depositary-collecting bank's principal defense was this rule:

> [A] representative, *including a depositary or collecting bank*, who has in good faith and in accordance with the reasonable commercial standards applicable to the business of such representative dealt with an instrument or its proceeds on behalf of one who was not the true owner is not liable in conversion or otherwise to the true owner beyond the amount of any proceeds remaining in his hands.

3–419(3) (1989 Official Text) (emphasis added). According to the usual interpretation of 3–419(3), a depositary-collecting bank acted as a *representative* when it took checks for deposit and collection from a thief who had stolen them and forged the payee's indorsement, even though the person represented was not the owner of the items. So, when the payee sued the bank for conversion, the section operated as a defense, except to the extent of proceeds remaining in the bank's hands. As usually interpreted, however, "remaining proceeds" meant funds attributable to the forged checks that remained available in the wrongdoer's account. The bank thus was not liable for amounts attributable to the checks that had been withdrawn from the account. Ordinarily, most of the funds had been withdrawn, and 3–419(3) thus operated as a complete, or almost complete, defense for the bank. There were contrary interpretations of 3–419(3) that very narrowly defined the term "representative," or the "remaining proceeds" language, so that 3–419(3) did not apply to any extent as a defense for the depositary-collecting bank. Most cases, however, rejected these interpretations, with the ultimate effect that the payee's direct action against the depositary-collecting bank was usually fruitless—except where the wrongdoer had left tainted funds in her account, or where the peculiar circumstances of the particular case made the 3–419(3) defense unavailable by its own terms.

2. Change in Law Denies Defense to Depositary Bank

In 1990, 3–419(3) became 3–420(c) and more than the number was changed. The section was rewritten to provide:

> A representative, *other than a depositary bank*, who has in good faith dealt with an instrument or its proceeds on behalf of one who was not the person entitled to enforce the instrument is not liable in conversion to that person beyond the amount of any proceeds that it has not paid out.

3–420(c) (emphasis added). This change in substance denies to depositary banks the defense of having acted reasonably and in good faith in dealing with converted items. The reason for the change is clear and sound, inasmuch as former law allowed the payee to shift the loss directly or indirectly to the payor bank which could shift it ultimately to the depositary bank:

> The depositary bank is ultimately liable in the case of a forged indorsement check because of its warranty to the payor bank under Section 4–208(a)(1) and it is usually the most convenient defendant in cases involving multiple checks drawn on different banks. There is no basis for requiring the owner of the check to bring multiple actions against the various payor banks and to require those banks to assert warranty rights against the depositary bank.

3–420 comment 3.

3. OTHER DIRECT ACTION SUITS

A. PAYEE VERSUS PAYOR BANK

1. Basis of the Action

In the typical check fraud case involving a payee's unauthorized indorsement, there is no doubt that the payee can recover directly from the payor bank for conversion if the check is paid. Paying a check over a forged indorsement amounts to conversion. 3–420(a). Because the payee is the owner of the check and is entitled to its proceeds, she is a proper party to complain of the wrong by the payor bank. Section 3–420 covers any case in which a check is paid over an unauthorized or missing indorsement.

2. Inapplicability of the 3–420(c) Defense

The defense of 3–420(c), which bars or limits a conversion action against a "representative" who deals with converted checks in good faith, is not available to the payor bank. The payor bank is not a "representative" within the meaning of the section, which has no applicability here whatsoever.

B. DRAWER VERSUS DEPOSITARY-COLLECTING BANK

The traditional view is that in the typical unauthorized indorsement case, the drawer of the check cannot directly recover from the depositary-collecting bank for conversion, money had and received, or otherwise. Article 3 expressly adopts this view, at least with respect to conversion. It provides that "[a]n action for conversion of an instrument may not be brought by * * * the issuer or acceptor of the instrument * * *." 3–420(a). The explanation is that the drawer of the check is not the holder or owner of the item, and has no right to the proceeds of it. Moreover, even though the check was paid and the drawer's account charged with the item, this charge was not authorized or effective against the drawer because the check was not properly payable, inasmuch as it carried an unauthorized indorsement. Therefore, any wrong committed by the depositary-collecting bank in dealing with the check violated no valuable property or other rights of the drawer. The drawer's recourse is to recover from the payor bank for paying an item that was not properly payable.

CHAPTER 7

BANK CHECKS

All of the earlier chapters in this part of the book deal with ordinary checks on which the drawer is a customer of the payor bank. The payor bank is drawee only, has not signed it in the beginning, does not accept it later, and is therefore never liable on the check under Article 3. Any liability the payor bank incurs is a result of some misstep and liability under Article 4.

This chapter deals with checks that a bank signs and for this reason is liable—on the checks themselves—under Article 3. To some extent Article 4 applies, too, and adds risks of further liability for violating rules of bank deposits and collections that apply to bank checks.

The bank checks discussed here are fully negotiable instruments in their standard forms. Otherwise, Article 3 has no application. Also, when put in circulation and deposited and collected, bank checks are subject to Article 4. Yet, Articles 3 and 4 apply differently to them in important respects, and these differences are the focus here—mainly as they affect rights and liabilities of ordinary customers who use bank checks, instead of ordinary checks, in transactions between them.

1. DIFFERENT TYPES: CERTIFIED, CASHIER'S, AND TELLER'S CHECKS

A **certified check** is really a hybrid. It begins life as an ordinary check and later becomes a bank check because the drawee signs, accepts, and thereby certifies it. The official definition is a "check accepted by the bank on which it is drawn." 3–409(d). The acceptance is the certification.

In real life, banks hardly ever certify a customer's check. The process is too expensive. Instead, when a customer needs the bank's liability on an instrument, the bank will sell the customer a **cashier's check**. It is a check drawn by the bank on itself. 3–104(g). The bank is both drawer and drawee. Typically, just as the bank does not sign its customers' checks, a customer who buys a cashier's check does not sign it. The customer's name may appear on the check to identify who bought it. In this role the customer is known as the **remitter**, 3–103(a)(15); but being named as remitter does not equate with having signed the cashier's check.

Banks maintain accounts among themselves. They often swap funds through these accounts by electronic transfers but can and do write checks against some of these accounts. A **teller's check** "means a draft drawn by a bank (i) on another bank, or (ii) payable at or through a bank." 3–104(h).

Bank checks do **not** generally include **money orders** sold by banks, depending on the form of the item. In truest form, a bank money order is really a check drawn by the customer against the general credit of the bank rather than against an account the customer owns. The bank commits to the customer to pay the check, just as the bank promises in a deposit agreement to pay checks the customer draws against her own account. However, just as the bank is not liable on the customer's checks against her account, the bank is not liable on the money order it sells the customer. It's very much a special, one-check checking account with a balance that equals the amount of the money order which is pre-cut in the same amount. Bank money orders are properly treated as ordinary checks.

2. HOW THEY WORK—THEIR INCIDENTS AND EFFECTS

A. CERTIFIED CHECKS

Suppose B buys goods from S and wants to pay by check. S is worried about the possibility of dishonor. So, B draws a check payable to S, takes the check to her bank, the drawee, and asks the drawee to certify the check. Remember: a drawee bank is never liable on a check unless and until it accepts. 3–408. By getting the bank to certify the check, the bank thereby accepts and becomes liable on the check as "acceptor." 3–409(d). The bank's liability on the check increases S's willingness to take B's check.

Note that the customer asking the bank to certify her check is not presenting for payment or any other purpose. The request neither imposes nor triggers any obligations or liabilities. "The drawee of a check has no obligation to certify the check, and refusal to certify is not dishonor of the check." 3–409(d). The reason a bank agrees to certify is to accommodate the customer and maybe earn a fee.

Acceptance is defined as "the drawee's signed agreement to pay a draft as presented." 3–409(a). The means of the acceptance are simple: "[i]t must be written on the draft and may consist of the drawee's signature alone." Id. Typically, the bank accepts after the customer has fully completed the check, but "[a] draft may be accepted although it has not been signed by the drawer, is otherwise incomplete, is overdue, or has been dishonored." 3–409(b).

A bank is highly unlikely to accept a customer's check that is incomplete, especially if the amount is left blank, because by signing the check the bank becomes liable on it. It is not liable as the drawer or an indorser. Rather, it is liable as an "acceptor" whose contract of liability on the instrument is "to pay the draft":

- according to its terms at the time it was accepted, even though the acceptance states that the draft is payable "as originally drawn" or equivalent terms,

- if the acceptance varies the terms of the draft, according to the terms of the draft as varied, or

- if the acceptance is of a draft that is an incomplete instrument, according to its terms when completed, to the extent stated in 3–115 and 3–407.

3–413(a). The obligation is owed to a person entitled to enforce the draft or to the drawer or an indorser who paid it.

When B pays S with the certified check, S thereby becomes a holder and so a person entitled to enforce the instrument. The bank's liability as acceptor thus runs to S.

B, however, is not liable on the certified check, even though she signed the check as drawer. "If a draft is accepted by a bank, the drawer is discharged, regardless of when or by whom acceptance was obtained." 3–414(c). Moreover, B's obligation on the underlying transaction between her and S is also discharged. 3–310(a). So, S is left with only the liability of the bank as acceptor of the check. On the other hand, the risk of bank insolvency is very small, and the risk of other nonpayment or stop payment is small, too. See discussion below.

B. CASHIER'S CHECKS

Suppose B's bank is unwilling to certify B's check (as is generally the case) and offers instead to sell B a cashier's check, which S agrees to take for the obligation B owes her. This instrument is signed by a bank official who is authorized to bind the bank. This official signs on behalf of the bank—fully disclosing the principal as principal and her representative capacity. Typically, S's name is filled in as the person to whose order the cashier's check is payable. Typically, also, the check names B as remitter, but she does not sign it.

Having signed the cashier's check, the bank is "obliged to pay the instrument"

- according to its terms at the time it was issued or, if not issued, at the time it first came into possession of a holder, or
- if the issuer signed an incomplete instrument, according to its terms when completed, to the extent stated in 3–115 and 3–407.

3–412. This obligation is equivalent to the obligation of maker of a note in that the liability of the issuer of a cashier's check, like the liability of the maker of a note, is not conditioned on dishonor.

The bank's liability is owed to a person entitled to enforce the instrument or to an indorser who paid the instrument under 3–415. After getting the cashier's check S becomes a person entitled to enforce it and thus the bank's obligation on the check runs to her.

The effect of S taking the cashier's check for the underlying transaction between her and B is to discharge B's obligation on the transaction. 3–310(a). Because B has not signed the check, B has no liability to S on the instrument. Again, however, as in the case of a certified check, the risk of bank insolvency is virtually non-existent, and the risk of other nonpayment or stop payment is small, too. See discussion below.

Now, it's possible for B to sign the cashier's check and incur personal liability on it. The bank could issue the cashier's check to B's order, and B would become liable by indorsing and negotiating the check to S. Or, even if the check is issued to S's order originally, B could sign the check in the margin on the front or on the back when delivering the check to S. Although B's signature was not necessary in this case for negotiation or any other purpose, the effect is the same: she is liable as an indorser. In either case, B's liability as indorser is triggered should the bank dishonor the cashier's check. B still has no liability on her underlying obligation, 3–310(a) (last sentence), which was discharged when S took the cashier's check. 3–310(a) (first sentence).

C. TELLER'S CHECKS

Our interest in teller's checks is a particular use of the instrument. Less so today than years ago, some financial services companies that are "banks" within the meaning of Articles 3 and 4 do not maintain accounts that their customers can access by check or similar means. So, when a customer of such a bank makes a withdrawal from her account, her bank gives her a check on an account that her bank maintains in its own name at a commercial bank. There are also other reasons why a bank of any kind sometimes pays its own obligations with checks drawn on another bank.

It would appear that a teller's check is exactly like an ordinary check, except that the drawer is a bank which might draw checks against an account at the same payor bank where you have an account. There are differences, however.

The obligation on the instrument of the bank issuing a teller's check is exactly the same as the obligation of the drawer of an ordinary check, i.e., to pay the instrument upon dishonor. 3–414(b). Yet, a teller's check is treated like a cashier's check—not like an ordinary check—in terms of the effect when taken for an underlying obligation. Suppose obligated bank issues a teller's check drawn on payor bank to S to pay some obligation owed her. S's taking the teller's check discharges the obligated bank's underlying obligation. 3–310(a).

On the other hand, as in the case of an ordinary check, the obligated bank remains liable on the teller's check as drawer of the instrument. Also, the payor bank is not liable on the teller's check because the payor bank's role is drawee only. The payor bank's dishonor of the teller's check triggers the obligated bank's liability as drawer. Here, though, is another difference from an ordinary check. The obligated bank on a teller's check incurs special, additional liability for stopping payment on or refusing to pay the instrument, which is beyond the usual liability of a drawer of an ordinary check. See discussion below.

3. STOPPING PAYMENT

In a very large number of cases the courts have considered if payment can be stopped on a cashier's check. This broad concern involves two entirely separate issues. The easier issue is whether the bank that issues the cashier's check becomes liable to the person who procured it, i.e., the remitter, by refusing to dishonor the instrument upon the remitter's request. The second and harder issue is whether an issuing bank that refuses payment of its cashier's check, either on its own or at the request of the remitter, can escape liability to the payee or other holder of the instrument.

Suppose that B buys goods from S who demands payment in the form of a cashier's check. B purchases a cashier's check from Bank and delivers the instrument to S. B quickly learns that the goods are defective and asks Bank not to pay the cashier's check and to return to B the money she paid Bank for the check. Must Bank honor B's request?

The answer is no, unless Bank and B have an enforceable agreement giving B the right to stop payment of the check. B does not have the right apart from such an agreement. 4–403 does not apply for two reasons: First, 4–403 is limited to checks drawn on the customer's account. A cashier's check is drawn by the issuing bank against the bank's own account. Second, a stop order comes too late, i.e., is ineffective, if received after the item it covers has been accepted. See 4–303(a)(1). A draft drawn by the drawer on itself is accepted upon issuance. Therefore, there can never be a timely stop order of a cashier's check.

A bank that issues a cashier's check may wish to dishonor the item either as a courtesy to the remitter who requests that payment be stopped, or for the bank's own reasons. The problem in doing so is that the bank, as issuer of the check, is liable on the instrument to the payee or a subsequent holder. 3–412. In a conflict between the bank and a holder of the cashier's check, is the bank always and inevitably liable, or can the bank raise defenses to its liability on the instrument? The courts disagree on this issue.

Some courts have suggested, in applying a variety of technical justifications, that the bank that issues a cashier's check is strictly, absolutely liable thereon to any holder of the instrument. The rationale for this view is that a cashier's check is regarded in the commercial world as the equivalent of cash, and to allow the issuing bank to assert defenses to payment would undermine the useful purposes of cashier's checks as substitutes for money.

A far preferable view is that an issuing bank can raise defenses to the payment of a cashier's check according to the usual rules governing an obligor's liability on a negotiable instrument. Unless the holder is a holder in due course, the bank can raise the full range of its defenses permitted under 3–305 and 3–306, including the defenses of want or failure of consideration and all other defenses of the bank which would be available in an action on a simple contract. If the holder enjoys "due course" status, the bank can raise only its real defenses. Yet, even if the holder lacks due-course status, the bank can assert only its own defenses. It cannot raise defenses that are personal to the remitter, such as breach of contract between the remitter and the payee of the cashier's check. Such matters are properly left for decision in an action between those parties.

Here are examples:

1. B satisfied an obligation to S by giving S a cashier's check B procured from Bank. In exchange for the cashier's check, B had given Bank her personal check drawn on another financial institution. B's personal check bounced. For this reason Bank dishonored the cashier's check when S presented it for payment. S sued Bank on the cashier's check. Bank can raise its defense of lack or failure of consideration unless S is a holder in due course who did not deal with the Bank. S may be a holder in due course even though she is the payee of the cashier's check.

2. S sold goods to B who paid for them using a cashier's check issued by Bank. The goods were defective, and B asked Bank to stop payment of the check. Because B was a valued customer, Bank dishonored the cashier's check when S presented it for payment. S sued Bank on the instrument. Bank should not be allowed to assert B's breach of contract claim as a defense.

Issues about stopping payment of certified checks arise less often, but the analysis is fundamentally the same. The drawer lacks the right herself to stop payment, and the bank's right—as acceptor—to assert defenses seems limited to the same extent as the defensive rights of a bank that issues a cashier's check.

The analysis for a teller's check is different. The check is drawn on an account owned by the obligated bank and maintained with the payor bank. The obligated bank is the payor bank's customer with respect to the check. So, the obligated bank can stop payment, and the payor bank incurs no liability for following the order and dishonoring the check. Indeed, the payor bank is obliged to obey its customer's orders.

On the other hand, the dishonor triggers the obligated bank's liability as drawer, and this liability is enhanced by special rules that apply to all bank checks. See discussion below.

4. ENHANCED LIABILITIES OF BANKS ON BANK CHECKS, 3–411

Even when banks are liable as issuers of cashier's check, drawers of teller's checks, or acceptors of certified checks, they retain the power to deny their liability and refuse payment even when they lack the right to do so. This power is held by anybody who is liable on an instrument, but there is more of a problem when the payor is a bank. The expectation of payment is higher when a bank is obligated on an instrument, and it leads to extraordinary reliance equally on cashier's, teller's, and certified checks.

To discourage and compensate for abuses of this power, Article 3 broadens the liability of an "obligated bank" which means "the acceptor of a certified check or the issuer of a cashier's check or teller's check bought from the issuer." 3–411(a). In essence, an obligated bank that refuses payment without good reason is liable for special or consequential damages caused the person asserting the right to enforce the check. The rule is:

> If the obligated bank wrongfully (i) refuses to pay a cashier's check or certified check, (ii) stops payment of a teller's check, or (iii) refuses to pay a dishonored teller's check, the person asserting the right to enforce the check is entitled to compensation for expenses and loss of interest resulting from the nonpayment and may recover consequential damages if the obligated bank refuses to pay after receiving notice of particular circumstances giving rise to the damages.

3–411(b). This extraordinary liability is excused if:

- the bank suspends payments,
- the obligated bank asserts a claim or defense of the bank that it has reasonable grounds to believe is available against the person entitled to enforce the instrument,
- the obligated bank has a reasonable doubt whether the person demanding payment is the person entitled to enforce the instrument, or
- payment is prohibited by law.

3–411(c).

5. WHEN BANK CHECKS ARE LOST OR STOLEN

Article 3 deals specially with another problem of cashier's, teller's and certified checks—enforcement when the check is lost, destroyed or stolen. In the typical situation, a person claims the right to receive the proceeds of a check that she has lost. The risk to the bank which honors the claim is that the check will end up in the hands of a holder in due course who can force the bank to pay the check. The bank will have paid twice. Perhaps the bank can recoup from the original claimant but the bank risks this person's solvency. The bank can protect itself by requiring the original claimant to provide security for any payment to her, but this imposes a large burden on this person.

Section 3–312 attempts to accommodate the interests of the bank and original claimant. The statute allows the claimant to make a claim for payment by providing the bank with a declaration of loss. The claim is enforceable at the later of the time the claim is made or the 90th day following the date or certification of the check. If the claim becomes enforceable before the check is presented for payment, the bank is obliged to pay the claim and is discharged of all liability with respect to the check. The claim is legally ineffective prior to the time the claim become enforceable, and the bank must pay the check if the check is presented prior to the time of the claim's enforceability. The reasoning seems to be that if 90 days pass without presentment of the check, the claim of loss is probably legitimate and the possibility is small that someone will appear as a holder in due course of the instrument. In the unlikely event that such a person appears after the bank has honored an enforceable claim, the claimant is accountable for the check.

PART III

PAYING AGAINST ORDINARY DRAFTS AND DOCUMENTS

A check is not an entirely reliable means of paying for property or services. A seller who takes the buyer's check in exchange for property or services is not certain to get payment from the drawee-bank. The check can be dishonored for a variety of reasons (insufficient funds, stop order, etc.) that leave the seller-payee with nothing more than a cause of action against the buyer-drawer. The result is that, although the seller intended a cash deal, she ends up having sold on credit. To make matters worse, this unintended credit is probably unsecured.

The seller could virtually eliminate these risks by asking the buyer to pay with a cashier's check. The problem is that this means of payment shifts risks to the buyer, who may therefore refuse the deal or require compensation.

A seller of goods can insure that she is actually paid by not delivering the property until she gets cash, or its equivalent, in hand. Of course, the typical buyer will not wish to pay for the goods in advance of delivery. The answer is a simultaneous exchange of goods for cash. When the seller and buyer are located far apart, this kind of exchange is made possible through the use of a documentary draft and a payment scheme known as "payment against documents."

In this scheme, the seller ships the goods by carrier to the buyer's city. The carrier gives the seller a receipt for the goods which is known as a bill of lading. A bill of lading is a kind of document of title and, as such, it represents the goods and controls their disposition. The seller attaches this document to a draft drawn by her against the buyer. The set of two writings is called a documentary draft, which is handled for collection by banks. The seller's bank will take the documentary draft and, as agent for the seller, send it to a bank in the buyer's city. The latter bank, upon receiving the documentary draft, will present it to the buyer for payment. Upon paying it, the buyer gets the document of title and thereby gets control of the goods. The payment is then sent by the presenting bank to the seller's bank and deposited in the seller's account.

Payment against documents is fully discussed in Chapter 9 *infra*, beginning with a short lesson on some of the law of documents of title. You cannot understand the former until you understand the latter. More fundamentally, understanding payment against documents requires that you know something about ordinary drafts. You know about checks, which are a form of draft. Chapter 8 discusses the major, special concepts and rules that attend drafts that are not checks—ordinary drafts.

CHAPTER 8

ORDINARY DRAFTS UNDER ARTICLES 3 AND 4

UCC Article 3 governs negotiable instruments. There are two basic types of negotiable instruments: note and draft. Earlier chapters of this book explain the most common form of draft: check.

This chapter explains a little about drafts that are not checks. Let's call them "ordinary drafts." The explanation is little because law school courses typically give some—but relatively small—attention to drafts that are not checks, except documentary drafts which are discussed in the next chapter. Indeed, the main purpose of the coverage of ordinary drafts here is so you will better understand documentary drafts covered later. So, here are the very basic basics of ordinary drafts and the fundamental rules of Articles 3 and 4 that apply differently to them compared to ordinary checks.

1. SIMPLE DEMAND OR SIGHT DRAFT

Suppose Ellen owes Thomas $100, and Thomas wants his money. Ellen could pay him in cash. She could "pay" by giving him her check drawn on an account with a payor bank. Ellen also could "pay" Thomas with an ordinary draft drawn on a person that is not a bank.

For example, let's say that on the basis of an entirely separate deal, Mohammad owed Ellen $100. Ellen could pay Thomas by writing and signing a draft ordering Mohammad to pay Thomas or his order $100 on demand. A draft payable on demand is also called a "sight draft."

This writing is a negotiable instrument in the form of an ordinary draft. Ellen is the drawer. Thomas is the payee. Mohammad is the drawee. Ellen is liable on the draft as drawer, but neither Thomas nor Mohammad is liable on the draft because neither of them signed it. Thomas would collect by presenting the draft to Mohammad.

If the instrument were a check drawn on a bank, the bank is obligated by contract (i.e., the deposit agreement) with Ellen to pay the check. If the bank dishonors the check, the bank is not liable to Thomas but is liable to Ellen for breach of the deposit contract.

In this case, Mohammad is not a bank and the instrument is not a check. Absent some extraordinary agreement with Ellen, Mohammad is not obligated to pay the draft. If he does pay the draft, however, Ellen's liability on the draft is discharged and also her liability on the underlying obligation to Thomas. At the same time Mohammad's underlying obligation to Ellen is discharged.

If Mohammad refuses to pay the draft, i.e., dishonors it when Thomas presents the draft, Mohammad is not liable on the draft and is not liable to Ellen for dishonoring it.

Ellen, however, is liable. She is the drawer who is obliged to pay the instrument upon dishonor by the drawee. Thomas would sue Ellen on the draft or on the underlying obligation Ellen owes Thomas.

Separately and unrelatedly, Ellen would collect the debt Mohammad owes her.

2. TIME OR ACCEPTANCE DRAFT

Instead of ordering Mohammad to pay the draft on demand, Ellen could write the draft ordering Mohammad to pay at a definite future time. In this case Thomas would have to wait until the time for payment before he could present the draft to Mohammad for payment.

Thomas may be worried about Mohammad honoring the draft. Remember: Article 3 does not require Mohammad to pay the draft on which he is drawee and does not obligate Mohammad on the draft itself. The draft names him as the drawee, but he did not sign it.

Thomas can reduce his worry by presenting the draft to Mohammad before the time for payment. This earlier presentment, however, is not for payment. It is for acceptance, which means Mohammad signs the draft and becomes liable on it as an acceptor. Then, if Mohammad does not pay the draft when the draft is due, Mohammad is liable to Thomas on the instrument as "acceptor."

Mohammad's acceptance does not let Ellen off the hook. She remains liable on the draft and is obliged to pay. So, if Mohammad accepts and dishonors the draft when payment is due, Thomas can sue Mohammad or Ellen on the instrument. If Thomas sues Ellen, she in turn can sue Mohammad on the instrument. The effect of Mohammad's acceptance of the draft changed Ellen's liability on the draft from her original liability as drawer to the liability of an indorser. 3–414(d). An acceptor who dishonors a draft is liable to an indorser.

3. COLLECTING DRAFTS THROUGH BANKS

How does Thomas present the draft to Mohammad for payment or acceptance? He could present the draft directly himself—in person or through some form of snail mail.

Another possibility is presenting through banking channels. Article 4 applies to items, which includes checks but is not limited to them. " 'Item' means an instrument or a promise or order to pay money handled by a bank for collection or payment." 4–104(a)(9).

Thomas takes the draft to his bank which sends the draft to Mohammad's bank. The purpose is not to present the draft to Mohammad's bank for payment. Mohammad's bank is not the drawee. Rather, the purpose of sending the draft to Mohammad's bank is "for collection." Mohammad's bank then presents the draft to Mohammad for payment by him.

On these facts both banks act as Thomas's agents for purposes of collecting the "item." Both banks are collecting banks with Thomas's bank as depositary bank and Mohammad's bank as presenting bank.

Neither of them is a drawee or payor bank, as neither of them is ordered to pay the draft.

The banks treat the item differently from a check. A check is treated as a cash item for which credit is given when the item is deposited and transferred between banks. An ordinary draft is treated as a noncash item. There are no credits following in the wake when Thomas gives the draft to his bank for collection and this bank forwards it to another bank for further collection. However, if the draft is paid, the proceeds will be remitted back through banking channels to Thomas; or, if the draft is dishonored or accepted, the item will follow the same path back to Thomas.

Also, each bank's duty to Thomas is to act reasonably in handling the item. 4–202. In the event of unreasonable conduct, i.e., negligence, the bank is liable for damages. 4–103(e). In no event, however, is the bank per se or strictly liable for the amount of the draft because of the negligence. The bank is liable only for damages that Thomas proves he suffered as a result of the negligence.

Collecting ordinary drafts is expensive and is not a public service. Thomas will pay a fee to the banks.

CHAPTER 9

TYING DRAFTS TO DOCUMENTS OF TITLE

1. DOCUMENTS OF TITLE

Checks and other negotiable instruments embody rights to the payment of money. Documents of title represent title to goods.

The principal source of state law on documents of title is U.C.C. Article 7, which is the basis of what is said here about documents. Be aware, however, that preemptive federal law often applies. See, e.g., United States Warehouse Act, 7 U.S.C.A. § 241 et seq. (governing the licensing and regulation of warehouses that store agricultural products for interstate or foreign commerce.); Pomerene Bills of Lading Act, 49 U.S.C.A. § 80101 to 80116 (interstate shipment of goods); Carriage of Goods by Sea Act, (see note to 46 U.S.C.A. § 30701) (shipments of goods from and to U.S. ports in foreign trade). These federal laws and Article 7 share many basic principles.

Under Article 7, a *document of title* (or its short-form synonym, *document*) is a record which "in the regular course of business or financing is treated as adequately evidencing that the person in possession or control of the record is entitled to receive, control, hold, and dispose of the record and the goods the record covers. . . ." 1–201(b)(16). Examples are: "bill of lading, transport document, dock warrant, dock receipt, warehouse receipt, and order for delivery of goods." Id. Among these examples, the most common and familiar are the bill of lading and the warehouse receipt, which explains why the balance of this discussion focuses exclusively on them. A certificate of title covering a motor vehicle is NOT a document of title within this definition.

A *bill of lading* is a "document of title evidencing the receipt of goods for shipment issued by a person engaged in the business of directly or indirectly transporting or forwarding goods * * *." 1–201(b)(6). Railroads and trucking lines, for example, issue bills of lading, as do other kinds of businesses which carry, i.e., transport, goods from one location to another. A *warehouse receipt* is "a document of title issued by a person engaged in the business of storing goods for hire." 1–201(b)(42). A farmer who stores grain in an elevator gets a warehouse receipt covering her crop. A law student who wins a mansion full of furniture on Wheel of Fortune gets a warehouse receipt upon storing the goods in a terminal near her law school. (There is no space for the booty in her studio apartment.) Notice that both kinds of documents originate with professional bailees, that is, people whose business—at least in part—is shipping or storing other people's goods.

In more general terms, a bill of lading or a warehouse receipt is, basically, evidence of a *bailment* that sets out the major terms of the contract between the bailor and bailee, including when and to whom the bailee should release the goods. A bill or receipt is also indicia of title to the bailed goods so that third parties can acquire ownership of, or other interests in, the goods by addressing the document rather than the goods themselves. In these roles, bills of lading and warehouse receipts serve two principal, closely related functions: controlling access to the goods and controlling ownership of them.

How a document serves these functions, and its effectiveness in doing so, are largely determined by whether the document is negotiable or non-negotiable.

A. DISTINGUISHING NEGOTIABLE DOCUMENTS

1. The Test for Negotiability

Recall (fondly?) the issue of determining whether a writing is negotiable under Article 3. U.C.C. 3–104(a) lists the requisites of Article 3 negotiability, but another dozen or so provisions in Part 1 of Article 3 amplify the listing. A chunk of Chapter 2, *supra*, is devoted to explaining those provisions as applied to checks.

Deciding if a document is negotiable under Article 7 is much easier. Except in overseas trade, the test is whether "by its [the document's] terms the goods are to be delivered to bearer or to the order of a named person." 7–104(a). That's it! "A document of title other than one described in subsection (a) is non-negotiable." 7–104(b). Restated in language you learned in studying Article 3, an Article 7 document is negotiable if it contains "words of negotiability." If these words are missing, the document is non-negotiable.

2. Article 7's Coverage of Non-Negotiable Documents

If a right to the payment of money is not negotiable under the provisions of Article 3, the consequences are that the writing is not an instrument and Article 3 is altogether inapplicable. Article 7 is different in this regard. It generally applies to both negotiable and non-negotiable documents. Making the distinction is important only in applying particular rules within Article 7, not in deciding whether the statute, as a whole, is the general source of governing law.

B. HOW DOCUMENTS CONTROL ACCESS TO THE GOODS

The bailee of goods who has issued a document of title, whether a bill of lading or a warehouse receipt, is generally obligated to "deliver the goods to a *person entitled under a document of title* * * *." 7–403(a) (emphasis added). The meaning of "person entitled under the document," which is the key to deciding who is entitled to the goods, depends on whether the document is negotiable or not.

1. When the Document Is Non-Negotiable

The person entitled to the goods under a non-negotiable document is "the person to which delivery of the goods is to be made by the terms of, or pursuant to instructions in a record * * *." 7–102(a)(9). Such written or electronic instructions, directed to a bailee who has issued either a warehouse receipt or a bill of lading, are referred to as a *delivery order,* 7–

102(a)(5), which is itself a document of title. 1–201(b)(16).

O stores goods with W who issues a non-negotiable warehouse receipt providing that the goods are "Received for the account of O." (There are no words of negotiability.) X steals the receipt and presents it to W. W would act wrongfully as against O by releasing the goods to X. W must deliver the goods to O or pursuant to O's instructions, and O has not instructed delivery to X.

Same facts except that O gives X a delivery order instructing W to deliver the goods to X. X presents this order to W. W is justified in releasing the goods to X.

A delivery order can be seen as Article 7's version of a check. A bank holds monetary credit that belongs to a customer. By her check the customer orders the bank to pay the credit to someone else. A warehouser or carrier, who is the bailee, holds goods that belong to the bailor. By a delivery order the bailor orders the bailee to deliver the goods to a third person.

The person named in a delivery order may not wish to take possession of the goods. Of course, the bailee is not bound to hold the goods for such person's account. If, however, the bailee agrees to hold the goods for the account of the person named in the delivery order, this agreement can be established by the bailee accepting the order, much as a drawee of a draft becomes liable thereon by accepting the instrument. "When a delivery order has been accepted by the bailee it is for practical purposes indistinguishable from a warehouse receipt." 7–102 comment 3. Thereafter, the bailee is obligated to deliver to the person entitled under the accepted delivery order.

O stores goods with W who issues a non-negotiable receipt. O writes a delivery order instructing W to deliver the goods to X. W accepts the order, which is itself non-negotiable. W is now obligated to deliver the goods to X or pursuant to the instructions of X.

2. When the Document Is Negotiable

The person to whom the bailee is obligated to deliver goods covered by a negotiable document is the *holder* of the document. 7–102(a)(9). The term "holder" has the same basic meaning here that it has for purposes of Article 3, except that documents are held instead of instruments: "Holder" means "the person in possession of a negotiable tangible document of title if the goods are deliverable either to bearer or to the order of the person in possession." 1–201(b)(21)(B). Deciding if a person is a holder depends, as under Article 3, on whether the paper is order or bearer paper.

a. Upon Issuance

If the bailee issues a negotiable document running to the order of a named person, only this person can be a holder upon issuance, and she acquires the status upon getting possession of the document which names her. If the document runs to bearer, any person in possession of it is a holder.

b. Subsequent Holders

A person can become the holder of a document issued to the order of someone else only if the person named in the document indorses it. If the indorsement is a blank indorsement, which means that the named person signs her name without specifying a person to whom delivery should be made, the document becomes bearer paper, and anybody in possession of it is a holder. If the indorsement is a special indorsement, meaning that the named person identifies someone to whom delivery should be made, no one can thereafter become a holder without the indorsement of the special indorsee. If the special indorsee indorses in blank, the document becomes bearer paper, and anyone in possession of it is a holder.

Of course, as is true with respect to instruments, a bearer document can be converted into order paper by a special indorsement. This is true whether the document was issued as bearer paper, or became bearer paper through a blank indorsement. In either event, after the special indorsement, no later taker could become a holder without the special indorsee's signature on the document.

Notice that these rules are essentially the same as the rules on the negotiation of instruments. Compare 3–201 and 3–205 with 7–501(a)–(c).

3. Bailee's Accountability for Non- or Misdelivery

A bailee is obligated to surrender goods to a person entitled to their delivery under a document covering the goods. A bailee who refuses to deliver the goods to such a person or is unable to do so because the goods have been lost or destroyed (nondelivery), or who cannot deliver them because she has given the goods to someone else (misdelivery), is liable, usually for conversion, to the person entitled to delivery.

2. HOW PAYING AGAINST DOCUMENTS WORKS

Now that you understand the basic principles of documents of title law, you can better appreciate and more critically evaluate the payment scheme known as "*payment against documents*." This scheme permits a simultaneous exchange of goods for cash or other payment, even when the buyer and seller are located far apart, by addressing payment to documents covering the goods rather than to the goods themselves.

A. HOW THE PAYMENT SCHEME WORKS

1. Step One: Creating the Documentary Draft

Upon shipping the goods to the buyer, the seller has the carrier issue a negotiable bill of lading to the seller's order. The bill of lading is, of course, a document of title, as discussed above. The bill will probably direct the carrier to notify the buyer when the goods arrive in the buyer's vicinity. Yet, because the bill is a negotiable document, the carrier cannot properly deliver the goods to anyone except a holder of the document. 7–403(a) & 7–102(a)(9). So, even though the carrier is asked to notify the buyer of the arrival of the goods, the carrier cannot surrender the goods to the buyer unless the buyer holds the bill of lading.

At the time of shipment, the holder of the bill is the seller. 1–201(b)(21)(B). It was issued to her order, and she is in possession of it. So, even though the seller has shipped the goods, she remains in control of them because she holds the negotiable document covering the goods and thereby holds the key to getting possession of them from the carrier. Moreover, by shipping the goods under a negotiable document to her own order, the seller effectively retains, by law, a security interest in the goods, 2–505(1)(a). This interest is important to the seller because, if the contract is a shipment contract, title to the goods will pass to the buyer when they are shipped despite the seller having procured a negotiable document covering the goods. See 2–401(2)(a).

The seller will attach the bill of lading to an Article 3 draft, in the amount of the price of the goods, drawn against the buyer. The seller is both the drawer and payee of the draft, which is payable at sight or on demand. The draft with the accompanying bill of lading is referred to as a *documentary draft*. 4–104(a)(6). The seller will not send the documentary draft directly to the buyer. Rather, she will ask her bank to send the draft through banking channels for the purpose of collecting it from the buyer.

2. Step Two: Sending the Documentary Draft for Collection

The collection activities of banks, and the scope of Article 4, are not limited to checks. Banks collect, and Article 4 regulates, other kinds of items. " '*Item*' means an instrument or a promise or order to pay money * * *." 4–104(a)(9). A documentary draft is an item, and a seller who seeks payment against documents can have her bank collect the documentary draft she has drawn against the buyer. Part 5 of Article 4 deals with the collection of documentary drafts.

The seller will indorse both the draft and document that comprise her documentary draft and transfer them to her bank. The bank's treatment of the draft, however, is very different from its treatment of a check. A check is treated as cash, and the depositor's account is credited with the amount of the item immediately upon deposit because the bank assumes that the item will be paid. Banks thus commonly refer to checks as *cash items.* There is no assumption that a documentary draft will be paid. So, when the bank takes a documentary draft for collection, the seller's account is usually not credited with the item. Thus, instead of referring to the draft as a cash item, it is labeled a *collection item,* which means that credit will be given to the seller's account only if and when the draft is actually collected, that is, when payment by the buyer is made and remitted to the depositary bank.

Upon taking a documentary draft for collection, the seller's bank, which in Article 4 terms is the depositary-collecting bank, "shall present or send the draft and accompanying documents for presentment * * *." 4–501. The bank, however, does not send the documentary draft to the buyer. Rather, it is sent, through banking channels, to a bank where the buyer is located for the purpose of having the latter bank present the item to the buyer for payment. In this regard Article 4 requires the seller's bank, which is a collecting bank, to "exercise ordinary care in * * * sending [the item] for presentment," 4–202(a)(1), which requires the bank to "send [the item] by a reasonably prompt method," 4–204(a), and to send the item before the bank's midnight deadline. 4–202(b).

The documentary draft will end up in the hands of a bank where the buyer is located. This bank is known as the *presenting bank,* see 4–105(6), which is not a payor bank. The presenting bank is not the drawee of the draft. The buyer is the drawee. The presenting bank is acting solely as the agent, or sub-agent, of the owner of the item, i.e., the seller, for the purpose of collecting the item from the buyer. So, like the seller's bank, the presenting bank is a collecting bank whose duties are very different from a payor bank.

3. Step Three: Presenting the Documentary Draft for Payment

The presenting bank is obligated to present the documentary draft to the buyer-drawee for payment. The bank can, and probably will, make presentment by sending the buyer, who is the drawee, a written or electronic notice that the bank holds the item for payment. See 4–212(a). In this event, the draft is deemed presented when the notice is received by the buyer-drawee. 3–501(b)(1). Upon receiving payment of the draft, the presenting bank is obligated to deliver the documents to the drawee. 4–503(1).

Here is the exact point at which the simultaneous exchange of goods for cash takes place. The buyer tenders actual payment, which is cash or a cash equivalent in the form of a bank obligation and not just the buyer's own commitment. This payment is sent back down the collection chain to the seller's bank which will credit it to the seller's account. In return, the buyer gets the bill of lading covering the goods. Remember that the bill was indorsed in blank by the seller to whose order the bill was issued. Thus, the buyer, by taking possession of the bill, becomes the holder of the document, and thus the holder of the key to the goods, because the carrier-bailee's obligation to deliver the goods now runs to the buyer qua holder of the negotiable bill of lading. 7–403(a) & 7–102(a)(9).

B. BUYER'S PROTECTIONS

The buyer who pays against documents actually gets, at the time of payment, a piece of paper which, in itself, is worthless. The credibility of the document, and the value in it, are based on rights which accompany the transfer of the document to her and provide some protection, i.e., some insurance that the buyer will get the goods she bargained for.

1. Exclusive Access to the Goods

By taking possession of the negotiable bill of lading which the seller has indorsed in blank, the buyer becomes the holder of the document, 1–201(b)(21)(B) & 7–501(a), and is the only person to whom the carrier can rightfully deliver the goods. 7–403(a) & 7–102(a)(9). The carrier would therefore become liable to the buyer for misdelivery should the carrier deliver the goods to the seller or otherwise follow the seller's orders after the buyer has taken up the document. The carrier is also liable to the buyer for loss or damage to the goods caused by the carrier's negligence.

2. Title to the Goods

If title to the goods has not already passed to the buyer by the time she gets the document of title, see 2–401, transfer of the document to her will pass the seller's title, that is, the buyer will thereby acquire the title and rights the seller had or had actual authority to convey. 7–504(a).

3. Rights Acquired Through Due Negotiation

The document is not merely transferred to the buyer. It is negotiated to her, 7–501(a), and in the typical case she will undoubtedly acquire the document in good faith, for value, without notice, and in the regular course of business. Thus, the buyer will be a holder through "due negotiation." 7–501(a)(5). As a result, she will take title to the document and also title to the goods free of claims to them that arose after the document was issued. 7–502.

4. Warranties

a. Upon Issuance of the Document

Ordinarily, when the sales contract provides for payment against documents, the buyer is not entitled to inspect the goods before paying for them. 2–512(1) & 2–513(3). So, when the seller's draft is presented to the buyer for payment, the buyer will inspect the document of title to insure that the bill describes goods of the kind and quantity she ordered. The credibility of this description is backed by what is, in effect, a warranty by the issuer of the document that the issuer has the goods described and that the goods are as described in the document. This warranty is stated in terms of the carrier's liability for nonreceipt or misdescription:

> A consignee of a nonnegotiable bill of lading which has given value in good faith, or a holder to which a negotiable bill has been duly negotiated, relying upon the description of the goods in the bill, or upon the date shown in the bill, may recover from the issuer damages caused by the misdating of the bill or the nonreceipt or misdescription of the goods, except to the extent that the bill indicates that the

> issuer does not know whether any part or all of the goods in fact were received or conform to the description, such as a case in which the description is in terms of marks or labels or kind, quantity, or condition or the receipt or description is qualified by "contents or condition of contents of packages unknown," "said to contain," "shipper's weight, load and count" or words of similar import, if that indication is true.

7–301(a) (applicable to bills of lading). For similar liability with respect to warehouse receipts, see 7–203.

In turn, the shipper (i.e., the seller) warrants to the carrier "the accuracy at the time of shipment of the description, marks, labels, number, kind, quantity, condition and weight, as furnished by the shipper * * *." 7–301(e).

b. Upon Negotiation of the Document

In negotiating the bill of lading to the buyer, the seller warrants, in addition to any warranty made in selling the goods, that

- the document is genuine; and
- he has no knowledge of any fact which would impair its validity or worth; and
- his negotiation or transfer is rightful and fully effective with respect to the title to the document and the goods it represents.

7–507. This warranty is not made by the seller's bank, the presenting bank or any other intermediary in the collection chain. Such a party warrants "only its own good faith and authority." 7–508.

c. Upon Sale of the Goods

The seller also makes warranties with respect to the goods themselves. 2–313 (express warranties), 2–314 (merchantability) & 2–315 (fitness for a particular purpose).

5. Contract Remedies

In the event the goods, or the seller's performance, fail to conform to the sales contract, the buyer may pursue against the seller the remedies that Article 2 provides for breach of contract, including breach of warranty. See 2–711 & 2–714.

C. SELLER'S PROTECTIONS UPON BREAKDOWNS IN THE SCHEME

1. Buyer Dishonors

a. Procedure upon Dishonor

The buyer dishonors the documentary draft by refusing to pay it, or by not paying it within the prescribed time. 3–502(c). If the presenting bank has made presentment by sending the buyer-drawee notice, 3–501(b)(1), the draft is deemed dishonored if the buyer does not respond by the close of business on the third banking day after notice was sent. 3–502(c) & 4–212(b).

In the event of dishonor, the presenting bank "must use diligence and good faith to ascertain the reason for dishonor, must notify its transferor of the dishonor and of the results of its effort to ascertain the reasons therefor and must request instructions." 4–503(2). "[U]pon learning that the draft has not been paid or accepted in due course," the bank which took the documentary draft for collection, i.e., the seller's bank, "shall seasonably notify its customer [the seller] of the fact * * *." 4–501.

b. Seller's Reaction

The buyer's dishonor is a breach of contract which triggers the seller's Article 2 remedies. See 2–703. In most instances the seller will react by reselling the goods and suing the buyer for the difference between the contract price and the resale price. See 2–706.

There is no problem, of course, in the seller getting access to the goods for the purpose of reselling them. The goods are still in the seller's control because, through the collecting and presenting banks, she retains possession of the document of title and is the holder of it. The carrier is thus obligated to deliver the goods to her. 7–403(a) & 7–102(a)(9). The seller may have the goods returned to her, or she may sell them where they sit. The resale may occur, without the goods themselves being moved, by the seller delivering to the new buyer the document of title covering the goods.

The presenting bank, however, is not obligated to act, on its own, with respect to the goods. The bank's only duties are to request instructions and to follow any reasonable instructions seasonably received. 4–503. In the absence of such instructions, the presenting bank may, but need not, "store, sell, or otherwise deal with the goods in any reasonable manner." 4–504(a). If the bank takes action with respect to the goods pursuant to instructions from the seller, the bank has a right to reimbursement for its expenses. Indeed, the bank can require prepayment or indemnity for such expenses. 4–503. If the bank takes action in the absence of instructions, it acquires, by law, "a lien upon the goods or their proceeds." 4–504(b).

2. Bailee Misdelivers Goods

Payment against documents reduces the seller's risks because she controls the goods until the buyer pays for them by honoring the documentary draft. The seller's control, however, depends on the carrier fulfilling its obligation to deliver only to a person entitled under the document, which is the seller in the case of a negotiable document still in possession of the seller or her agent. If the carrier violates this obligation, as by delivering the goods to the buyer before the buyer gets the document, the seller's insurance for payment is altogether lost. In this event, the carrier is liable to the seller for misdelivery.

3. Presenting Bank Misdelivers Documents

The seller's control of the goods until the buyer pays is also undermined if the presenting bank surrenders the document prior to the buyer honoring the draft. With the document in hand, the buyer is a holder of it, and the carrier can rightfully surrender the goods to her. The presenting bank, however, is liable to the seller for violating 4–503, under which the bank can deliver the document to the buyer only upon payment of the draft. This violation amounts, at the very least, to a breach of the presenting bank's duty of ordinary care which the bank, as a collecting bank, owes to the seller as the owner of the documentary draft. See 4–202 & 4–103(e).

4. Depositary Bank Is Negligent

The seller's bank, which is the depositary bank, owes the seller a duty of ordinary care in handling the documentary draft for collection. If the bank violates this duty, as by delaying in sending the draft for collection or by acting unreasonably in giving the seller notice of dishonor or in forwarding instructions to the presenting bank, the depositary bank is liable for damages. In the absence of bad faith, however, the seller's maximum recovery is the amount of the draft less "an amount that could not have been realized by the exercise of ordinary care." 4–103(e). Bad faith by the bank exposes it to liability for consequential damages. Id.

D. VARIATIONS IN THE SCHEME

1. Discounting Documentary Drafts

Typically, when a depositary bank takes a documentary draft for collection, the amount of the draft is not credited against the seller-customer's account until the draft is actually paid by the buyer-drawee and payment is remitted through banking channels to the depositary bank. The seller, however, may convince her bank to purchase the draft from her rather than simply take it for collection. This arrangement is referred to as *discounting the draft.*

Obviously, by discounting a documentary draft, the depositary bank assumes the risk of the buyer's dishonor. This risk is well insured, however. In effect, the goods become collateral for the bank's advance, inasmuch as the bank acquires a security interest in the document, 4–210(a); and the bank enjoys the control and rights of a holder of the document who acquired it through due negotiation. Also, upon the buyer's dishonor and notice to the seller-drawer, the latter party becomes liable on the draft to the bank. Arguably, though not certainly, the bank has the 4–214(a) right to charge back the amount of the item to the seller's account, see 4–201(a) (last sentence). In any event, because the seller will be liable to the bank as drawer of the draft should the buyer dishonor it, the bank can debit the seller's account through its common-law right of setoff, whether or not the 4–214(a) right of charge back is available to the bank.

2. Shipping Under a Non-Negotiable Document

So far, the discussion of payment against documents has assumed that the goods are covered by a negotiable document. Payment against documents can be structured, however, so that the goods are shipped under a non-negotiable bill of lading. In this event, the seller retains control of the goods by consigning them to herself or her agent so that the carrier is obligated to deliver the goods according to the seller's instructions. 7–403(a) & 7–

102(a)(9). The seller or her agent will instruct the carrier to surrender the goods to the buyer upon the buyer's payment of the draft.

This variation is less acceptable to the buyer for two basic reasons: First, paying the draft does not give the buyer exclusive control of the goods, as is true when she pays and gets a negotiable document covering them. Even after a buyer pays a draft against a non-negotiable document, the carrier can rightfully deliver the goods to whomever the seller instructs (at least if the carrier has not received notice of the buyer's claim). This is true even if the buyer receives, upon paying the draft, a delivery order in her favor. Second, a buyer who pays against a non-negotiable document cannot have the rights of a holder who takes through due negotiation. These rights are possible only when a negotiable document is negotiated. Thus, the buyer would have no protection against preexisting claims to the document or the goods themselves.

3. TRADE ACCEPTANCES

Payment against documents requires the buyer to pay the documentary draft upon presentment to her. The seller may agree, however, that the buyer can acquire the documents accompanying the draft by accepting the instrument upon presentment instead of paying it. " 'Acceptance' means the drawee's signed agreement to pay a draft as presented," and is accomplished by the drawee signing the draft. 3–409(a). The buyer qua acceptor "is obliged to pay the draft * * * according to its terms at the time it was accepted * * *." 3–413(a). A draft accepted by a buyer in a sale of goods arrangement such as that described here is referred to as a *trade acceptance*. The arrangement as a whole could be labeled, quite accurately, credit against documents because the effect is an extension of credit to the buyer for a period of time specified by the terms of the draft. For example, if the draft provides for payment "60 days after sight," the drawee turned acceptor must pay the draft, to the payee or her transferee, 60 days after accepting it.

The procedure for getting the buyer's acceptance is basically the same as that involved in getting payment from the buyer when she is to pay against documents. There are only two basic differences, both of which are obvious: First, in credit against documents, the seller draws a time draft, rather than a demand draft, ordering the buyer to pay the instrument following a specified period after acceptance. Second, although the documentary draft is routed to the buyer through banking channels (just as in the case of a draft requiring payment), the presenting bank presents the draft for acceptance rather than for payment. See 4–503(1).

The obvious question is why the seller would insist on a trade acceptance instead of simply sending the goods to the buyer on unsecured credit and relying on the buyer's Article 2 obligation to pay the price. In either case the seller depends on the buyer's promise to pay. The difference is that a trade acceptance captures the buyer's promise to pay in a negotiable form, which is easier to enforce (even for the seller-payee) than a mere contractual promise, see 3–308, and for which there may be a wider market should the seller-payee decide to discount her rights against the buyer.

In the event the seller discounts the draft, the purchaser will acquire the buyer's obligation thereon as acceptor, 3–413(a), and also the obligations of the seller as both drawer and indorser. 3–414(b) & 3–415(a). Moreover, the typical purchaser would satisfy the requirements for holder-in-due-course status, see 3–302(a), so that she would acquire the draft free from claims and defenses. 3–305(b) & 3–306. Thus, the purchaser of the draft could enforce it against the buyer-acceptor notwithstanding that the seller breached the underlying sales contract between her and the buyer.

From the buyer's perspective, credit against documents is preferable to signing a note at the time the sales contract is made because, in accepting a documentary draft, her engagement on an instrument is concurrent with acquiring control of the goods. In signing an instrument beforehand, as when the contract is made, the buyer risks having to pay a holder in due course for goods she never received.

PART IV

PAYING WITH CREDIT

CHAPTER 10

LETTERS OF CREDIT

Seller and Buyer are negotiating a contract for the sale of goods. Seller is unwilling or unable to commit herself without payment in advance. Buyer does not wish to pay for the goods until she gets them. This impasse can be broken by the buyer having her bank issue the seller an Article 5 letter of credit.

1. INTRODUCTION

An Article 5 *letter of credit* is "a definite undertaking * * * by an issuer [the buyer's bank] to a beneficiary [the seller] at the request or for the account of an applicant [the buyer] * * * to honor a documentary presentation by payment or delivery of an item of value." 5–102(a)(10).

This undertaking, which is an enforceable promise even without consideration, runs directly to the person named as beneficiary in the letter of credit, which would be the seller in the hypothetical case described here. The letter of credit undertaking is an independent obligation of the issuer to the beneficiary. The obligation is separate from the sales contract between the buyer and seller and separate from the bank's relationship with its customer who requested the credit. The seller thereby acquires, up front, a bank's promise to pay her upon the seller satisfying conditions described in the letter of credit.

These conditions are decided by the buyer and seller, although nothing requires the buyer's bank to issue a credit on conditions that are objectionable to it. Typically, the principal condition is the presentation of documents of title covering goods the customer has ordered from the seller. Satisfaction of the conditions of the credit triggers the issuer's obligation to pay without the seller first looking to the buyer for payment. In this sense, the issuer's obligation to the seller is primary rather than secondary, which distinguishes a letter of credit from a guaranty.

Under the letter of credit arrangement the seller does not get payment in advance, but she gets the next best thing: A virtually undeniable promise by a person likely to remain solvent that the seller will be paid once control of the goods passes to the buyer by the transfer of appropriate documents.

The buyer is required to reimburse the issuer for paying the letter of credit. In effect, therefore, the buyer is paying for the goods when the bank honors the seller's demand for payment under the letter of credit. Thus, the buyer must pay for the goods before actually getting them. The buyer, however, gets the next best thing. She gets control of the goods upon payment because the bank will not pay the seller unless the seller transfers documents covering the goods.

If the goods are nonconforming, the buyer can sue the seller for breach of contract. Herein, however, is the ultimate effect of using a letter of credit. Ordinarily, a buyer is not required to pay for goods until after she has inspected them following delivery. The seller thus bears the risk of the buyer's dissatisfaction and the burden of having to sue to recover the price or other damages if the buyer breaches by rejecting conforming goods.

When a letter of credit is used, the seller is paid regardless of the buyer's dissatisfaction with the goods. The buyer must sue to recoup her damages if the seller has breached the contract, as by shipping nonconforming goods. In effect, therefore, using a letter of credit shifts—from the buyer to the seller—the advantage of holding the price of the goods pending the resolution of contractual disputes between the parties. Significantly, the risk of insolvency also shifts. The buyer, rather than the seller, gambles that the other party will have available assets from which to satisfy her damages in the event she is the victim of a breach of contract.

The foregoing overview illustrates the traditional use of a letter of credit, which is facilitating sales of goods (especially in international transactions) by insuring payment of the price to the seller-beneficiary upon her performance in accord with the terms of the letter of credit. A letter of credit so used is referred to as a *commercial credit.* The remainder of this chapter is primarily concerned with filling in the most important details about commercial credits. Some attention is paid, however, to *standby credits.* A standby credit is a letter of credit that insures payment to the beneficiary not for her performance in a sale or other transaction with the customer, but for the customer's default in the transaction.

The principal source of law for the discussion here is U.C.C. Article 5. In practice, an equally important source of law is the Uniform Customs and Practice for Commercial Documentary Credits (UCP), promulgated by the International Chamber of Commerce. The UCP often governs rights and duties under letters of credit, and the interpretation of their terms, either because the credit itself declares that it is issued subject to the UCP, or because the courts rely on the UCP as evidence of trade usage and common understanding with respect to letters of credit. In most important respects, Article 5 and the UCP are consistent.

2. DEFINING BASIC TERMS AND RELATIONSHIPS

A. COMMERCIAL CREDITS

1. The Main Players

In the commercial letter of credit, the *issuer,* 5–102(a)(9), usually a commercial bank, issues the *credit,* which is shorthand for *letter of credit,* 5–102(a)(10), in favor of the seller of goods. The bank acts in response to a request or application of the buyer, who is known as the *applicant.* 5–102(a)(2). The seller is known as the *beneficiary* of the credit. 5–102(a)(3). The *credit* is a signed writing or other authenticated record in which the issuer engages that it will honor a documentary presentation, which usually means paying or accepting drafts or other demands for payment that comply with the terms of the credit. See 5–102(a)(10); 5–102(a)(8); 5–104. Typically, the terms require the seller to present documents, which usually consist of the seller's invoice; a shipping document (e.g., bill of lading, airway bill); an insurance certificate; various additional certificates (e.g., of inspection or origin); and consular documents, if necessary. The terms of credit also typically require presenting the documents together with a draft, or other form of a demand, ordering the issuer to pay or accept.

A credit that requires presentation of only a draft is commonly called a *clean credit*. A credit requiring a draft and presentation of documents is called a *documentary credit*.

The nature of the draft gives rise to an important distinction in credit law: The distinction between *payment credits* and *time*, *usance*, or *acceptance credits*. With a payment credit, the beneficiary presents a sight or demand draft calling for payment, and the issuer honors the credit by paying the draft. With a time, usance, or acceptance credit, the beneficiary draws a draft payable at a specified future date after presentation, and the issuer honors the draft by accepting it, thereby creating a *banker's acceptance. In either case, the seller-beneficiary gets her money sooner or later, but the delay in payment under an acceptance credit is a cost to the seller which she may shift to the buyer in negotiating the price of the goods. This cost is incurred whether the seller holds the accepted draft until maturity or sooner discounts the draft to a third party.*

The terms of a letter of credit, including the required documents and whether drafts are presented for payment or acceptance, are really decided by the seller and buyer. They decide how little, or how much, is required of the seller in order to get payment or acceptance of drafts drawn under a credit. The buyer then asks her bank, through an *application agreement,* to issue a letter of credit containing the terms agreed to by the seller. In this role the buyer is known, technically, as the *applicant.* 5–102(a)(2).

If the buyer's bank is unwilling to establish a credit on the terms agreed to by the buyer and seller, they must find another bank willing to accept their terms or change the terms to suit the bank.

2. The Relationship Between Issuer and Beneficiary: Duty to Honor

A letter of credit becomes effective as regards the beneficiary, meaning that the issuer becomes liable thereon to the beneficiary, when the credit is issued, which means the "issuer sends or otherwise transmits it to the . . . beneficiary." 5–106(a). A credit that has been issued cannot be modified or revoked unilaterally by the issuer unless the credit is a *revocable credit.* See 5–106(b). Practically speaking, however, a revocable credit is not really a letter of credit because it has no legal significance. So nothing more will be said here about revocable credits. The entire discussion before and after this paragraph refers to *irrevocable credits,* which cannot be modified or revoked as regards the customer or the beneficiary without her consent.

Once a credit is issued, the issuer is burdened with a statutory *duty to honor* owed directly to the beneficiary. This duty is stated in 5–108, which is the heart and soul of Article 5 and the statute's most important provision: "an issuer shall honor a presentation that, as determined by the standard practice * * *, appears on its face strictly to comply with the terms and conditions of the letter of credit." This duty is virtually absolute and applies, with some limited exceptions, *whether or not* the goods or documents actually conform to the underlying contract for sale or other contract between the applicant (the buyer) and the beneficiary (the seller).

The separation between the documents presented to the issuer and the actual facts of the underlying transactions between the applicant and beneficiary is known as the *independence principle,* which was described this way in an earlier version of Article 5:

> The letter of credit is * * * independent of the underlying contract between the customer [buyer] and the beneficiary [seller]. * * * [T]he issuer is under a duty to honor the drafts or demands for payment which in fact comply with the terms of the credit without reference to their compliance with the terms of the underlying contract. * * * The duty of the issuer to honor where there is factual compliance with the terms of the credit is also independent of any instructions from its customer once the credit has been issued and received by the beneficiary.

The current Article 5 nails down the point: "An issuer is not responsible for . . . the performance or nonperformance of the underlying contract, arrangement, or transaction. . . ." 5–108(f)(1).

An issuer that violates the duty to honor is guilty of *wrongful dishonor* and is liable to the beneficiary for "the amount that is the subject of the dishonor. . . ." 5–111(a). The issuer is also liable to the applicant for compensatory and incidental damages the wrongful dishonor causes her, "less any amount saved as a result. . . ." of the dishonor. 5–111(b). Consequential damages are not allowed.

3. The Relationship Between Issuer and Customer: The Right of Subrogation

The application or other agreement between the issuer and the applicant invariably provides not only for a fee for the credit but also some form of reimbursement or other insurance if and when the issuer honors a presentation under the credit.

In any event the law protects the issuer by providing that upon honoring a presentation under a credit, the issuer is subrogated to the rights of the beneficiary against the applicant, and also the rights of the applicant against the beneficiary, with respect to the underlying transaction between them. 5–117(a). This provision does not create a new or distinct right of subrogation. Rather, it recognizes and adopts subrogation to the extent that other law would subrogate the issuer if the issuer were a secondary obligor of the obligations the buyer and seller owe each other. 5–117(a); 5–117 comment 1.

Assume, therefore, that buyer gets bank to issue a credit in favor of seller to facilitate a sale of goods. The credit requires the seller to present a draft and appropriate documents covering the goods. Upon honor, the issuer—as a secondary obligor of buyer's obligation to seller and having honored the credit—would be entitled under other law to recover from the buyer. If it turns out that the goods were not as warranted in the contract between buyer and seller, the buyer would have a defense or counterclaim and the issuer's subrogation rights against buyer would be concomitantly limited. Issuer, however, would also be subrogated to the buyer's breach of warranty claims against the seller. So, in theory, the issuer is made whole.

In practice, the issuer by contract will have made easier, cheaper, and more certain arrangements for reimbursement.

B. STANDBY CREDITS

The main players, and the basic rights and duties of the issuer, are the same in both commercial and standby letters of credit. Yet, a standby credit differs fundamentally from a commercial credit. While the traditional commercial credit directs a bank to pay the beneficiary upon the shipment of goods or other performance by her in favor of the customer, the standby credit "directs the bank to pay the beneficiary not for his own performance but upon the customer's default, thereby serving as a guarantee device." Note, *"Fraud in the Transaction": Enjoining Letters of Credit During the Iranian Revolution*, 93 HARV. L. REV. 992, 993 (1980). For this reason, standby credits are often referred to as *guaranty letters of credit*. A standby credit differs from a common-law guaranty, however, in "that the former is a direct obligation to pay upon 'specified documents showing a default' while the latter is a secondary obligation requiring 'proof of the fact of default'." *American Nat'l Bank & Trust Co. v. Hamilton Industries Internat'l, Inc.*, 583 F.Supp. 164, 169 (N.D. Ill. 1984); rev'd on other grounds, 767 F. 2d 380 (7th Cir. 1985).

3. DETERMINING COMPLIANCE WITH THE CREDIT

An issuer's fundamental and principal duty under Article 5 is to "honor" a compliant presentation. 5–108(a). Then, the issuer is entitled to recover from the applicant or otherwise. Honor basically, practically means having paid or accepted a draft only in compliance with the terms of the credit. So, a critical issue is the standard that applies to determine if a presentation is in compliance with the credit. The standard is equally important in the opposite case: the issuer dishonors on the belief that the presentation is not in compliance with the credit. Obviously, the procedure and substance of compliance are central to credit law both with regard to the relationship between the issuer and the beneficiary and the relationship between the issuer and the customer.

A. WHAT DETERMINES COMPLIANCE

The most important point to remember about credit law is that the issuer deals only in documents (and other papers), not in performance. The issuer's duty to honor turns on whether the presentation complies with the terms of the credit. This means that the issuer's duty to honor depends exclusively on whether the beneficiary has presented the kinds of documents and other papers called for in the credit, not on whether the beneficiary has otherwise satisfied the underlying contract with the customer. Thus, when a demand is made under a credit, the issuer simply compares what the beneficiary actually presents with what she is required to present by the terms of the credit. A match here triggers the issuer's duty to honor regardless of whether the goods or documents conform to the underlying contract for sale or other contract between the customer and beneficiary.

B. DEGREE OF COMPLIANCE

The standard for deciding if a presentation is in compliance with the relevant credit is whether, "as determined by the standard practice," the presentation "appears on its face strictly to comply with the terms and conditions of the letter of credit." 5–108(a).[1] It is a rule of strict compliance that explicitly rejects the lesser, riskier standard of

---

[1] These other conditions include an expiration date, also known as *expiry date*, upon which the issuer's duty to honor terminates. This date is part of the terms of the credit, and any draft or demand for payment that violates the date is not in compliance with the credit even though the documents are in perfect form and otherwise satisfy the terms of the credit. "A letter of credit that states that it is perpetual expires five years after its stated date of issuance, or if none is stated, after the date on which it is issued." 5–106(d). In the absence of an expiry date or "other provision that determines its duration, a letter of credit expires one year after its stated date of issuance or, if none is stated, after the date on which it is issued." 5–106(c).

substantial compliance that some courts and commentators have occasionally advocated.

The statute seeks certainty and tolerates ambiguity only in two respects. Strict compliance is defined in terms of "standard practice of financial institutions that regularly issue letters of credit." 5–108(e). Also, determining whether or not in a particular case the issuer observed "standard practice is a matter of interpretation for the court" based on evidence of standard practice offered by the parties. Id. On the other hand, it is hoped and expected that giving this issue to judges and not juries will result in comparatively "more consistency in the outcomes and speedier resolution of disputes." 5–108 comment 1.

C. TIMING OF COMPLIANCE

As a general rule, the issuer is allowed a "reasonable time after presentation" to honor "but not beyond the end of the seventh business day of the issuer after the day of its receipt of documents." 5–108(b).

4. RIGHTFUL DISHONOR DESPITE FACIAL COMPLIANCE

A. REASONS JUSTIFYING DISHONOR DESPITE COMPLIANCE

An issuer must honor a presentation that complies with the terms of the relevant credit. Compliance means that the draft or demand, and the documents presented with it, appear on their face strictly to satisfy the terms of the credit. Thus, as a general rule, an issuer is guilty of wrongful dishonor, and is accordingly liable to the beneficiary and applicant, by refusing to honor a facially compliant presentation. There are, however, a few exceptions, themselves qualified, which justify an issuer dishonoring a letter of credit despite facial compliance with the credit's terms.

The exceptions are:

- a required document is forged or materially fraudulent, or
- honor of the presentation would facilitate a material fraud by the beneficiary on the issuer or applicant.

5–109(a).

Remember! For purposes of the immediate discussion, the assumption is that the presentation, i.e., the draft and accompanying documents, appear on their face strictly to comply with the terms of the credit. The reasons for dishonor under 5–109(a) involve latent or hidden problems that the issuer is not usually obligated to search for when a demand is made. How then will the issuer know of these problems so that, on the basis of them, it can dishonor? The informant is usually the customer who asks the issuer to dishonor a credit because, the customer alleges, there is a hidden defect or problem that justifies dishonor under 5–109.

All's well if the customer is right because "the issuer, acting in good faith," may dishonor the presentation. 5–109(a)(2).

If the customer is wrong, however, the issuer will have wrongfully dishonored and thus will be liable to the beneficiary. The credibility and overall utility of credits would be seriously undermined if the issuer were allowed to dishonor solely on the basis of the customer's allegations, or if the issuer were required, or even allowed, to suspend a credit while it investigated the customer's allegations because these matters frequently involve situations in which the determination of the fact of the non-conformance may be difficult or time-consuming.

Article 5 resolves this problem, in the first instance, against the customer by providing that despite what the applicant says, "the issuer . . . may honor . . . the presentation. . . ." 5–109(a)(2). This means that when an issuer honors a credit despite the customer's warning of a hidden defect, the issuer nevertheless has its rights of reimbursement and subrogation against the customer even though, in fact, the customer was right. The only requirement is that the issuer must have acted in good faith, which is judged by a subjective standard. See 5–102(a)(7).

The customer is not completely without recourse in this situation. Upon the issuer deciding to ignore the customer's warning and honor the credit, "a court of competent jurisdiction may * * * enjoin the issuer from honoring a presentation or grant similar relief against the issuer or other persons" upon certain findings. 5–109(b).

B. REASONS NOT JUSTIFYING DISHONOR

It is very important to understand that the reasons for justifiably dishonoring a credit when the presentation appears compliant on its face are very, very few and narrow, as described above. They DO NOT INCLUDE breach or other nonperformance of the underlying contract, arrangement, or transaction between the applicant and beneficiary. The issuer's duty to honor is independent of such tackiness.

Look at it this way: The very purpose of the letter of credit is to insure that the money is in the seller's hands during any period of dispute between the buyer and seller as to performance of their underlying contract. The risk of recovering for nonperformance is therefore on the buyer. She agrees to assume this risk by agreeing to the letter of credit arrangement. So, breach of contract is not a reason justifying dishonor of a credit. The buyer does not accept, however, the risk of recovering the price in circumstances where the seller hoodwinked her. Putting the money in the seller's care in such a case is thus beyond the purpose of the letter of credit, and therefore dishonoring the credit in such a case does not undermine its legitimate commercial utility.

The reasons for justifiably dishonoring a facially compliant credit also DO NOT INCLUDE any separate, distinct notion of "fraud in the transaction."[2] This kind of fraud was included in

---

[2] The source of the phrase is well known. It codifies the holding of *Sztejn v. J. Henry Schroder Banking Corp.*, 177 Misc. 719, 31 N.Y.S.2d 631 (Sup.Ct.1941). In the *Sztejn* case, Schroder had issued, for the account of Sztejn, an irrevocable credit in favor

earlier versions of Article 5 as a basis for dishonoring a facially compliant credit. The current Article 5 DOES NOT include it in so many words. If conduct justifying dishonor in cases decided under the old law on the basis of fraud in the transaction is conduct justifying dishonor today, it has to be because the tackiness fits the language of the current law: namely, a required document is forged or materially fraudulent, or honor of the presentation would facilitate a material fraud by the beneficiary on the issuer or applicant. And it is possible—even likely—that these two statutory bases together are more narrow than the old "fraud in the transaction," so that not all of the situations justifying dishonor under old law will justify dishonor under the current law.[3]

Neither the *Sztejn* case nor the phrase "fraud in the transaction" justifies dishonor simply because of a breach of warranty or other breach of contract in the underlying transaction between the customer and the beneficiary. What is required is *intentional, active fraud on the part of the seller.* Moreover, the

---

of Transea Traders. The credit required the beneficiary to present, among other things, a bill of lading covering a quantity of bristles. The issue in the case was whether the issuer was required to honor the credit if the beneficiary presented a document in perfect order, that is, a genuine bill of lading describing the goods as bristles, when, in fact, the seller-beneficiary had shipped cowhairs and other worthless materials. The court decided that, on these facts, payment of the credit should be enjoined.

[3] One recent case stated that the standard under which fraud in the transaction must be measured requires that "the beneficiary have no colorable claim or basis in fact for asserting its rights under the letter of credit." *Hook Point LLC v. Branch Banking & Trust Co.*, 725 S.E.2d 681, 686 (S.C. 2012).

fraud must be serious, that is, *of such an egregious nature as to vitiate the entire transaction.*

There may be some continuing, indirect value of the old cases finding and justifying dishonor on the basis of "fraud in the transaction." Those cases and that basis for dishonor required conduct of such *egregious nature as to vitiate the entire transaction.* This requirement of egregiousness may survive as a test for the materiality that is required under current law when dishonor is justified on the basis of "a required document is forged or *materially* fraudulent, or honor of the presentation would facilitate a *material* fraud by the beneficiary on the issuer or applicant." 5–109(a) (emphasis added).

CHAPTER 11

CREDIT CARDS

A basic definition of credit card is "[a]ny card that may be used repeatedly to borrow money or buy products and services on credit."[1] Really, a credit card is the symbol of and sometimes the key to a typically revolving account between the issuer of the card and the cardholder. The account is established by contract. The essential terms are that the cardholder can charge certain purchases or cash advances to the account; the issuer will finance these purchases and advances; and the cardholder will repay the principal plus certain interest, fees, and other finance charges.

There are two basic types of credit cards. The older type is the two-party card (a/k/a "private-label" or "proprietary" card) that a retailer or business issues to customers for financing the customer's purchases from the business itself. Bank credit cards are newer and general purpose: the cards can be used to buy stuff from anybody authorized by the issuer to accept the card as a means of payment. So, these cards are commonly known as general bank credit cards, general purpose cards, or, simply, bank cards.

Four major systems, or networks, provide authorization and settlement services for the bank cards in the United States: Visa, MasterCard,

---

[1] *Credit card,* InvestorWords.com—Online Investing Glossary, http://www.investorwords.com/1199/credit_card.html (last visited Nov. 5, 2014).

American Express and Discover. Banks are behind or associated with all of them. American Express and Discover are often referred to as **closed-loop** systems. Basically, the same firm issues the card to cardholders and enrolls merchants to accept the card; and to a larger degree the issuer itself vertically controls and handles all transaction and payment operations associated with the use of the card.

Visa and MasterCard are **open-loop** systems. Thousands of banks operate horizontally under each association's banner independently issuing cards and signing up merchants. Because the issuer of a card and the merchant who accepts it are often tied to different banks, an interchange system settles accounts between them; and third-party processors typically act as intermediaries for merchants and banks in the card payment network.

Visa and MasterCard members issue credit cards, debit cards, and other payment products with the Visa and MasterCard brands. American Express and Discover issue credit and charge cards[2] with their brand names but have only recently begun to issue

---

[2] Traditionally, a distinction has been made between charge and credit cards. A charge card requires the cardholder to pay his or her full balance upon receipt of a billing statement from the issuer of the card. A credit card permits cardholders to pay only a portion of the balance due on the account after receipt of a billing statement. Such different accounts still exist and some laws (especially disclosure laws) distinguish between them; but most people have dropped the refined terminology and refer to cards for either kind of account as a credit card. This book, too, ignores tradition and uses the term credit card to mean either kind of account, though you must remember that the details of some laws may apply differently to the different types of accounts.

prepaid cards and gift cards. Although debit cards are similar to credit and charge cards in that they may be used at unrelated merchants, the fact that upon use they promptly access money directly from a cardholder's checking or deposit account strongly differentiates them from credit cards.

WARNING! Don't confuse credit and debit cards. Different laws apply. Even when a card is multi-purpose, which law applies depends on whether the card is used for credit or to debit a checking or other asset bank account. This chapter is about credit cards or using a multi-purpose card for credit. A later chapter discusses debit cards.

FURTHER WARNING!! The chapter is not limited to bank cards. Later discussions about the law of credit cards applies pretty much equally to two-party credit cards. The market and workings of bank cards, however, are more complicated. So, the chapter begins by explaining how the dominant bank cards—Visa and MasterCard—work.

1. HOW BANK CARDS WORK

Together, Visa and MasterCard hugely dominate the market, and by a long shot Visa is the biggest.[3] Also, because they are open systems, their workings

---

[3] The website maintained by the staff of CreditCards.com recently reported the following credit card purchase volume statistics (in billions): American Express U.S.—$424.3 (2011); Discover—$106 (2012); MasterCard U.S.—$534 (2012) and Visa U.S.—$981 (2012). *See* Credit Card Statistics—Credit Card Purchase and Transaction Volume, http://www.creditcards.com/credit-card-news/credit-card-industry-facts-personal-debt-statistics-1276.php (last visited Oct. 8, 2014).

are somewhat more complicated than other bank cards. So, this section explains how Visa and MasterCard work. In large part, the two systems, though separate, work very much the same, and the following explanation applies generally to both Visa and MasterCard and ignores differences, which are not important for our purposes. For ease of writing and reading, therefore, the term bankcard association means either of them. Later discussions about the law that affects credit cards applies to all bank cards and also to two-party credit cards.

A. BANK JOINS BANKCARD ASSOCIATION

As just explained, Visa and MC are associations of banks. Neither the Visa nor MC association issues any credit cards. Banks issue them, but only a bank that is a member of the bankcard association can issue the association's card. So, the first step in the working of a Visa or MC credit card is that the bank joins the bankcard association. As a member, the bank regularly pays membership fees and agrees to an elaborate set of by-laws which include very detailed operating regulations. These bankcard association by-laws and regulations are extensive, and were formerly kept confidential. Once Visa and MasterCard became publicly traded companies, however, their operating rules were made publicly available. *See* http://usa.visa.com/merchants/merchant-support/international-operating-regulations.jsp; http://www.mastercard.us/merchants/index.html (MasterCard).

The operating regulations serve the same purpose for processing of credit-card transactions that Article 4 serves for the collection of checks. A big difference is that the credit-card operating regulations are not enacted law. The system these regulations create is private law in the form of an inter-bank agreement among the association members. Disputes among members are handled by arbitration or other ADR means; and the ultimate penalty for failing to comply is expulsion from the bankcard association.

The association itself operates largely unseen to the public. It works behind the scenes managing the affairs and workings of the association for the members, maintaining and building the networks that carry and settle credit-card transactions, and marketing (on a wholesale level) the various card products. The marketing has dual purposes: to convince the public to use the products and to convince merchants to honor the products as means for the public to pay for the property and services the merchants sell.

Dealing with the public at the retail level is the responsibility of the member bank. The bank sells or issues credit cards to its customers who will use them in paying for stuff. In this role the bank is the credit card **issuer** or **issuing bank**; and the customer is the **cardholder**, which may be a consumer or a business operating in any form.

The bank also sells, opens, and maintains credit card accounts for businesses that have agreed to honor the card as a means of payment for whatever they sell. In this role the business is the **merchant**, and the bank is the **merchant bank** (a/k/a **acquiring bank**). Nobody selling anything can participate in the bankcard payment system without operating through a **merchant account**. Either the merchant herself must maintain such an account, or she must process her credit card payments through a third person who owns such an account with a merchant bank.

B. BANK ISSUES CARDS TO CARDHOLDERS

You get a bankcard by making application for a card to a bank that issues the kind of card you want.[4] It's not hard to apply and, as you well know, it's not hard to qualify. The requirements of creditworthiness are comparatively low, and it's not a requirement that you maintain a checking or other asset account with the bank.

It's important to understand, however, that if you do maintain an asset account with the issuer, the credit card account is separate in accounting and legal terms. True, the plastic card in your pocket or purse is a multi-purpose device. You can use it to charge something to your credit card account or to

---

[4] In real life almost all banks offer bank cards. Also in real life, most banks completely or to some extent outsource their credit card operations. They contract with a super bank or other large-scale processor to handle operations and "share" revenue, costs, and risks. This arrangement is seamless and unnoticed by cardholders who contract directly with—and retain all their legal rights against—the bank that issues the card to them. These super banks not only operate in the background on a wholesale basis with other banks. The super banks also issue their own cards on a regional or national, retail basis directly to their own customers who are cardholders.

access your checking account as an ATM card or a point-of-sale debit card. The particular use, however, channels the transaction either to the credit card account or the checking account, depending on how you used the card. You know: the clerk at the store asks you—"Debit or credit?"—or the machine you're using requires the same choice. How you use the card also determines whether the law that applies is credit-card law (which is basically the federal Truth In Lending Act (TILA) and similar state laws) or the mainly and different federal law that governs electronic funds transfers (see Chapter 13 *infra*). Use also determines, of course, which contract between you and the bank applies—the agreement with the bank pertaining to the credit card or the agreement pertaining to your use of ATMs and debit cards. The agreements—like the accounts—are separate.

When the bank issues a credit card and you accept it, you will also accept, i.e., "agree to," a **cardholder agreement**. It is a contract between you and the bank and is equivalent to—but different from—the deposit agreement that covers your bank checking account. They are different in their terms and in the governing law. UCC Article 4 governs checking accounts and regulates deposit agreements but has no application to credit card accounts. Credit card accounts are regulated mainly by the cardholder agreement, which incorporates the operating procedures of the bankcard association.

Checking and credit card accounts are also fundamentally different in their purposes and the kinds of relationships they create. A checking account is the balance of monetary value that belongs to you. The bank is your debtor with respect to this balance and reduces the obligation by paying checks you write against the account.

A credit card account is, essentially, a line of credit. The bank agrees to pay charges to your credit card account; and you agree to repay the bank with interest and also to pay other fees associated with your account.

The cardholder agreement details these basic obligations and also provides lots of other terms. Surely you have studied the fine print of your own cardholder agreements.

C. MERCHANTS OPEN ACCOUNTS AT BANK

Merchants who are members of the bankcard system agree to honor the cards of the system or systems in which they enroll. A merchant makes this agreement in opening a credit-card merchant account with a bank that is a member of the bankcard association. In this role the bank is sometimes known as the **acquiring bank** because the bank acquired the account. Again, the merchant's contract is with the bank, not the bankcard association; but this contract incorporates the association's operating rules.

In exchange the merchant gets the bank's commitment to give the merchant credit for purchases of property and services that a customer makes using a system card. In effect, the merchant bank finances the merchant's accounts receivable by discounting the merchant's sales slips, after which the issuing bank collects payments from the cardholders on a deferred, revolving credit basis. So, the banks in the middle of credit card transactions win and win: the acquiring bank gets a fee from the merchant, and the issuing bank collects interest from the cardholder. The acquiring bank may also pay a fee to the issuing bank because the latter bank's customer used her card at the former bank's merchant. It's called an **interchange fee**.[5] The best situation is when the bank both issued the card used to make the purchase and acquired the merchant account of the business where the card was used. See why credit card earnings "have been almost always higher than returns on all commercial bank

---

[5] "The interchange fee is usually a percentage of the transaction amount (an *ad valorem* fee). The interchange fee allows open schemes [such as Visa and MasterCard] to operate effectively and to promote effective competition in the activities of issuing and acquiring. Interchange fees paid to issuers serve to: provide issuers with incentives to issue credit cards and to encourage their use; and allow issuers to recover their full costs in doing so, given constraints as to the level of costs that cardholders are willing to bear.

"In open schemes [such as Visa and MasterCard] the card issuing and merchant signing members have a mutually dependent relationship. If revenue produced by cardholders is insufficient to cover card issuing costs, the card issuing service will be cut back or eliminated. The result would be a decline in card use and a reduction in the number of merchants signing up to the system, leading to a decline in acquiring revenues. The interchange fee allows the effective operation of competition in issuing and acquiring in an open system by overcoming the complex coordination and incentive problems inherent in the joint venture arrangements." 51 Frontier Economics, Joint Bank Review of Credit Card Membership and Interchange Fees: Report on Credit Card Interchange Fees to Review Banks (Jan. 2001).

activities"? [Report to the Congress on the Profitability of Credit Card Operations of Depository Institutions (Board of Governors of the Federal Reserve System (June 2014) at 5, *available at* http://www.federalreserve.gov/publications/other-reports/credit-card-profitability-2014.htm]. Despite the 2008 crisis and subsequent recession, the profitability of credit card operations for 2013 surpassed the average rate of return during the 2001–2013 time frame (although not as high as levels reached in several years prior to that recession). Id at 3.

The merchant agreement with the bank (or third-party merchant processor acting as an intermediary) is very comprehensive. It covers everything from the procedures the merchant must use for handling credit card transactions to the details of presentation, payment and repayment of sales slips. It also incorporates appropriate bankcard association rules, especially including merchant account operating procedures. Collectively, the total of terms, rules, conditions, and the like is a huge and mostly standard form.

Two pieces are especially important to your understanding of issues covered below in discussing the workings of credit card systems: authorization and chargeback. **Authorization** means that the merchant, before accepting a customer's use of a card, should get the issuer bank—directly or indirectly—to approve the charge. It is this authorization that triggers this bank's obligation to pay the charge. The authorization, however, is limited in effect to signaling that the cardholder's credit line is sufficient for the authorized charge. It is not a warranty against a chargeback for other reasons.

Chargeback refers to the issuer dishonoring—not paying for—a charge to a cardholder's account that the merchant accepted because the merchant failed to follow the terms of the merchant agreement, association rules, operating procedures and the like. Failing to obtain authorization before accepting the charge is a reason for chargeback. The effect is that the merchant must look directly to the customer-cardholder for payment on the basis of the law governing the underlying transaction between them.

There are lots and lots of other reasons for chargeback. Some of them are based on violations of purely internal procedures. Other reasons are based on complaints or problems by the cardholder who wants to push back against the issuer—that is, charge back or reverse—the charges associated with the underlying transaction between the cardholder and the merchant.

Bottom line: lots of risks are allocated to the merchant in its relationships with the banks in the card network.

It's very important to understand that chargeback is part of the merchant's contract with the merchant bank and, indirectly, with the association and other banks in the association. The cardholder is not a party to this contract, and the separate contract the cardholder makes does not include avoiding credit card cards, as against her issuer, for all the reasons that a merchant can suffer a chargeback. Also, though less likely, cardholders may have rights to push or charge back against the issuer that are not reasons for a chargeback against the merchant, which would mean that the issuer assumes these risks. Cardholder's rights to push back against the issuer are provided for in the cardholder agreement with her issuer, discussed above, and also by law, discussed below.

D. CARDHOLDERS USE CARDS TO PAY FOR STUFF MERCHANTS SELL

These days, of course, a cardholder can use her credit card to buy stuff in person at a physical store, by telephone, or on line. Security of the data varies; but the merchant agreement with the acquiring bank and the cardholder agreement with the issuing bank allow use of the card in all of these ways. In fundamental respects, and for our purposes, these agreements don't really care whether the sales are made and the card is used face-to-face between the merchant and cardholder or electronically between them.[6] Also, the means for settling accounts among

---

[6] An important exception that doesn't much concern us but really concerns the merchant is the higher costs to her. The risk of fraud is higher with Internet and phone sales between cardholders and merchants, which are sometimes called "card-not-present" transactions and include mail order sales. So, the discount a merchant pays for credit card charges she collects in these kinds of sales—and the reserve she is required to maintain—may be higher compared to charges she collects in face-to-face sales. Also, collecting charges electronically may require a separate merchant account that builds in these and other differences and can require the merchant to satisfy higher standards of trust and creditworthiness to qualify for the account.

the merchant, cardholder, and banks are fully electronic, even in face-to-face sales in physical stores. See below.

In a face-to-face transaction between the cardholder and merchant, the cardholder will usually sign a credit card sales slip by writing her signature on paper or on an electronic pad. That sales slip is commonly referred to by member banks and merchants as a draft. Actually, however, the slip is not a draft or other negotiable instrument within the scope of UCC Article 3. The writing does not fulfill the requisites of negotiability spelled out in § 3–104(a). Rather, the slip evidences the sale transaction and authorizes the issuer to charge the amount of the slip to the cardholder's credit card account. Although written authorization is safer, it is not required. Issuers are increasingly permitting credit card holders to forego the signature requirement, especially for smaller purchases or at inconvenient locations (such as gas pumps). Technological innovations such as Apple Pay are also increasingly permitting cardholders to utilize contactless technology which excuses any physical presentation of the card at all.[7]

The sale aspects of the transaction between the merchant and cardholder are governed by state law applicable to the transaction, which usually means common law in the case of services and UCC Article 2 in the case of goods. In the latter case Article 2 obligates the cardholder to accept the goods and pay

---

7 *See* Apple Pay, http://www.apple.com/apple-pay/?cid=wwa-us-=kwm-features-com (last visited Nov. 6, 2014).

the price according to the contract of sale between her and the merchant. U.C.C. 2–507(1); 2–709(1).

When the cardholder pays for the goods using her credit card, the merchant captures the information about the cardholder's credit card account either by swiping the card through an electronic device that reads the information encoded on the card, by utilizing some type of contactless technology, or by the cardholder telling the merchant the information. The account number is 16 digits, although only the last five digits are permitted to be printed on any receipt provided to the cardholder at the point of sale. 15 U.S.C.A. § 1681c(g). The first ten digits identify the issuing bank. The other six digits identify the cardholder's credit card account at the bank. These numbers are important in processing the slip through the interchange network. See below. In sum, they help in getting the merchant's account credited with the amount of the sales slip; sending the slip to the issuer for payment; sending the payment to the merchant's bank; and charging the cardholder's credit card account.

In order to complete the transaction whether or not face-to-face, the merchant will electronically tap into the bankcard network (directly or indirectly through a third party) to contact the issuer or its agent for authorization to allow the cardholder to charge the price of the goods to her credit card. (Each bankcard association maintains an authorization system to which member banks can subscribe directly or through a third party.) Whether or not this authorization is forthcoming depends on the available credit that the issuer has agreed to extend the cardholder with respect to her credit card account. If authorization is given, the merchant will receive and record an authorization code for the transaction.

The sale is done. Now the question is how the merchant gets her money.

E. MERCHANTS COLLECT THROUGH SETTLEMENTS OR INTERCHANGE NETWORK

The credit card charges that a merchant accumulates are transmitted in one way or another to the merchant's acquiring bank, which credits the merchant's account for the total amount less a discount paid to the bank. This process may happen directly between the parties or through intermediary, processing agents between them. The credit may be available for withdrawal immediately or—more often—after some time, depending on the merchant agreement and also on the terms of any arrangement with intermediary processors.

The charges are then forwarded by or for the merchant bank to the issuing bank for payment through an interchange network connecting member banks. The inter-bank collection of credit card charges is not accomplished through the same channels of the Federal Reserve or other systems for collecting checks, but largely through entirely different and independent, completely private interchange networks maintained separately by the bankcard association.

These bank card collection networks are not governed by UCC Article 4 or federal law, except for the possibility that card collection somehow piggybacks on federally regulated networks. Rather, bankcard collection networks are mainly governed exclusively by contract, primarily by the by-laws and operating regulations of the bankcard association. Although VISA and MasterCard operate separately in collecting credit card charges, the essentials of the two systems' interchange networks are very similar, and both networks are equally or more efficient than the processes used to collect checks under Article 4 and through the Federal Reserve System.

The association network electronically records the credit card charges received from member banks. Intra-association settlements are then determined and effected through accounts that association member banks maintain for this purpose.

A national switch is the central bookkeeper or clearing house for the entire system. It determines daily net settlements among member banks, addressing the banks directly or through regional processing centers. The system maintains a settlement account, and each member bank, or a representative of the bank, maintains its own clearing account for inter-bank settlement. If a bank's net settlement position is a credit, the switch will transfer funds from the system's settlement account to the bank's clearing account. If the bank's net settlement position is a debit, the switch will request the bank to transfer funds to the system settlement account. Transfers of funds are typically accomplished electronically by wire or otherwise, and funds transferred between banks are usually same day (collected) funds in United States dollars. (The switch also determines, collects, and distributes interchange reimbursement fees as part of effecting net settlements. See above.)

Remember that the bank credit card interchange system is largely truncated: any paper sales slips are impounded by the acquiring bank or its agent, and the remaining operations are handled electronically. So the issuer will not in the ordinary course receive any paper sales slip a cardholder signs when using her credit card. Rather, the issuer will learn of the transaction when the information about the transaction is relayed electronically to the issuer by the bankcard association switch or otherwise through the interchange network, which received the information in the same fashion.

The issuer will then charge the amount of credit card purchases to the cardholder's credit card account. The cardholder is bound to pay this charge, plus interest and other fees, by the terms of the cardholder agreement between him and the issuer.

F. INTERLOCKING AGREEMENTS PROVIDE CREDIBILITY

What is it about the bankcard system that gives credibility to payment by credit card so that merchants readily accept Visa or MasterCard credit cards as a means of payment? It is nothing in the UCC.

Even if the cardholder signs a paper sales slip, it is not a draft or other instrument within the scope of Article 3. Clearly then, the issuer's authorization for the charge card does not amount to acceptance of the sales slip within the meaning of U.C.C. 3–409(a). Also, neither the cardholder agreement nor the issuer's authorization of a particular purchase by a cardholder amounts to a letter of credit under UCC Article 5. So, the merchant is not a beneficiary of a letter of credit that is entitled to the issuer commitment to pay under Article 5. Finally, the merchant bank does not independently commit to the merchant for credit card charges; the merchant swapping the credit card charges for credit to its merchant account does not amount to a sale of accounts covered by UCC Article 9. In this role the merchant bank acts essentially as an agent for collection only.

The credibility behind a cardholder's authorized use of his bank credit card comes from the merchant agreement between the merchant and acquiring bank and also from the agreement among the acquiring bank, issuing bank, and the bankcard association as parties to the association by-laws. Through the merchant agreement the acquiring bank promised, upon certain conditions, to "make payment to the Merchant for sales slips physically presented by the Merchant to the Bank." By agreeing to the association by-laws the issuer agreed to pay authorized credit card charges by persons holding credit cards the bank issued. Moreover, the association promises member banks that it will indemnify and reimburse them for loss or expense they suffer by reason of any member's failure properly to honor any credit card charges processed in accordance with association by-laws and regulations.

So the merchant will gladly accept the authorized use of a credit card in payment for goods, other property or services because the merchant has the commitment of the acquiring bank to give the merchant credit, less a discount, for credit card sales. The merchant bank makes this commitment because the issuing bank is bound by contract to pay the credit card charges; and, if the issuer breaches this contractual obligation, the bankcard association will indemnify the acquiring bank. The issuer will not likely breach, however, because it expects to collect the charges, plus interest, from the cardholder. Moreover, if the issuer breached by failing to pay the merchant bank, it could be expelled from the bankcard system—a terrible penalty because the issuer wants to continue as a member in good standing of the association. Participation produces serious revenues. The issuer earns interest from cardholders who use credit cards the bank issued to them; and the issuing bank earns an interchange fee from the acquiring bank every time one of the issuer's cardholders uses her credit card in a transaction with a merchant with an account at the acquiring bank.

2. WHAT LAW APPLIES

A. STATE LAW AND CHOICE OF LAW

Common-law contract fundamentally governs all of the relationships that are involved in the use of two-party credit cards and bank cards. None of the relationships is governed by a comprehensive, integrated statute of federal or state law. Statutory law most significantly supplements and displaces contracts law in defining the rights and liabilities of cardholders in their relationships with card issuers and, to a lesser extent, the remedial rights of cardholders against merchants when a credit card is used as the means of payment. Special credit card law adds nothing substantive to the main issue between cardholder and merchant, which is the quality of the performance in the underlying transaction between them. This issue is governed by whatever law ordinarily applies to the kind of transaction involved (such as UCC Article 2 in the case of a sale of goods).

States statutory regulation of credit cards, especially the consumer protection aspects, is neither large nor uniform. Some states have adopted the aged Uniform Consumer Credit Code (UCCC) (1974) or something or pieces akin to it. To a significant extent, however, these state laws duplicate or are less generous than applicable federal law, which is discussed below; and the federal law will preempt at least to the extent the federal law provides greater rights.

Some pieces of states consumer protection laws, however, are stronger than federal law and not so clearly preempted. Moreover, state law sets the maximum rates of interest and other charges that issuers can charge cardholders. For these and other reasons, including that the basic law governing all the relationships in a credit card system is local contract law, there is an incentive for credit card contracts to include choice-of-law clauses whereby the parties effectively pick which state's law will govern their transaction.

As a general rule, choice-of-law clauses are perfectly legal and enforced as long as there is a reasonable relation between the transaction and the chosen state. Citibank, which is among the largest card issuers in the world, operates some of its credit card programs out of South Dakota for reasons that are favorable to both the bank and the state. Because of Citibank's location in the state, and because applicants for credit cards apply to this location, a reasonable relation exists between the bank and the state with respect to cardholder agreements. Moreover, being located in South Dakota would trigger the usual default rule—without the need for a choice-of-law agreement—that the law governing the terms of a contract is the place where the contract is accepted, which means South Dakota because applicants apply to the issuer and acceptance occurs there. Bottom line: "Most major credit card issuers are based in states without usury laws and without interest rate caps on credit cards. Banks and credit card issuers based in these states can charge any interest rate they wish—as long as the rate is listed in the cardholder agreement and the borrower agrees."[8]

Some states with consumer protection laws attempt to limit the effect of choice-of-law rules and clauses favoring credit card issuers. Especially with respect to interest rates, and finance charges, the statutes effectively provide that local law applies and protects cardholders without regard to where the issuer is located and without regard to any choice-of-law clause in the cardholder agreement.

These laws limiting choice-of-law clauses are not very effective with respect to credit cards, especially bank cards. The main reason is preemptive federal law. Interpreting the National Banking Act, 12 U.S.C.A. § 85, the Supreme Court held, in *Marquette National Bank of Minneapolis v. First of Omaha Service Corp.*, 439 U.S. 299 (1978), that a national bank can "export" higher interest rates from the state where the bank was located to customers in other states with lower limits. 12 U.S.C.A. § 1831d(a). Congress later extended this benefit to *all federally insured institutions*. See 12 U.S.C.A. § 1831d(a).

The Court extended *Marquette* in *Smiley v. Citibank (South Dakota), N.A.*, 517 U.S. 735 (1996). In Smiley, a resident of California held credit cards issued by Citibank (South Dakota). The issuer imposed late-payment fees that are legal under South Dakota law but illegal in California. The

---

[8] Lucy Lazarony, Credit Card Companies Sidestep Usury Laws, Center for Credit Counseling Services, Inc. Document Library, *available at* http://arnoldbatsonturner.com/Bankrate%20article.htm (last visited Nov. 5, 2014).

cardholder led a class action challenging the imposition of the fees on California residents. The Court held that the preemptive exportation of interest rates that the National Bank Act and *Marquette* allows applies equally to the kinds of fees challenged in the case.

B. FEDERAL TILA

The most significant statute defining cardholders' rights is the federal Truth In Lending Act (TILA), 15 U.S.C. § 1601–67f, which governs some important aspects of credit card transactions mainly involving consumers. The implementing regulations originally promulgated by the Board of Governors of the Federal Reserve System are collected in and known as Regulation Z (Reg Z), 12 C.F.R. part 226. Pursuant to the Dodd-Frank Wall Street Reform and Consumer Protection Act of 2010, Pub. L. 111–203, Title X, § 1022, 124 Stat. 1376 (July 21, 2010) however, consumer financial protection functions were transferred to the newly created Bureau of Consumer Financial Protection (CFPB). The CFPB thereafter promulgated its own version of Regulation Z, set out at 12 C.F.R. Part 1026, which applies if a consumer transaction is involved.[9] TILA, as amplified by Regulation Z, is an early flagship of modern consumer protection legislation.

[9] Hereafter, citing references will therefore be made only to the CFPB version of Regulation Z. Corresponding cites to the FRB Regulation Z are generally correspondingly numbered in 12 C.F.R. Part 226.

Congress enacted TILA in 1970 largely in response to a particular problem. Both national and state banks have the power to issue credit cards, and for a long time the law has allowed a single bank to issue both VISA and MasterCard. When credit cards were initially issued in the 1960s, unsolicited mailings to potential cardholders created troublesome questions of offer and acceptance. The mailing itself seemed to constitute an offer to the recipient which was accepted by the recipient's use of the card. This use of the card triggered all the terms and conditions of the cardholder agreement itself. However, if the recipient did not use the card, then there was arguably no contract formed. This meant, for example, that fraudulent use of the card by a thief might not subject the intended holder to a provision in the card that placed fraudulent losses on the holder until the issuer was notified.

To clarify issues such as this and many others, Congress enacted TILA which applies generally to consumer credit transactions, including open-end credit plans. An open-end plan under TILA is defined as "a plan under which the creditor reasonably contemplates repeated transactions, which prescribes the terms of such transactions, and which provides for a finance charge which may be computed from time to time on the outstanding unpaid balance." 15 U.S.C.A. § 1602(j). A credit card is a quintessential open-end credit plan for TILA purposes.

TILA not only expressly prohibits the issuance of unsolicited credit cards to consumers *and businesses* but, more importantly, in connection with Regulation Z, requires initial and periodic disclosures to *consumer* cardholders. TILA requires issuers, even as early as the marketing of credit cards, to make certain detailed disclosures about the terms of the plan as part of credit card applications and in solicitations. 15 U.S.C.A. § 1637(c). Then, before a consumer uses a credit card account, the issuer must disclose certain information, such as: when a finance charge will be imposed, how the balance subject to the finance charge will be computed, how the finance charge will be computed, and the annual percentage rate calculated and stated according to a standardized formula.[10] 15 U.S.C.A. § 1637(a). Additionally, the issuer must send the cardholder a billing statement for each billing cycle at the end of which there is an outstanding balance or during which a finance charge is imposed, disclosing such information as the beginning balance, all transactions that occurred during the billing cycle, the ending balance, the amount of finance charges imposed, how the finance charge was computed, and the amount and due date of any required minimum payment. 15 U.S.C.A. § 1637(b).

Even though TILA and related federal statutes require disclosing lots of stuff, they were primarily

---

[10] Significantly, TILA does not limit interest rates that creditors can charge in connection with credit card or other accounts (although national usury limits have periodically been proposed. See, e.g., S. 673, 113th Cong., 1st Sess. (2013)). State law regulates maximum rates, which may vary even in the same state depending on the purpose for which a card is used. The role of TILA is to require accurate, meaningful disclosure of the rates charged by creditors and limited by local law.

disclosure laws. In response to continued consumer complaints about unfair and deceptive credit card practices, however, Congress went further in adopting the Credit Card Accountability Responsibility and Disclosure Act of 2009 (the CARD Act) (Pub. L. No. 111–24, 123 Stat. 1734 (2009).

First, the CARD Act addressed two major cardholder concerns. To protect cardholders from immediate increases in interest rates for future purchases, the CARD Act imposed a 45-day notice requirement before the effective date of any increase. 15 U.S.C.A. § 1637(i)(1). To protect cardholders from increases in interest rates on existing balances, the CARD Act adopted a general rule prohibiting such increases. 15 U.S.C.A. § 1666i–1(a). That rule was subject to several exceptions, including a limited right to increase the rate as a result of missed payments. 15 U.S.C.A. § 1666i–1(b)(4). However, the issuer may only increase the rate if the payment is more than 60 days late, and the increase must terminate at the end of six months if the cardholder pays on time during the interim. Id. Furthermore, the listing of those specific exceptions precluded issuers from using other triggers to increase rates on existing balances. One significant result was that issuers were no longer permitted to increase those rates as a result of the cardholder's default on *other*, unrelated obligations (universal default provisions).

Secondly, the CARD Act addressed concerns regarding improvident extensions of credit. The Act now requires issuers to consider the ability of consumers to make the required payments, based on reasonable estimates. 15 U.S.C.A. § 1665e; 12 C.F.R. § 1026.51(a). It further regulates marketing to persons under 21 years of age. 15 U.S.C.A. § 1637(c)(8).

Thirdly, the CARD Act addressed concerns regarding exorbitant fees. The Act first adopted a standard requiring that any penalty fee imposed for a violation of the credit card contract be "reasonable and proportional to such omission or violation." 15 U.S.C.A. § 1665d(a). The implementing regulations set a safe harbor fee, currently adjusted to $26 for first violations, and $37 for repeat violations. 12 C.F.R. § 1026.52(b)(1)(ii). The Act further adopted a new provision requiring the express permission of the cardholder before the issuer could charge an over-the-limit fee (a fee for exceeding the dollar amount of credit authorized on the card). 15 U.S.C.A. § 1637(k)(1).

Fourthly, the CARD Act restricted a variety of techniques which issuers had used to increase the likelihood of late payment. Issuers cannot treat payments as late unless they have adopted procedures ensuring that statements are mailed 21 days before payment is due [15 U.S.C.A. § 1666b(a)], and are restricted in imposing late fees due to their own changes in handling procedures [15 U.S.C.A. § 1666c(c)]. Furthermore, payments are required to be due on the same day each month [15 U.S.C.A. § 1637(o)(1), and payments received when the issuer is closed may not be treated as late if received the next day [15 U.S.C.A. § 1637(o)(2)].

Fifthly, the CARD Act adopted a handful of provisions designed to make the billing statement more cardholder friendly. The statement must now include a warning that making only minimum payments will increase interest and time to repay [15 U.S.C.A. § 1637(b)(11)(A)]. It must further include calculations relating to repayment if only minimum payments are made (plus the total cost of doing so) [15 U.S.C.A. § 1637(b)(11)(B)], and the payment required to eliminate the balance in 36 months Id. The billing statement must further conspicuously disclose the date on which payment is due, together with any late fee [15 U.S.C.A. § 1637(b)(12)(A)]. If late payment will increase the APR, notice of that fact and the increase must be disclosed in close proximity to the due date [15 U.S.C.A. § 1637(b)(12)(B).

Finally, the CARD Act adopted a variety of other provisions regulating deceptive introductory and promotional rates [15 U.S.C.A. § 1666i–2(a–b)], prohibiting fees for method of payment [15 U.S.C.A. § 1637(*l*)], mandating the internet posting of credit card agreements [15 U.S.C.A. § 1632(d)(1), available on the CFPB website at http://www.consumerfinance.gov/credit-cards/agreements/], and mandating that any payment above the minimum be applied to balances bearing the highest rate of interest [15 U.S.C.A. § 1666c(b)(1)].

The CARD Act appears to have had a significant impact on some of the targeted techniques, but some commentators fear that issuers may be compensating for those decreased revenues by increasing interest rates or other permitted fees.

The next several sections discuss these rights and a few other, closely related issues beyond the clear scope of TILA, but this discussion is prefaced with a short explanation as to why disputes about these rights and other disagreements about credit cards very rarely appear in reported judicial decisions.

C. ARBITRATION

What law applies in deciding disputes about credit card rights and liabilities is different from the venue where the dispute is decided. Although the practice does not appear to be as widespread as previously thought, many credit card contracts continue to mandate arbitration as the appropriate venue. Further, waivers of class actions are nearly universal. [See Peter Rutledge & Christopher Drahozal, Contract and Choice, 2013 B.Y.U.L. Rev. 1 (relying on website postings of current credit card contracts)]. If an agreement provides for arbitration, and if the transaction involves interstate commerce (as is often true in credit card transactions) the Federal Arbitration Act (FAA) applies and preempts state law that would otherwise block arbitration.

Part of the reduced numbers of arbitration clauses likely result from settlements, such as one in 2009 by means of which four of the largest credit card issuers agreed to remove arbitration clauses and class action bans from their contracts for a period of 3 ½ years. *Ross v. Bank of America, N.A. (USA)*, 524 F. 3d 217 (2d Cir. 2008) (Settlement agreement *available at*

Documents, https://www.arbitration.ccfsettlement.com/documents/ (last visited Oct. 8, 2014)). The CFPB is in the process of soliciting information regarding the use of such arbitration clauses for the purpose of possible future regulation. [77 F.R. 25148–05 (April 27, 2012)]. Preliminary results indicate that "just over 50% of credit card loans outstanding are subject to" arbitration clauses," but that "[n]early all the arbitration clauses studied include provisions stating that arbitration may not proceed on a class basis." CFPB, Arbitration Study Preliminary Results 12–13 (Dec. 12, 2013), *available at* http://files.consumerfinance.gov/f/201312_cfpb_arbitration-study-preliminary-results.pdf (last visited Oct. 8, 2014).

3. CARDHOLDER RIGHT TO PAYMENT—"WRONGFUL DISHONOR"

TILA does not provide in so many words that an issuer is obliged to pay credit card charges that are properly payable under the terms of the cardholder agreement. The source of this obligation is the agreement itself, though not in those exact or clear terms. The obligation is more inferred than expressed. So, what happens if an issuer mistakenly or otherwise wrongfully refuses to authorize a credit card charge?

UCC Article 4 explicitly addresses and punishes a payor bank's wrongful dishonor of a customer's check. Liability includes actual and consequential damages, including damages for arrest or prosecution of the customer. 4–402(b). In contrast, when an issuer of a letter of credit wrongfully dishonors its obligation to pay, Article 5 imposes liability for actual and incidental damages but not consequential damages. 5–111(a). Wire transfers are handled similarly. In the case of a payment order that the receiving bank accepts from the originator but fails to execute, the bank is liable "to the originator for its expenses in the funds transfer and for incidental expenses and interest losses. . . ." 4A–305(b); see also 4A–305(d). Consequential damages are recoverable only if provided for in an express written agreement of the bank. 4A–305(c). The clear reason for this rule with respect to wire transfers are two: the common-law rule of HADLEY V. BAXENDALE, 156 Eng. Rep. 145 (1854), and the broader notion that imposing liability for consequential damages on banks would destroy the speed and low costs associated with wire transfers. 4A–305 comment 2.

None of these rules applies to the dishonor of a credit card. Presumably, the usual rule of damages for breach of contract applies with its usual constraints, including *Hadley*, on extraordinary damages.

Even this conclusion assumes that a breach of contract occurs when an issuer refuses to authorize a properly payable charge. Cardholder agreements sometimes include provisions that seemingly purport to allow the issuer to reduce the credit limit, refuse to make an advance, or terminate the account at any time for any reason. Arguably, such a free way out of the cardholder agreement is limited to some extent by the common-law obligation of good faith, if not by an explicit or implied requirement of prior notice.

In *Gray v. American Express Co.*, 743 F.2d 10 (D.C. Cir. 1984), Mr. and Mrs. Oscar Gray had enjoyed a wedding anniversary dinner, and he tendered his American Express card for payment. The restaurant informed Gray that American Express had refused to authorize the charge and had instructed the restaurant to keep and destroy his card. Gray sued, alleging that this conduct violated the cardholder agreement between him and American Express. The defense was a provision in the agreement allowing the issuer to revoke the right to use the card at any time with *or without notice.* The district court granted summary judgment to American Express. The court of appeals reversed.

The basis for reversal was nothing like unconscionability or adhesion. It was good, old, reliable, close construction of the contract. The issuer was free to decide internally to cancel. No notice of this cancellation was required. On the other hand, the issuer was bound to accept irreversible obligations incurred with the credit card before the cardholder knows the card has been canceled. "The right to cancel 'without giving you notice' means that the decision to cancel can be entirely unilateral and instantaneous. It cannot, however, be an internalized decision which is never communicated to the cardholder . . . [for otherwise] the underlying contractual relationship [is] illusory." Id. at 18–19.

Be careful here! Even the court in *Gray* recognized the right of the issuer to cancel freely—with or without notice—*prospectively*, that is, kill off the card with respect to future purchases made after the cardholder knows of the cancellation. This free right was confirmed in *Shwartz v. American Express Travel Co.*, 2002 WL 1684440 (E.D. La. 2002). The cardholder, Michael Shwartz, resisted by arguing that such a right to cancel was limited by an obligation of good faith. The court disagreed because courts should not imply an obligation of good faith and fair dealing to override or replace express contractual terms. "The cancellation language of the [cardholder] agreements expressly allowed [the issuer] to cancel Shwartz's accounts for *any* reason. Thus, this Court will not rewrite either of the contracts to impose an obligation of good faith and fair dealing that was not agreed to by the parties." Id. at 4.

Be more careful! A different but related case implies caution about concluding that good faith does not limit an issuer's right to terminate. In *Table Steaks v. First Premier Bank*, 650 N.W.2d 829 (S.D. 2002), MasterCard and the local merchant bank became suspicious that the merchant, Table Steaks, which is a restaurant and bar with pool tables and video games, was involved in some sort of fraudulent card scheme. So, the bank terminated the merchant's credit card account. The effect was that no customer—no matter where she got her MasterCard—could use her card at Table Steaks.

Table Steaks sued. The bank argued that its contract with Table Steaks allowed either party to terminate at will. The bank lost. The court affirmed liability on the basis of the jury's finding that the bank did not act reasonably or in good faith in abruptly terminating the credit card contract with Table Steaks. It is important to note, however, that this case is limited by an important fact: nobody contacted Table Steaks about anything prior to the termination. In this respect the case is more like *Gray* than *Shwartz*. The result in *Table Steaks* might have been different if the bank terminated the agreement prospectively, that is, after notice to the merchant.

Though acknowledging that "no . . . case raises or resolves the question of wrongful dishonor of credit cards," a recent commentator argues that liability for wrongful dishonor should be extended to credit cards on the basis that "the card issuer creates market expectations that the issuer will pay the cardholder's authorized charges. The cardholder uses the card in contractual reliance. . . ." L. Ali Khan, A Theoretical Analysis of Payment Systems, 60 S.C. L. Rev. 425, 479, 481 (2008). Professor Kahn rejects the argument that dishonoring a check relates to "my money" while refusing to pay a credit card charge relates to "their money," acknowledging that money in your checking account also belongs to the bank.

4. CARDHOLDER SECURING PAYMENT

The typical cardholder agreement allows the cardholder to terminate prospectively, too. On the other hand, the agreement is crystal clear that in any event the cardholder remains liable for charges already incurred and associated future expenses. The language of the cardholder in the agreement that "I shall pay my bill" is much clearer and more certain than language of the issuer that "Bank shall pay your charges."

Also, the cardholder's promise to pay her credit card bill is sometimes backed by provisions in the agreement purporting to secure this promise with collateral, including:

- securing the promise with a security interest in anything purchased with the card;
- collateral securing other loans the cardholder has with the issuer;
- and the cardholder's checking, savings, and other asset accounts held with and by the issuer.

With respect to goods purchased with the card or securing other loans, the validity of the first two claims of security by the issuer will be governed by UCC Article 9. The last claim, too, at least to the extent it purports to create a consensual lien on a deposit account, is also governed recently by Article 9. Even if Article 9 can and is satisfied, however, TILA imposes additional requirements to the effectiveness of a security interest to secure credit card indebtedness:

> [A] security interest must be affirmatively agreed to by the consumer and must be disclosed in the issuer's account-opening disclosures. . . . The security interest *must not be the functional equivalent of a right of offset*; as a result, routinely including in agreements contract language indicating that consumers are giving a

> security interest in any deposit accounts maintained with the issuer [is not adequate].

12 C.F.R. pt. 1026, Supp. I, Part 1, Official Staff Interpretations 12(d)(2)(1) (emphasis added).

The reference to a "right of offset" is the benchmark because TILA is clear that offset cannot be used to satisfy card indebtedness. What is this right? Beyond and apart from the possibility of a consensual lien, a bank enjoys a state, common-law **right of setoff** as a remedy for settling mutual debts: the bank owes you money in your checking or other asset account; you owe the bank because of a credit card debt or other loan; the bank can satisfy the latter by setting off the former.

TILA severely limits—effectively disallows—using setoff. An issuer cannot offset a consumer cardholder's indebtedness against funds of the cardholder held on deposit with the issuer unless:

> (1) such action was previously authorized in writing by the cardholder in accordance with a credit plan whereby the cardholder agrees periodically to pay debts incurred in his open end credit account by permitting the card issuer periodically to deduct all or a portion of such debt from the cardholder's deposit account, and
>
> (2) such action with respect to any outstanding disputed amount not be taken by the card issuer upon request of the cardholder.

15 U.S.C.A. § 1666h. So, setoff as a unilateral creditor's remedy is prohibited, "either before or after

termination of credit card privileges." 12 C.F.R. § 1026.12(d)(1).[11] This prohibition includes " '[f]reezing' or placing a hold on funds in the cardholder's deposit account [which] is the functional equivalent of an offset." 12 C.F.R. pt. 1026, Supp. I, Part 1, Official Staff Interpretations 12(d)(1)(1.). Periodic, consensual, authorized debits against the cardholder's deposits as a way of routinely paying down credit card debt is okay.

Some other "exceptions" to the prohibition against using setoff are also created. The possibility of a consensual security interest, with limits discussed above, is excepted. Also excepted from the prohibition against setoff are actions to:

- attach or otherwise levy upon the funds, and
- obtain or enforce a court order relating to the funds.

12 C.F.R. § 1026.12(d)(2). So, "if an order of a bankruptcy court required the card issuer to turn over deposit account funds to the trustee in bankruptcy, the issuer would not violate the regulation by placing a hold on the funds in order to comply with the court order." 12 C.F.R. pt. 1026, Supp. I, Part 1, Official Staff Interpretations 12(d)(1)(1.). This exception would not allow the issuer acting in its own interest to freeze the funds upon and because of the cardholder's bankruptcy. Doing so is okay under bankruptcy law as an exception to the

---

[11] "If the indebtedness was incurred after termination, the prohibition does not apply." 12 C.F.R. pt. 1026, Supp. I, Part 1, Official Staff Interpretations 12(d)(1)(4.).

automatic stay but only if the issuer otherwise enjoys the right to setoff under all other applicable law.

5. CARDHOLDER "STOPPING PAYMENT"—WITHHOLDING PAYMENT ON BASIS OF DEFENSES AGAINST MERCHANT

The drawer of a check enjoys the little fettered right to stop payment of the instrument so long as she acts timely and follows required procedures. The reason for stopping payment is irrelevant as between the drawer and the payor bank. If the drawer acts quickly enough and follows the rules, the payor bank is obliged to follow the stop order. The main purpose of this right, however, is to give the drawer some protection in the event she discovers flawed performance in the underlying transaction soon after paying for it. She remains liable on the check but keeps her money and forces the payee to sue her, at which time the drawer can raise defenses and counterclaims based on the payee's failure to perform.

The law does not recognize the same, broad right to stop payment for a cardholder who has charged something to her credit card account. The reason is not that the process always works too quickly to accommodate a stop order. Sometimes the time between using a credit card and settling hard debits and credits between participants in the network is longer than the time between writing a check and final payment by the payor bank. The reason for the absence of a stop-payment right for cardholders is neglect or, more likely, a considered policy decision against the right in credit card systems.

TILA nevertheless provides a very limited right for a cardholder to keep her money on the basis of defenses and counterclaims against a merchant. 15 U.S.C.A. § 1666i. It's a tiny right to withhold payment to the issuer for credit card charges incurred in connection with transactions that give the cardholder defenses and counterclaims against the merchant. Please understand that this right is beyond the common law and so is extraordinary; but it is also very small.

Let's start by understanding the relevant common law. Under the common law, and also under UCC Article 9, an assignee stands in the shoes of an assignor. So, if an obligee sells or otherwise assigns to an assignee the obligee's right to payment from the obligor, the obligor can ordinarily assert against the assignee whatever defenses the obligor has against the obligee-assignor. For example, suppose OR buys goods on credit from EE. The parties sign a simple contract that explains their deal, including OR's obligation to pay the price to EE. EE then assigns the contract to Bank. Bank notifies OR of the assignment and is free to collect payment from her. It turns out, however, that EE breached some warranty in selling the goods to OR. This breach gives OR a defense to payment or counterclaim under UCC Article 2. Bank is subject to this defense or counterclaim.

Suppose, however, that OR paid for the goods using a credit card issued by Bank. Can OR avoiding paying Bank what she owes on her credit card to the extent the balance represents the value of her claim or defense against EE? The answer under the common law and UCC is no. In this situation, Bank is not an assignee asserting OR's right to payment. Rather, Bank is suing on a separate, independent obligation OR made in her cardholder agreement with Bank to pay all charges OR incurs using her credit card.

TILA creates a special, limited right of cardholders to assert against issuing banks the cardholders' claims and defenses against merchants arising out of the underlying transactions between them. TILA allows claimants whose transactions exceed $50 and who have made a good faith attempt to obtain satisfactory resolution of the problem, to assert non-tort claims and defenses arising out of the credit card transaction, *if the place of the initial transaction is in the same state as the mailing address the cardholder provided the issuer or within 100 miles of the address*. 15 U.S.C.A. § 1666i. Assert means that "[t]he cardholder may withhold payment up to the amount of credit outstanding for the property or services that gave rise to the dispute and any finance or other charges imposed on that amount." 12 C.F.R. § 1026.12(c). "The geographical limitation serves to protect banks from consumers who may expose them to unlimited liability through dealings with merchants in far-away states where it is difficult to monitor a merchant's behavior." *Izraelewitz v. Manufacturers Hanover Trust Co.*, 465 N.Y.S.2d 486, 488 (N.Y.City Civ. Ct. 1983).

So, does this right apply when you sit at home and use your credit card to pay for stuff by phone with a merchant far, far away?

The available case law on this issue is scarce, and resolution depends upon which party is classified as the offeror under contract law. In *In re Standard Financial Management Corp.*, 94 B.R. 231 (D. Mass. 1988), for example, a bankruptcy court held that a distant telemarketer selling coins by telephone was the offeror. When the customer provided his credit card information, the court found that he accepted the offer "in the comfort of his own home," Id. at 239. Thus, the transaction took place in his home state.

However, in *Plutchok v. European American Bank*, 540 N.Y.S.2d 135 (Nassau Co. Dist. Ct. 1989) a Florida marketer selling memberships in a vacation discount club by phone was held to be merely soliciting an offer from the cardholder. When the cardholder relied on 1666i to resist paying the credit card issuer, the cardholder lost:

> The question of where the transaction occurred is to be determined by State law. * * * Under New York State law, a contract is transacted in the State where there is an acceptance and completion of a contract, and completion of a contract may be made by telephone. * * *
>
> In the instant case, the plaintiff, a resident of New York State, received a mail solicitation from "Holiday," a Miami corporation. "Holiday's" mail solicitation was an invitation for plaintiff to make an offer of membership for $249.00. The

> solicitation, through advertising, constitutes a request for offers, and once the offers are tendered, the seller has the option to accept or reject any or all of them. * * * Plaintiff's telephone conversation, where he purchased membership by giving his credit card number, constituted an offer which was accepted by "Holiday." * * * Consequently, the transaction occurred in Florida and outside the 100 mile requirement of 15 U.S.C.A. section 1666i since the transaction was complete when "Holiday" accepted plaintiff's membership offer.

Id. at 137.

So, how does 1666i apply when you use your credit card on the Internet? Where is the seller located—where does the transaction occur—if seller's business, its input computers, and its host servers are all in different states or countries? The courts have still not decided this issue under 1666i. However, numerous cases have now considered the issue of personal jurisdiction over a person operating through a website. Although initially reluctant to base jurisdiction solely on Internet contacts, courts now permit jurisdiction on the basis of different tests. Some courts have adopted a sliding scale test, which depends on the passive or interactive nature of the website [e.g. *Zippo Manufacturing Co. v. Zippo Dot Com, Inc.*, 952 F. Supp. 1119 (W.D. Pa. 1997)]. Other courts have adopted a more traditional test, looking at such factors as whether the defendant has purposely availed itself of the privilege of conducting activities within the forum state. [e.g. *Chloe v. Queen*

Bee of Beverly Hills, LLC, 616 F. 3d 158 (2d Cir. 2010)]. *See generally* Pavan Mehrotra, Back to the Basics: Why Traditional Principles of Personal Jurisdiction Are Effective Today and Why Zippo Needs to Go, 12 N.C. J. L. & Tech. 229 (Fall 2010); Joanna Taatjes, Downloading Minimum Contacts: The Propriety of Exercising Personal Jurisdiction Based on Smartphone Apps, 45 Conn. L. Rev. 357 (Nov. 2012). Those approaches indicate that whether making a purchase over the Internet locates the transaction in the cardholder's home state is not a simple issue.

However, the scarcity of case law may be based on the reluctance of card issuers to raise the geographic defense. A recent commentator indicates that "the Visa and MasterCard networks do not rely upon" that geographic limitation. Ronald Mann, Making Sense of Payments Policy in the Information Age, 93 Geo. L. J. 633, 648 at n. 71 (Jan. 2005). A second issue raised by the jurisdiction cases is whether a cardholder who cannot use 1666i against her bank with respect to charges for failed Internet transactions will face difficulty in suing the merchant directly. Remember that the inapplicability of 1666i only means that the cardholder cannot withhold payment for the disputed charges as against the issuer. The cardholder must pay the issuer for the charges. The cardholder nevertheless retains her rights to pursue and recover damages directly from the merchant for breach of contract. Whether the cardholder will be able to establish local jurisdiction over the merchant will depend upon whether the merchant's maintenance of its website meets the tests for minimum contacts adopted by that jurisdiction as discussed above.

The dollar amount and geographical limitations do not apply—therefore claims and defenses against the merchant are widely good against the issuer—as to any transaction in which the person honoring the credit card:

- is the same person as the card issuer,
- is controlled by the card issuer,
- is under direct or indirect common control with the card issuer,
- is a franchised dealer in the card issuer's products or services, or
- has obtained the order for such transaction through a mail solicitation made by or participated in by the card issuer in which the cardholder is solicited to enter into such transaction by using the credit card issued by the card issuer.

15 U.S.C.A. § 1666i(a).

Even when the 1666i right applies, the law limits the extent to which the cardholder's claim and defenses against the merchant can be asserted against the issuer. First, tort claims cannot be asserted against the issuer. 15 U.S.C.A. § 1666i(a). Second, "[t]he amount of claims or defenses asserted by the cardholder may not exceed the amount of credit outstanding with respect to such transaction at the time the cardholder first notifies the card issuer or the person honoring the credit card of such claim or defense." 15 U.S.C.A. § 1666i(b).

6. CARDHOLDER LIMITED LIABILITY FOR UNAUTHORIZED USE

Under TILA, a cardholder is liable for unauthorized use of his credit card only if: 1) the credit card has been accepted by the cardholder for his use; 2) the liability does not exceed $50; 3) the issuer gives adequate notice of the potential liability; 4) the issuer provides the cardholder with a description of a means by which the issuer may be notified of loss or theft of the card; 5) the unauthorized use occurs before the cardholder has notified the issuer of the loss or theft; and 6) the issuer has provided a means to identify (i.e., signature or photograph) the person, the cardholder, who is authorized to use the card. 15 U.S.C.A. § 1643(a)(1).

Thus, unlike when cash is stolen, the cardholder's liability is limited to $50 for unauthorized use if the card was an "accepted" credit card, the issuer gave the cardholder "adequate notice" of the potential liability and the "means by which the card issuer may be notified of loss or theft" and the unauthorized use occurred before the issuer has been notified that an unauthorized use has or might occur. Moreover, TILA expressly defers to any state statute that is even more consumer-protective. 15 U.S.C.A. § 1643(c). Finally, for marketing purposes, card issuers commonly waive even the $50 liability. The gross benefits of advertising a card with no liability for unauthorized are much greater than the net loss of holding cardholders liable for the $50 which costs much more to collect in many individual cases and always costs more in the total of all cases.

Because section 1643 was enacted as an amendment to the Truth in Lending Act, which expressly excludes from its scope "[c]redit transactions involving extensions of credit primarily for business, commercial, or agricultural purposes * * * or to organizations," 15 U.S.C.A. § 1603(1)[12], card issuers have argued in the past that the section's limitation on liability for unauthorized use did not apply when the cardholder was a corporation, or when a credit card was used by an individual for business purposes. Yet, in 1974 Congress amended TILA expressly to provide that the exemption of section 1603(1) does not apply to the provisions relating to the issuance of credit cards and their unauthorized or fraudulent use. 15 U.S.C.A. § 1645. As a result, the 1643 limitation of liability applies to any person—including organizations—to whom a credit card is issued for any purpose, including business. 12 C.F.R. pt. 1026, Supp. I, Part 1, Official Staff Interpretations 12(b)(1.).

Importantly, however, section 1643 is not applicable where the cardholder voluntarily and knowingly allows another to use his card and that person goes on a spending spree of her own. Unauthorized use triggering 1643 occurs only where

---

[12] Proposals have been made to extend TILA protections to credit cards issued to certain qualified small businesses. See, e.g., H.R. 2419, 113th Cong., 1st Sess. (2013).

the card is used by a person other than the cardholder "who does not have actual, implied, or apparent authority for such use, and from which the cardholder receives no benefit." 12 C.F.R.§ 1026.12(b)(1)(i). Authority is determined by local law, not TILA. 12 C.F.R. pt. 1026, Supp. I, Part 1, Official Staff Interpretations 12(b)(1)(ii)(1.).

If the cardholder authorizes somebody to use the card but limits the person's use, the limitation is not effective against the issuer. Any authorization is, as against the issuer, unlimited authorization. *American Express Bank v. Kayatta*, 118 Cal. Rptr. 3d 462 (Cal.App.2010). It is the equivalent of signing and giving someone a blank check, in which case the drawer is stuck with whatever the other person fills in. The drawer has no good complaint against the payor bank which pays the check unless the payor bank has prior notice that the check was completed for a larger amount than authorized. 4–401(d)(2).

So, can the cardholder protect herself when she has given her card to someone for use by notifying the issuer of some limit on use or that the authority given has been exceeded? The answer is maybe, sort of. TILA and Regulation Z are worded such that a cardholder can argue that the limitation of liability and even liability itself end upon certain notice to the issuer. 12 C.F.R. § 1026.12(b)(1)(i). The statute says that a "cardholder shall be liable for the unauthorized use of a credit card only if" certain conditions are satisfied, including "the unauthorized use occurs before the card issuer has been notified that an unauthorized use of the credit card has occurred or may occur as the result of loss, theft, or otherwise. . . ." 15 U.S.C.A. § 1643(a)(1)(E). The necessary notice is given when the cardholder takes steps

> "as may be reasonably required in the ordinary course of business to provide the card issuer with the pertinent information about the loss, theft, or possible unauthorized use of a credit card, regardless of whether any particular officer, employee, or agent of the card issuer does, in fact, receive the information. Notification may be given, at the option of the person giving it, in person, by telephone, or in writing. Notification in writing is considered given at the time of receipt or, whether or not received, at the expiration of the time ordinarily required for transmission, whichever is earlier."

12 C.F.R. § 1026.12(b)(3).

The courts disagree, however, whether or not giving this notice lets the cardholder off the hook for subsequent misuse of the card. The courts holding that notice does not prospectively free the cardholder from liability read 1643(a) to apply only to unauthorized use; and they refuse to read the statute to mean that a cardholder's notice of misuse converts previously authorized use to unauthorized use thereafter.

Ordinarily, however, when the cardholder notifies the issuer of misuse, the issuer blocks or cancels the card. Therefore, no merchant can safely accept the card because the card network will deny authorization for everybody or anybody using the card. In this event, the cardholder's notice to the issuer practically and functionally—if not legally—protects the cardholder against further liability for misuse. If the issuer is asked to cancel and fails to do so, the issuer may be liable to the cardholder for breach of contract or otherwise; but this issue has not arisen in the cases holding that notice of misuse alone is insufficient to end the cardholder's liability for further misuse of the card.[13]

The self-help remedy of the cardholder simply retrieving the card is a less complete solution. Credit card accounts are accessible these days using only the information from the card, though perhaps any later use of the information from a retrieved card is—without fresh authority—unauthorized.

Can unauthorized use turn into authorized use when a cardholder fails to examine her statements and continues to pay the relevant charges? Three circuits have now said yes—on the basis of apparent authority. In *Minskoff v. American Express Travel Related Services Co., Inc.*, 98 F. 3d 703 (2d Cir. 1996), the Second Circuit held that the cardholder's failure to examine credit card or bank statements over a

---

[13] A related issue has been raised: whether the issuer or the cardholder is liable for an agent's authorized charges that exceed the credit limit on the card. The court said in *Michigan Nat'l Bank v. Olson*, 723 P.2d 438 (Wash Ct. App. 1986), that this situation creates genuine issues of fact as to whether such a limit creates a duty by the issuer to the cardholder and whether the duty was breached. For comparison, with respect to checks, a customer who writes overdrafts against her account that the bank pays is liable for the overdrafts to the bank, even in the absence of an overdraft agreement. 4–401(a).

period of 28 months created as a matter of law "apparent authority for [the assistant's] continuing use of the cards," based on American Express's "continuing impression that nothing was amiss" with the account. Id at 710. The court noted that nothing in TILA was intended to "sanction intentional or negligent conduct by the cardholder that furthers the fraud or theft of an unauthorized card user." Id at 709.

Two other Circuits have agreed, but utilize a narrower approach. Rather than faulting the cardholder for merely failing to inspect monthly statements, those courts found apparent authority on the basis of the cardholder's continuous payment of the charges over a period of time. *DBI Architects, P.C. v. American Express Travel-Related Services Co., Inc.*, 388 F. 3d 886 (D.C.Cir. 2004) ($133,000+ over 10 months); *Azur v. Chase Bank, USA (N.A)*, 601 F. 3d 212 (3d Cir. 2010) ($1 million+ over 7 years). Those courts reason that the cardholder is in a better position than the issuer to discover such fraudulent charges. This approach, of course, requires the trier of fact to make the additional (and difficult) determination of *when* that apparent authority arose.

Be careful! Even if the card is used by someone whom the cardholder has not authorized in terms of state law, the card is not necessarily "unauthorized" for purposes of section 1643 and its limitation of liability. Triggering the protection of 1643 requires not only lack of authority for the use but also requires that the cardholder received no benefit from the use.

In *Citibank v. Gifesman*, 773 A.2d 993 (Conn. App. 2001), the cardholder, Gifesman, requested a secondary card for use by a friend's acquaintance. The friend, Kharkover, had promised to repay the cardholder for any use by the person, Popov. Also, Kharkover paid Gifesman $25 a month for the arrangement. Well, Popov or somebody else ran up a huge bill. The issuer sued the cardholder for the balance, and the cardholder relied on section 1643.

The problem with this defense is seemingly that giving a secondary card to Popov is authority to use it. Interestingly, however, the court did not decide the case on this basis. Rather, the basis for upholding judgment for the issuer was: the cardholder "received a benefit for his role in the procurement of the Popov card," 773 A.2d at 996, which was the $25 a month Kharkover paid Gifesman.

Be more careful! Even if use is unauthorized and the cardholder received no benefit from the use, the cardholder may still be liable if the card credit card account is a joint account and the use is by the other person to the account. We're not talking about the case in which a person opens an account on which she is solely liable and then requests the issuer to issue a secondary card to another person. In such a case the cardholder is liable, if at all, because the use is authorized. The different case we're talking about here is the case in which two people open the credit card account and agree in the cardholder contract that each of them is liable for the other's use of the card. In this event, each person is liable for all charges to the account whether or not she authorized the other person's use or benefited from it. *Dunkinson v. Citigroup, Inc.*, 2012 WL 32573 (D.N.J. 2012).

Be even more careful! Even if use is unauthorized, the cardholder received no benefit from the use, and there is no joint account liability, the issuer still may have the alternative argument of extra-statutory negligence in not discovering and reporting the unauthorized use to the issuer. This issue is better discussed below in connection with the TILA process for resolving billing errors and how this process relates to the 1643 limitations on liability for unauthorized use. See the related discussion later in this chapter.

In the case of unauthorized use when 1643 protects the cardholder, the unauthorized user of the credit card is then accountable to the card issuer under the law of **unjust enrichment** for charges incurred through the wrongful use of the card. *See Fifth Third Bank/Visa v. Gilbert*, 478 N.E.2d 1324 (Ohio Mun.Ct.1984). The unauthorized user also is accountable to society under federal and state criminal laws.

With respect to **procedure**, federal law applies when a card issuer sues to enforce liability for the use of a credit card. Federal law applies, and section 1643(b) changes the burden of proof very substantially. When a card issuer sues a cardholder, "the burden of proof is upon the card issuer to show that the use was authorized or, if the use was unauthorized, then the burden of proof is upon the card issuer to show that the conditions of liability for the unauthorized use of a credit card, as set forth in subsection (a) of this section, have been met." 15 U.S.C.A. § 1643(b). If the issuer meets the burden proving authorized use, the cardholder is naturally responsible for the charges.

7. CARDHOLDER RIGHTS AGAINST ISSUER FOR "BILLING" ERRORS (INCLUDING CHARGES "NOT PROPERLY PAYABLE")

A. RIGHTS AND PROCESS

A subset of TILA provisions, known as the Fair Credit Billing Act (FCBA), 15 U.S.C.A. § 1666–1666j, aims to prescribe an orderly procedure for identifying and resolving disputes between a cardholder and a card issuer as to the amount due at any given time. The trigger for this procedure, and the rights accompanying it, is a "billing error," which means, and is limited to, aspects of a cardholder's statement of account or the issuer's handling of the account that are wrong or otherwise trigger billing-error rights because:

- The charge was not made by the consumer or a person who has actual, implied, or apparent authority to use the consumer's credit card or open-end credit plan.

- The charge was not identified in accordance with the requirements of 12 C.F.R. § 1026.7(b)(2) and 1026.8.

- The charge was for property or services not accepted by the consumer or the consumer's designee, or not delivered to the consumer or the consumer's designee as agreed.
- The issuer failed to credit properly a payment or other credit issued to the consumer's account.
- There is a computational or similar error of an accounting nature that is made by the creditor.
- The cardholder requests additional clarification, including documentary evidence, concerning some charge to her account.
- The issuer failed to mail or deliver a periodic statement to the consumer's last known address if that address was received by the creditor, in writing, at least 20 days before the end of the billing cycle for which the statement was required.

12 C.F.R. § 1026.13(a).

If the cardholder believes that the statement contains a billing error, so defined, she then may send the issuer a written notice setting forth her belief, indicating the amount of the error and the reasons supporting her belief that it is an error. If the issuer receives this notice within sixty days of transmitting the statement of account, *and if the notice does describe a problem that is a billing error as § 1666(b) describes*, § 1666(a) then imposes two separate obligations upon the issuer:

- First, within thirty days, the issuer must send a written acknowledgment that it has received the notice.
- Second, within ninety days or two complete billing cycles, whichever is shorter, the issuer must investigate the matter and either make appropriate corrections in the cardholder's account or send a written explanation of its belief that the original statement sent to the cardholder was correct. The issuer must send its explanation before making any attempt to collect the disputed amount.

An issuer that fails to comply with these obligations forfeits its right to collect the first $50 of the disputed amount including finance charges. 15 U.S.C.A. § 1666(e). In addition, § 1666(d) provides that, pursuant to regulations of the Federal Reserve Board, a creditor operating an "open end consumer credit plan" may not restrict or close an account due to a cardholder's failure to pay a disputed amount until the creditor has sent the written explanation required by § 1666(a).

Other obligations also attach. First, if "appropriate corrections" are made, the card issuer also must credit any finance charge on accounts erroneously billed. 15 U.S.C.A. § 1666(a)(B)(i). Second, the card issuer must notify the cardholder on subsequent statements of account that she need not pay the amount in dispute until the card issuer has complied with § 1666. 15 U.S.C.A. § 1666(c)(2). Third, the card issuer may not report, or threaten to report, adversely on the cardholder's credit before the card issuer has discharged its obligations under § 1666, 15 U.S.C.A. § 1666a(a); and, if the cardholder continues to dispute the bill in timely fashion, the card issuer may report the delinquency only if it also reports that the amount is in dispute and tells the cardholder to whom it has released this information. 15 U.S.C.A. § 1666a(b). The card issuer is further obliged to report any eventual resolution of the delinquency to the same third parties with whom it earlier had communicated. 15 U.S.C.A. § 1666a(c). Finally, a card issuer that fails to comply with any requirements of the Act is liable to the cardholder for actual damages, twice the amount of any finance charge, and costs of the action and attorney's fees. 15 U.S.C.A. § 1640(a).

B. RELATIONSHIP TO UNAUTHORIZED USE AND CLAIMS AGAINST MERCHANT

Two important substantive disputes of cardholders are that somebody else used the card without the cardholder's authority or that the merchant with whom the cardholder dealt somehow breached the underlying transaction. In the former case, TILA limits the cardholder's liability in many cases, 15 U.S.C.A. § 1643, which is discussed above. In the latter case, TILA allows the cardholder in certain, limited cases to assert against the issuer the claims and defenses that the cardholder would have against the merchant for breach of contract, 15 U.S.C.A.

§ 1666i, which is also discussed above. When either of these rights applies, the effect is to give the cardholder a defense to paying the issuer.

Either problem may also be a treated as a billing error under § 1666 and trigger the accompanying process for resolving the error under § 1666a. Unauthorized use is always a billing error; and certain breaches of contract by the merchant are billing errors, too, whether or not 1666i applies to allow the cardholder to assert claims and defenses against the issuer.

Anyway, when § 1643 or § 1666i applies to give the cardholder a defense and the problem is also a billing error that triggers § 1666a, the right to assert the defense and the right to use the § 1666a process for resolving the billing error are cumulative rights.

C. RELATIONSHIP TO ISSUER CHARGEBACK AGAINST MERCHANT

A card issuer retains, by contract, a right of chargeback against a merchant in a bankcard system. American Express, Discover, and other like systems also provide for chargeback or something similar to it. Chargeback is essentially a right not to pay charges the merchant has accepted. It is part of the merchant's contract, not statutory; and, as the earlier discussion shows, the reasons for chargeback are almost endless. They far exceed the contractual and legal bases why a cardholder can defend against paying the issuer for charges to her credit card account.

So, the question arises whether or not a cardholder can rely on chargeback as a defense against the issuer when the defense is unavailable to the cardholder by law or by the terms of her own contract with the issuer. More precisely, does the cardholder have a legally enforceable right to piggyback on chargeback? The answer is no.

The cardholder is not a party to the merchant's contract that creates and defines chargeback. She lacks privity of contract and is not an intended third-party beneficiary. As thoroughly explained by Visa:

> What is important to understand about chargebacks is that they are contractual rights and obligations between the financial institutions that issue Visa Cards and the financial institutions that sign merchants to accept Visa Cards, and that these rights and obligations derive from their Visa membership and their exchange of Visa-branded transactions. They give no direct rights to consumers, and their exercise is optional for issuers; however, they do provide a standard worldwide level of consumer protection that issuers in any country can exercise on behalf of their Visa cardholders.
>
> Visa's chargeback rules do not attempt to track all of the possible consumer protection laws around the world, although some chargeback rights do correspond with statutory rights granted to consumers in particular countries, such as the rights granted under Federal Reserve Board Regulation Z to dispute certain

credit card transactions. The chargeback reasons permitted under Visa's rules for international transactions have been adopted to enable issuers of Visa Cards to address the fundamental consumer concerns of their cardholders, and incidentally to reinforce the reputation of Visa Cards as the best way to pay.

There may be additional rights available to a consumer under local law for which the issuer of the consumer's Visa Card has no supporting chargeback right in Visa's rules. Even in the absence of any chargeback right, in a domestic transaction the merchant will be directly liable to a consumer under applicable consumer protection laws. However, the key advantage of chargeback rights in international transactions is that they provide a consistent and standard level of protection on behalf of consumers in situations where the merchant is beyond the reach of local law.

The Visa chargebacks for consumer/merchant disputes described above cover most of the disputes that typically arise between consumers and merchants in both domestic and international transactions. Visa's chargeback rules do not correspond in every respect with each country's consumer protection laws because chargeback processing is expensive and complex, and as a private adjudicative process, the rules must be clearly and consistently defined for every participant.

> The chargeback system would break down if each issuer in every country around the world had a set of chargeback rights corresponding to the particular consumer protection laws in their country. The Visa Members signing merchants would encounter substantial problems in determining the validity of a chargeback based on the consumer protection laws of another country, and merchants doing business with consumers in other countries would have similar difficulties in determining what their liabilities might be under a wide variety of foreign laws. Finally, as the ultimate arbitrator, Visa would be required to acquire expertise in the laws of the nearly 180 countries in which Visa cards are issued.[14]

Of course, for business or other reasons, an issuer could let a cardholder off the hook for a charge against which the cardholder has no contractual or legal defense; and, the issuer could absorb the loss itself or transfer the loss to the merchant if the circumstances fit a reason for chargeback. Doing so, however, is solely within the issuer's discretion and is not required by law. What will most likely move an issuer or card systems to act in this way is a business judgment in the particular case or market forces operating to expand cardholders' push back rights, which would result from competitive efforts to

[14] Letter from Broox W. Peterson, Senior Vice President and Assistant General Counsel, Visa International Service Association to the Secretary, Federal Trade Commission, March 25, 1999 (regarding U.S. perspectives on consumer protection in the Global Electronic Commerce Marketplace, Comment, P994312).

increase share by catering to such a demand by cardholders.

PART V

PAYING WITH ELECTRONIC TRANSFERS OF FUNDS[1]

---

1 The usual name is "electronic fund transfers" (EFTs). This name is unnecessarily confusing. What is being transferred are funds, i.e., monetary value; and the funds are not any more electronic here than sitting in your checking account. The electronic part that is important with this payment system is causing the movement of funds electronically. So, this book alternately uses the name "electronic transfers of funds."

CHAPTER 12

COMMERCIAL FUNDS TRANSFERS

Together, checks and credit cards are still the most common form of payment as measured by the number of transactions per day.[1] However, commercial electronic fund transfers (a/k/a commercial or wholesale wire transfers) far exceed all other payment systems as measured by dollar volume on a daily basis. Each wholesale wire transfer is usually six figures or more, and total payments over the principal funds transfer services exceed $4 trillion per day.[2]

Electronic transfers of funds, or electronic fund(s) transfers (EFT), generally means using any electronic means to withdraw or move funds between accounts held at banks or other financial institutions. Commercial fund transfers are EFTs that affect only accounts held by businesses, including banks. They are B2B: moving funds from the account of a business to the account of another business through banking channels, i.e., networks and accounts owned by banks. The governing law is mainly UCC Article 4A, which applies according to its terms whether or not the means are electronic (but they usually are).

---

[1] However, the number of debit cards transactions now exceed both checks and credit cards as individually measured. See 2010 Federal Reserve Payment Study at 4, http://www.frbservices.org/files/communications/pdf/press/2010_payments_study.pdf. (last visited Oct. 22, 2014).

[2] The average daily volume over Fedwire alone totaled $2,841,874 million in 2013. http://www.federalreserve.gov/paymentsystems/fedfunds_ann.htm (last visited Oct. 22, 2014).

1. SCOPE OF ARTICLE 4A

In general, "Article 4A governs a method of payment in which the person making payment (the 'originator') directly transmits an instruction to a bank either to make payment to the person receiving the payment (the 'beneficiary') or to instruct some other bank to make payment to the beneficiary." 4A–104 comment 1.

In particular, the statute applies to "funds transfers." 4A–102. A "funds transfer" is:

> the series of transactions, beginning with the originator's payment order, made for the purpose of making payment to the beneficiary of the order. The term includes *any payment order* issued by the originator's bank or an intermediary bank intended to carry out the originator's payment order.

4A–104(a) (emphasis added). In turn, "payment order" means

> an instruction of a sender to a receiving bank, *transmitted orally, electronically, or in writing*, to pay, or to cause another bank to pay, a fixed or determinable amount of money to a beneficiary if: (i) the instruction does not state a condition to payment to the beneficiary other than time of payment, (ii) the receiving bank is to be reimbursed by debiting an account of, or otherwise receiving payment from, the sender, and (iii) the instruction is transmitted by the sender directly to the receiving bank or to an

agent, funds-transfer system, or communication system for transmittal to the receiving bank.

4A–103(a)(1) (emphasis added).

Well, if a paper payment order triggers 4A, how does it fit with checks under UCC Articles 3 and 4? True, a check is a paper writing but in the form of a "negotiable instrument", which has peculiar characteristics and prerequisites. See Chapter 2 *supra*. An Article 4A payment order is much simpler: just an instruction in any form telling a bank, directly and unconditionally, to pay somebody else with the understanding that the bank will get reimbursed by the person giving the instruction.

A check is a means to effect payment by a bank that also carries rights and liabilities reified in the instrument itself. A payment order is a means to effect payment by a bank but has no efficacy itself apart from its role in the payment process Article 4A provides.

Also, a check is given to the payee who then presents the instrument to the drawee bank and pulls the money from the obligor-drawer's account. A payment order under Article 4A works the opposite: the obligor (originator) gives the instruction directly to its bank (receiving bank) to push money to the beneficiary, usually through the beneficiary's bank.[3]

---

[3] Okay. Maybe it's possible that an Article 3 check could operate as a payment order. The obligor might draw a check to the beneficiary and, instead of delivering the check to the beneficiary, deliver it to the obligor's bank as an instruction to transfer funds to the beneficiary through the beneficiary's bank. On the other

You often hear that Article 4A governs only commercial or B2B funds transfers, but the statute does not positively limit itself to commercial transfers. The limitation happens because the statute excludes "a funds transfer any part of which is governed by the Electronic Fund Transfer Act" (EFTA), 4A–108. The EFTA is federal law comprehensively governing electronic transfers of funds (or electronic fund transfers (EFTs)) affecting consumer accounts. So, consumers' EFTs governed by the EFTA are out of Article 4A, which means that 4A is mainly left with commercial EFTs.

Some consumer EFTs are excluded from the EFTA; but they do not necessarily fall within Article 4A. Consumer EFTs that are excluded from the EFTA and are transmitted through Fedwire will be governed, to some extent, by Regulation J. See Chapter 13 *infra*. Some consumer EFTs, however, might fit within the letter or the principles and policies of Article 4A, and more certainly so when the means of transfer is not Fedwire.

Also, Article 4A is not limited to fund transfers effected electronically. The EFTA is so limited. So, Article 4A will govern consumer and commercial fund transfers that are not electronic and that otherwise satisfy the requirements for applying 4A.

In practice, however, most commercial fund transfers that fit within Article 4A are electronic. Moreover, this chapter focuses on electronic

---

hand, there is no possibility that a payment order is a check because it lacks the elements of negotiability Article 3 prescribes.

transfers. So, we'll assume from here on that all transfers discussed in this chapter involve electronically moving funds between the bank accounts of businesses; and Article 4A clearly applies, even though the scope of the statute is broader.

2. ELECTRONIC CHANNELS FOR ZAPPING FUNDS BETWEEN BANK ACCOUNTS

There are two principal wire transfer services through which commercial funds transfers are effected between banks: Fedwire and CHIPS (The Clearing House Interbank Payments System). In regard to Fedwire:

> The Federal Reserve Banks provide the Fedwire Funds Service, a real-time gross settlement system that enables participants to initiate funds transfers that are immediate, final, and irrevocable once processed. Depository institutions and certain other financial institutions that hold an account with a Federal Reserve bank are eligible to participate in the Fedwire Funds Services. In 2008, approximately 7,300 participants made Fedwire funds transfers. The Fedwire Funds Service is generally used to make large-value, time-critical payments.
>
> The Fedwire Funds Service is a credit transfer service. Participants originate funds transfers by instructing a Federal Reserve Bank to debit funds from its own account and credit funds to the account of another participant. Participants

may originate funds transfers online, by initiating a secure electronic message, or off line, via telephone procedures.

Fedwire Funds Services, About, http://www.federalreserve.gov/paymentsystems/fedfunds_about.htm. (last visited Oct. 22, 2014).

Federal Reserve Regulation J governs transfers made by Fedwire. 12 C.F.R. part 210. In a typical Fedwire transfer, Bank A (with an account at the Chicago Federal Reserve Bank) wants to pay Bank B (with an account at the New York Federal Reserve Bank). Bank A will send a payment order to Chicago Federal Reserve Bank which will then debit Bank A's account and credit the account of the New York Federal Reserve Bank. The Chicago Federal Reserve Bank will then issue an instruction to the New York Federal Reserve Bank to credit the account of Bank B and debit the account of the Chicago Federal Reserve Bank. The New York Federal Reserve Bank will then advise Bank B of the credit. If Addie is the originator and Pooch Pound is the beneficiary, then Fedwire will not only transfer the requested amount from Bank A to Bank B but will also simultaneously instruct Bank B to pay the requisite amount to Pooch Pound's account.

In contrast to Fedwire, CHIPS is a bank-owned, privately operated electronic payments system maintained by The Clearing House, a banking association headquartered in New York. *About CHIPS, Overview,* http://www.chips.org (last visited Oct. 22, 2014). It currently has 49 participants, and in 2012 settled an average of $1.5 trillion international and domestic payments *daily*. In regard to CHIPS:

> CHIPS provides a final intraday settlement system, continuously matching, netting, and settling queued payment orders throughout the business day. All CHIPS payment orders are settled against positive balances and are simultaneously offset by incoming payment orders, or some combination of both. To facilitate this process, the funding participants jointly maintain an account (CHIPS account) on the books of the Federal Reserve Bank of New York. Each CHIPS participant must fund this account via a Fedwire funds transfer to fulfill its pre-funded opening-position requirement. These required balances are then used to settle payment orders throughout the day.

FRB Commercial Bank Examination Manual, § 4125.1 at 2, (Effective April 2009), *available at* http://www.federalreserve.gov/boarddocs/SupManual/ (last visited Oct. 22, 214).

Commercial wire transfers can also pass through the ACH network, which is often the case for scheduled, recurring payments between businesses. See Chapter 13 *infra*, which explains the ACH network. The discussion there explains the network mainly in terms of its use for consumer transfers of funds which are affected by the Electronic Fund Transfer Act (EFTA), which has no application to B2B or commercial funds transfers whether or not the transfers pass through the ACH network.

The key to applying Article 4A and the EFTA is not the network or other channel used to move funds. The key is whether the transfer involves just businesses, in which case Article 4A applies, or involves a consumer, in which case the EFTA usually applies.

Commercial funds transfers are governed by UCC Article 4A as modified—by force of agreement or preemptive law—by the rules governing whatever networks the transfers travel through, including network operating rules and federal statute and regulations.

3. STAGES AND PLAYERS INVOLVED IN AN ARTICLE 4A FUNDS TRANSFER

WARNING! The very best writing anywhere in the entire UCC is the "Prefatory Note" to Article 4A. Nothing can be said here or anywhere else that better explains how a funds transfer work. So, read and study the whole Prefatory Note. It comes free with the copy of the UCC or selected statutes you probably had to buy for this or another law school course.

In a simple commercial funds transfer, a bank will make the transfer on behalf of a business customer to the account of another business at the same or another bank. It is a process that Article 4A breaks down into distinct stages with special names for the players or participants in the process. Suppose X, Inc., a debtor, wants to pay an obligation owed Y, Inc. Here's part of what the Prefatory Note says about how X pays Y using a commercial funds transfer governed by Article 4A:

Instead of delivering to Y a negotiable instrument such as a check or some other writing such as a credit card slip that enables Y to obtain payment from a bank, X transmits an instruction to X's bank to credit a sum of money to the bank account of Y. In most cases X's bank and Y's bank are different banks. X's bank may carry out X's instruction by instructing Y's bank to credit Y's account in the amount that X requested.

The instruction that X issues to its bank is a "payment order." X is the "sender" of the payment order and X's bank is the "receiving bank" with respect to X's order. Y is the "beneficiary" of X's order. When X's bank issues an instruction to Y's bank to carry out X's payment order, X's bank "executes" X's order. The instruction of X's bank to Y's bank is also a payment order. With respect to that order, X's bank is the sender, Y's bank is the receiving bank, and Y is the beneficiary. The entire series of transactions by which X pays Y is known as the "funds transfer."

With respect to the funds transfer, X is the "originator," X's bank is the "originator's bank," Y is the "beneficiary" and Y's bank is the "beneficiary's bank." In more complex transactions there are one or more additional banks known as "intermediary banks" between X's bank and Y's bank.

In the funds transfer the instruction contained in the payment order of X to its bank is carried out by a series of payment orders by each bank in the transmission chain to the next bank in the chain until Y's bank receives a payment order to make the credit to Y's account. In most cases, the payment order of each bank to the next bank in the chain is transmitted electronically, and often the payment order of X to its bank is also transmitted electronically, but the means of transmission does not have any legal significance. A payment order may be transmitted by any means, and in some cases the payment order is transmitted by a slow means such as first class mail. To reflect this fact, the broader term "funds transfer" rather than the narrower term "wire transfer" is used in Article 4A to describe the overall payment transaction.

UCC Article 4A, Prefatory Note.

4. RIGHTS, DUTIES, AND PAYMENT

Rights and obligations under Article 4A arise as a result of "acceptance" of a payment order by the bank to which the order is addressed. 4A–209. In the case of a payment order sent to a receiving bank *other than* the beneficiary's bank, acceptance occurs when the receiving bank "executes" the payment order of the sender by sending a payment order to some other bank intended to carry out the payment order received by the receiving bank. 4A–209(a); 4A–301(a). In the case of a payment order sent to the *beneficiary's bank*, acceptance usually occurs when the bank receives payment of the sender's payment order or when the bank pays the beneficiary or notifies the beneficiary of receipt of the payment order. 4A–209(b)(1) and (2).

Significantly, Article 4A itself does not require a receiving bank to accept a payment order. By law, the order is only a request that the receiving bank execute the sender's order. It is only by contract that the bank is obligated to accept and execute an order.

> A receiving bank has no duty to accept a payment order unless the bank makes an agreement, either before or after issuance of the payment order, to accept it, or acceptance is required by a funds transfer system rule. If the bank makes such an agreement it incurs a contractual obligation based on the agreement and may be held liable for breach of contract if a failure to execute violates the agreement. In many cases a bank will enter into an agreement with its customer to govern the rights and obligations of the parties with respect to payment orders issued to the bank by the customer or, in cases in which the sender is also a bank, there may be a funds transfer system rule that governs the obligations of a receiving bank with respect to payment orders transmitted over the system. Such agreements or rules can specify the circumstances under which a receiving bank is obliged to execute a payment order and can define the extent of liability of the receiving bank for breach of the agreement or rule.

4A–209 comment 3. This rule shouldn't surprise you. It's not unlike writing a check against a bank where you have no account. The drawee bank isn't obliged to pay the check for you unless you have a deposit agreement with the bank. If there is such an agreement, then the bank is obligated to pay checks you draw that are properly payable. If the bank doesn't pay consistent with the agreement, the bank is liable for wrongful dishonor.

Same notions apply here. You can send a payment order to any bank in the country right now. No bank, however, is obliged to accept and execute the order absent a contract with you to do so. If you have such a contract with the receiving bank, the bank must accept and execute any order consistent with the agreement and is liable to you for breaching the agreement if the bank fails to act on your order. It's the equivalent of wrongful dishonor, but under Article 4A the damages are limited to actual damages. Consequential damages are not possible unless the agreement with the bank expressly provides for them. See 4A–305.

When a payment order is accepted, the sender of the order must pay the amount of the order to the receiving bank. 4A–402(b) & (c). If the beneficiary's bank accepts a payment order, this bank incurs no obligation to the sender but is obligated to the beneficiary for the amount of the order and must pay the order to the beneficiary. 4A–209 comment 4; 4A–404(a). Acceptance by the beneficiary's bank also means that the funds transfer has been completed; when acceptance occurs, payment by the originator of the funds transfer to the beneficiary occurs. 4A–406(a).

Thus, under Article 4A, if a funds transfer is made to pay an obligation, the obligation is paid by the originator at the time the beneficiary bank incurs an obligation to pay the beneficiary and in the amount of the payment order accepted by the bank. 4A–406(b). Importantly, Article 4A imposes a duty on a beneficiary bank promptly to pay the beneficiary; breach of this duty may subject the beneficiary's bank to liability to the beneficiary for consequential damages in the appropriate circumstances. 4A–404(a).

IMPORTANT: "Pursuant to Section 4A–402(c), the originator is excused from the obligation to pay the originator's bank if the funds transfer is not completed, i.e., payment by the originator to the beneficiary is not made. Payment by the originator to the beneficiary occurs when the beneficiary's bank accepts a payment order for the benefit of the beneficiary of the originator's payment order. Section 4A–406. If for any reason . . . acceptance [by the beneficiary's bank] does not occur, the originator is not required to pay the payment order that it issued or, if it already paid, is entitled to refund of the payment with interest. This 'money-back guarantee' is an important protection of the originator of a funds transfer. The same rule applies to any other sender in the funds transfer." Article 4A, Prefatory Note.

If, by contrast, a bank other than the beneficiary's bank accepts a payment order, the obligations and liabilities are owed to the originator of the funds transfer. 4A–209 comment 1; 4A–302(a)(1). The primary obligation of the receiving bank to the originator is to issue a payment order to the beneficiary's bank on the execution date that complies with the sender's order. 4A–302(a)(1).

The "execution date" of a payment order is the day on which the receiving bank properly may issue a payment order executing the sender's order and refers to the time that the payment order should be executed rather than the day that it is actually executed. 4A–301(b). The sender by its instruction may set an execution date, but the date cannot be earlier than the day the order is received by the receiving bank. Id. If no payment date or execution date is set, the order usually is intended to be executed immediately. 4A–301 comment 2. In this instance, the execution date is the date the order is received. Id.

Significantly, absent an express written agreement to the contrary, consequential damages are not available to the originator if the receiving bank delays execution of an order, 4A–305(a), fails to complete an order it has accepted, 4A–305(b), or fails to execute a payment order it was obligated to execute under an express agreement with the originator or sender. 4A–305(d). Of course, the parties can otherwise agree. So, if a receiving bank fails to fulfill its obligations concerning acceptance, it may be liable for any and all damages, including consequential damages, "to the extent provided in an express written agreement" between the bank and its customer. 4A–305(c).

5. STOPPING PAYMENT

Stopping payment of a payment order is called cancellation. A sender can cancel by transmitting the cancellation orally, electronically, or in writing to the receiving bank. 4A–211(a). It is effective only if verified under any applicable security procedure or the bank agrees to the cancellation and it is "received at a time and in a manner affording the receiving bank a reasonable opportunity to act on the communication before the bank accepts the payment order." 4A–211(b).

Now, suppose that X, Inc. issues a payment order to its bank, which has already accepted the order and sent its own conforming payment order to the beneficiary's bank. In this case cancellation is not possible unless X's bank agrees or a banking rule provides otherwise. As a practical matter, X's bank will not agree unless there is time to cancel with the beneficiary's bank before the beneficiary's bank has accepted (4A–211(b) applies) or unless the beneficiary agrees to the cancellation.

Remember: "If a payment order does not specify a delayed payment date or execution date, the order will normally be executed shortly after receipt. Thus, as a practical matter, the sender will have very little time in which to instruct cancellation . . . before acceptance." 4A–211 comment 3. This fuse is very, very short because usually we're dealing with electronic transmissions, and the short fuse applies equally between the originator and its bank and also between the receiving bank and the beneficiary's bank. So, practically speaking, a payment order given is very quickly a payment order completed with a tiny or no gap for cancellation as a matter of right. Cancellation will require the banks' agreement.

The beneficiary's bank isn't likely to agree because, upon its acceptance of the payment order, the beneficiary's bank became liable to its customer, the beneficiary. But it's okay, and a cancellation would be effective against the beneficiary, if the beneficiary agrees or, even if the beneficiary objects, *maybe* if one of these unusual circumstances is present:

- the order was issued in execution of an unauthorized payment order, or
- because of a mistake by a sender in the funds transfer which resulted in the issuance of a payment order
  - ✓ that is a duplicate of a payment order previously issued by the sender,
  - ✓ that orders payment to a beneficiary not entitled to receive payment from the originator, or
  - ✓ that orders payment in an amount greater than the amount the beneficiary was entitled to receive from the originator.

4A–211(c)(2). Even in these circumstances, however, the beneficiary bank that cancels is entitled to recover from the beneficiary any amount paid to the beneficiary only to the extent allowed by the law governing mistake and restitution. Id.

As a result, a beneficiary bank even under these circumstances may be reluctant to cancel, and nothing here requires the bank to cancel regardless of the circumstances. If the beneficiary bank decides to take the risk and agree to the cancellation, "the sender, whether or not cancellation . . . is effective, is liable to the bank for any loss and expenses, including reasonable attorney's fees, incurred by the bank as a result of the cancellation . . . or attempted cancellation. . . ." 4A–211(f).

In the face of a likely uncooperative beneficiary bank, the originator can seek an injunction.

> For proper cause and in compliance with applicable law, a court may restrain (i) a person from issuing a payment order to initiate a funds transfer, (ii) an originator's bank from executing the payment order of the originator, or (iii) *the beneficiary's bank from releasing funds to the beneficiary or the beneficiary from withdrawing the funds.*

4A–503 (emphasis added). Otherwise, "[a] court may not . . . restrain a person from issuing a payment order, paying or receiving payment of a payment order, or otherwise acting with respect to a funds transfer". Id.

6. UNAUTHORIZED PAYMENT ORDERS

The payment order is Article 4A's equivalent of a check. See 4A–103(a)(1). In a large percentage of cases, the payment order of the originator of the funds transfer is transmitted electronically to the originator's bank. An important issue addressed in 4A–202 and 4A–203 is allocating the risk of loss from unauthorized payment orders. Suppose, for example, that a thief, T, manages to obtain X, Inc.'s payment order code (equivalent to a security PIN) and issues an unauthorized payment order, see 4A–202(a), to Receiving Bank and the funds are ultimately transferred from X's account at Receiving Bank to T's account in Beneficiary Bank. How is this loss allocated between X and X's bank?

First, the analysis depends upon whether X (the putative Sender) and Receiving Bank have agreed in advance that the authenticity of a payment order issued in Sender's name is to be verified by a commercially reasonable "security procedure." See 4A–201, which defines "security procedure," and 4A–202(c) which provides a test for commercial reasonableness. If such a security procedure is agreed, the unauthorized payment order is "effective" if the "bank proves that it accepted the payment order in good faith and in compliance with the security procedure and any written agreement or instruction of the customer restricting acceptance of payment orders issued in the name of the customer." 4A–202(b). The effect is to place the risk of loss on the customer when the receiving bank accepts an unauthorized payment order after verification by the bank in compliance with a commercially reasonable security procedure. 4A–203 comment 5.

In sum, absent such a security procedure, the bank takes the hit for unauthorized payment orders. The order in such a case is unauthorized and ineffective.

If such a procedure exists and the bank follows it, but the customer does not comply with the procedure, any unauthorized order is deemed effective. The customer takes the hit.

There are, however, two exceptions to allocating the risk of unauthorized but effective orders on the customer. Even if a payment order is unauthorized but "effective" under 4A–202(b), the bank still takes the hit if either of the conditions of 4A–203(a) is satisfied. The first exception is when, and to the extent, the bank by express written agreement has contracted for the risk of loss occasioned by unauthorized but effective payment orders. 4A–203(a)(1).

The other exception is when the customer can prove that the payment order was not caused, directly or indirectly, by a person

> (i) entrusted at any time with duties to act for the customer with respect to payment orders or the security procedure, or (ii) who obtained access to transmitting facilities of the customer or who obtained, from a source controlled by the customer and without authority of the receiving bank, information facilitating breach of the security procedure, regardless of how the information was obtained or whether the customer was at fault. Information includes any access device, computer software, or the like.

4A–203(a)(2). In effect, "[i]f the customer can prove that the person committing the fraud did not obtain the confidential information [necessary to breach the payment order security procedures] from an agent or former agent of the customer or from a source controlled by the customer, the loss is shifted to the bank." 4A–203 comment 5.

Note that 4A–203(a)(2) tracks the concept of a "responsible" employee employed in 3–405, which allocates fraud risks between the owner of a checking account and her bank. Under Article 4A, Receiving Bank cannot enforce an unauthorized but effective payment order unless an "entrusted" person caused the order or unless access to key transmission facilities was obtained from a "source controlled" by the customer. Thus, under this rule, Receiving Bank cannot enforce an unauthorized order caused, for example, by a computer "hacker" or other outsider to the process who is able to pierce the security procedure.

Finally, if the unauthorized payment order is neither "effective" under 4A–202 nor "enforceable" under 4A–203, the "bank shall refund any payment of the payment order received from the customer to the extent the bank is not entitled to enforce payment and shall pay interest on the refundable amount calculated from the date the bank received payment to the date of the refund." 4A–204(a). Remember: this rule applies where the parties have not agreed in advance to a commercially reasonable security procedure. In such a case an unauthorized order is always ineffective. So, in the absence of an agreed security procedure, the loss from an unauthorized payment order is treated like a forged check under Article 4—the Receiving Bank bears the loss.

The customer's right to recover interest under 4A–204 is lost is "if the customer fails to exercise ordinary care to determine that the order was not authorized by the customer and to notify the bank of the relevant facts within a reasonable time not exceeding ninety days after the date the customer received notification from the bank that the order was accepted or that the customer's account was debited with respect to the order." 4A–204(a). "Loss of interest is in the nature of a penalty on the customer designed to provide an incentive for the customer to police its account." 4A–204 comment 2. Otherwise, "[t]he bank is not entitled to any recovery from the customer on account of a failure by the customer to give [this] notification. . . ." 4A–204(a). Also, the customer's failure to notify does not affect the customer's recovery of the principal amount of the payment order. "There is no intention to impose a duty on the customer that might result in shifting loss from the unauthorized order to the customer." 4A–204 comment 2.

Whichever party takes the hit for the unauthorized payment order—either the customer or the bank—can pursue the tacky person responsible for the unauthorized payment order. The problem, of course, is that this person is always financially unavailable.

7. MISTAKES IN PAYMENT ORDERS

Another big risk that Article 4A allocates is the risk of mistakes in payment orders. Here the problem is not that a person originates a funds transfer to steal someone else's money. The problem is that in making a completely authorized funds transfer, someone in the chain makes a mistake—usually duplication of payment orders or a mistake in the amount of the transfer or the identity of the beneficiary. The mistake can be made by the originator or a bank in the process of effecting the funds transfer. The allocation of risks, as in the case of unauthorized payment orders, depends in some instances and to some extent, on the existence of a security procedure for detecting mistakes between the sender of the payment order (either the originator or an originator's bank that is not the beneficiary's bank) and the receiving bank.

A. ERRONEOUS PAYMENT ORDERS

A payment order is "erroneous" if the order: "(i) erroneously instructed payment to a beneficiary not intended by the sender, (ii) erroneously instructed payment in an amount greater than the amount intended by the sender, or (iii) was an erroneously transmitted duplicate of a payment order previously sent by the sender. . . ." 4A–205(a).

The rule is simple if the order was not transmitted pursuant to a security procedure for the detection of error: the sender takes the loss and must act on its own to recover from the beneficiary based on the law of mistake and restitution.

Assuming transmission pursuant to a security procedure, and assuming the sender can prove that it complied with the security procedure and the error would have been detected if the receiving bank had also complied, then the following rules apply:

> If the funds transfer is completed on the basis of an erroneous payment order described in clause (i) or (iii) of subsection (a), the sender is not obliged to pay the order and the receiving bank is entitled to recover from the beneficiary any amount paid to the beneficiary to the extent allowed by the law governing mistake and restitution.
>
> If the funds transfer is completed on the basis of a payment order described in clause (ii) of subsection (a), the sender is not obliged to pay the order to the extent the amount received by the beneficiary is greater than the amount intended by the sender. In that case, the receiving bank is entitled to recover from the beneficiary the excess amount received to the extent allowed by the law governing mistake and restitution.

Id.

It's important to note that a sender gets off under these rules despite its own negligence in making the mistake. "Although the customer may have been negligent in transmitting the erroneous payment order, the loss is put on the bank on a last-clear-chance theory." 4A–205 comment 2.

On the other hand, the statute imposes a duty on a sender who escapes liability for her errors under 4A–205 to exercise ordinary care to discover the error and notify the bank within a reasonable time not exceeding 90 days. 4A–205(b). "If the bank proves that the sender failed to perform that duty, the sender is liable to the bank for the loss the bank proves it incurred as a result of the failure," id., not to exceed the amount of the sender's order. But, "[w]hether the bank is entitled to recover from the sender depends upon whether the failure to give timely notice would have made any difference. If the bank could not have recovered from the beneficiary that received payment under the erroneous payment order even if timely notice had been given, the sender's failure to notify did not cause any loss of [to] the bank." 4A–205 comment 2.

B. MISDESCRIPTION OF BENEFICIARY

Erroneous payment orders covered by 4A–205, and discussed above, include the case in which the order is sent to a beneficiary not intended by the sender. For example, X, Inc. intended to pay Y, Inc. but by mistake addressed the payment order to Z, Inc. A different case is a payment order received by the beneficiary's bank on which "the name, bank account number, or other identification of the beneficiary refers to a nonexistent or unidentifiable person or account." 4A–207(a). This problem is called "misdescription" of the beneficiary and is handled very differently.

In this case "no person has rights as a beneficiary of the order and acceptance of the order cannot occur." Id. No acceptance. No liability. So, "each sender in the funds transfer that has paid its payment order is entitled to get its money back." 4A–207 comment 1. The rules are different and more complicated when the payment order carries conflicting identification of the beneficiary that refers to different persons. See 4A–207(b)–(c).

CHAPTER 13

CONSUMER FUNDS TRANSFERS

For most purposes a consumer electronic funds transfer means

- ✓ any transfer of funds,
- ✓ initiated through any electronic means (including terminal, telephone, or computer),
- ✓ for the purpose of getting a bank or other financial institution,
- ✓ to debit or credit a checking, savings or other *asset* account (but not a credit account),
- ✓ established by a *natural person*, and
- ✓ for *personal, family or household purposes*.

WARNING! We're talking here about electronically—by any means—reaching into an asset account at a financial institution: most commonly, your checking or savings account at a bank. We aren't talking here about using different or the very same electronic means to charge something to a credit account. The law with respect to credit cards—no matter how they are accessed or used—is discussed elsewhere, and the law discussed here does not apply.

I know. I know. The card you carry does lots of things. It is a credit card and also is an ATM and/or debit card that affects your checking account. Which chapter of this book and which law applies depends on how you use the card in each transaction. Crazy, ain't it?! Scary, too. Imagine what a law school final exam question can look like.

Consumer electronic funds transfers (EFTs) affecting asset accounts are common. One of the most familiar is a bank customer's use of her ATM (automated teller machine) card to get cash from her accounts at the bank. A close relative is the debit or check card used to pay for stuff at the point of sale. The customer gets these cards from her bank; but she can use her ATM card (for a fee) at other bank's ATM machines; and she can use her debit card to access her checking account at any place of business that accepts this form of payment.

ATM machines and point-of-sale registers are connected to networks that verify and debit funds in real time using encrypted personal identification numbers for authorization and security. Networks that are privately owned include Star and NYCE, as well as networks affiliated with MasterCard (Maestro, Cirrus), Discover (Pulse), and Visa (Plus and Interlink).

As recently recognized by the Federal Reserve Board, "Debit cards now play a prominent role in the U.S. payments system. Debit card payments have grown more than any other form of electronic payment over the past decade, increasing to 37.9 billion transactions in 2009. Debit cards are used in 35 percent of noncash payment transactions, and have eclipsed checks as the most frequently used noncash payment method." 76 FR 43394–01, 43395 (July 20, 2011).

There are two types of debit card authentication methods, with different infrastructures. PIN (personal identification number) based networks, which evolved from the ATM networks, and signature based networks, utilizing the credit card networks developed by such issuers as Visa and MasterCard.[1] PIN networks were originally cheaper, generally charging a fixed per-transaction interchange fee similar to an ATM fee. (Remember that interchange fees are the fees paid by the bank that signs up the merchant to the bank which issues the card. The important thing to remember here is that those interchange fees are usually also the basis for setting the discount fee paid by the merchants.) Signature networks generally charged a significantly higher interchange fee, based on a percentage of the transaction like a credit card. Id. at 43396. Those discrepancies were part of the reason for federal regulation of debit card interchange fees, as discussed *infra*.

Another common consumer EFT is the direct deposit to pay employees' wages and salaries. The backbone network for direct deposits is the

---

[1] Increasingly, however, issuers are permitting "PIN" debit transactions to be accomplished without a PIN, and "signature" debit transactions to be accomplished without a signature. In 2014, for example, Apple introduced a contactless payment technology labelled "Apple Pay," which permits cardholders to access debit cards by holding an iPhone, iPad or Apple Watch up to a sensor at the point of sale. As its website explains, " . . . your actual . . . debit card numbers are never shared by Apple with merchants or transmitted with payment." http://www.apple.com/apple-pay/?cid=wwa-us-kwm-features-com (last visited Oct. 29, 2014).

Automated Clearing House (ACH) Network. The ACH network is also increasingly providing the means for effecting other kinds of electronic payments to and from consumers and businesses. Therefore, this chapter provides a short explanation of the ACH network and the major, traditional and a few newer ways the network is used to make consumer funds transfers.

The ways and means of transferring consumer funds using ACH and, increasingly, other channels are many and growing. Traditionally separate, narrow systems are widening and expanding their services to handle new forms of consumer EFTs, mainly by using excess capacity in newer, more efficient technology and computer networks. Systems that traditionally used closed, private networks are partnering to share channels and capacity and are opening up to use the Internet.

The differences in these electronic payment systems are mainly in the underlying technologies; their functionalities; and—to some extent—how they are priced and how the contract between the issuer and user allocates risks and other costs. What they share are fundamental duties imposed by preemptive federal law whenever a consumer electronic funds transfer crosses their networks or otherwise uses their services to affect a consumer account. So, this chapter also explains the federal law.

1. AUTOMATED CLEARING HOUSE (ACH) NETWORK

A. WHAT IS THE ACH?

The automated clearing house (ACH) network is a batch-oriented, electronic funds transfer system for the interbank clearing of electronic payments for participating depository financial institutions. ACH transactions are basically payment instructions which direct a financial institution to either debit or credit a deposit account. First developed by bankers in California in the 1970s, the ACH Network currently moves "almost $39 trillion and 22 billion electronic financial transactions each year."[2] Originally transferring data by paper, magnetic tapes, and diskettes, the current network is an electronic payment system which in the U.S. "moves more than 20 percent of all electronic transactions each year."[3]

The current FFIEC Examination Handbook[4] explains the process:

> ACH transactions are sent in batches by financial institutions and third-party service providers to ACH operators for processing one or two business days before settlement dates. The

---

[2] *See* https://www.nacha.org/ach-network/timeline (last visited Oct. 29, 2014).

[3] Id.

[4] The Federal Financial Institution Examination Council provides standards for the federal examination of financial institutions by the relevant federal agencies. *See* http://ithandbook.ffiec.gov/ (last visited Oct. 29, 2014).

ACH operators deliver the transactions to the receiving institutions at defined times. The Electronic Payments Network (EPN), one of the two national ACH operators, is a private processor with a significant share of the national market.[5] The Reserve Banks process the remaining share of the market. ACH operators charge a small fee per-transaction to both the originating and receiving depository institutions.[6]

B. NACHA

The ACH Network is administered by the National Automated Clearing House Association (NACHA), a not-for-profit self-regulatory association representing more than 10,000 financial institutions. *See* https://www.nacha.org/about (last visited Oct. 29, 2014) In that capacity, NACHA establishes and enforces the rules that provide the legal foundation for the ACH network.

C. HOW ACH PAYMENTS WORK

The NACHA website provides the following description of an ACH payment:

1. An Originator—whether that's an individual, a corporation or another entity—

---

[5] EPN is a subsidiary of The Clearing House (formerly known as the New York Clearing House Association).

[6] *See* IT Booklets—Retail Payment Systems—Payment Instruments, Clearing, and Settlement—The Automated Clearing House (ACH)—The ACH Network, at http://ithandbook.ffiec.gov/ (last visited Oct. 29, 2014).

initiates either a Direct Deposit or Direct Payment transaction using the ACH Network. ACH transactions can be either debit or credit payments and commonly include Direct Deposit of payroll, government and Social Security benefits, mortgage and bill payments, online banking payments, person-to-person (P2P) and business-to-business (B2B) payments, to name a few.

2. Instead of using paper checks, ACH entries are entered and transmitted electronically, making transactions quicker, safer and easier.

3. The Originating Depository Financial Institution (ODFI) enters the ACH entry at the request of the Originator.

4. The ODFI aggregates payments from customers and transmits them in batches at regular, predetermined intervals to an ACH Operator.

5. ACH Operators (two central clearing facilities: The Federal Reserve or The Clearing House) receive batches of ACH entries from the ODFI.

6. The ACH transactions are sorted and made available by the ACH Operator to the Receiving Depository Financial Institution (RDFI).

7. The Receiver's account is debited or credited by the RDFI, according to the type of ACH entry. Individuals, businesses and other entities can all be Receivers.

8. Each ACH credit transaction settles in one to two business days, and each debit transaction settles in just one business day, as per the *Rules*.

About NACHA, ACH Network: How It Works, https://www.nacha.org/ach-network (last visited Nov. 7, 2014).

The only public-sector processor is the FED ACH, which is an electronic payment delivery system owned by the Federal Reserve. FED ACH exclusively handles all ACH transfers of federal funds. The Debt Collection Improvement Act of 1996 required the federal government to convert most of its nearly one billion annual payments from paper check to electronic funds transfers (EFT), including federal salary, benefit, vendor and miscellaneous payments disbursed either by the U.S. Department of the Treasury or by other agencies.

FED ACH also is the major player in handling batch electronic funds transfers originated and received by private parties through their financial institutions. In this respect FED ACH competes with the private-sector operator.

Federal law supplements NACHA rules in some respects. Mostly, however, the Federal Reserve works with NACHA to develop general rules within and for the entire association that the Federal Reserve mostly accepts and follows.

D. HOW ACH IS MAINLY USED—RECURRING PAYMENTS TO AND FROM CONSUMERS

The ACH payments system was designed to allow corporations and consumers to reduce or eliminate the use of paper checks to make routine payments. Therefore most of the payments transferred over the ACH network represent recurring credit payments intended for the accounts of the receivers. Typical payments are salaries, consumer and corporate bill payments, interest and dividends, and Social Security and other entitlement programs originated by the U.S. Treasury. However, because of the ACH's ability to process large volumes of payments efficiently and its ability to allow an originator to debit the banking account of the payer, it increasingly is used for other types of payments, such as insurance premiums, purchases of stock, and consolidation of corporate cash balances.[7]

The primary applications for ACH are direct deposits and direct payments. Direct Deposit gives a company the ability to credit the accounts of its employees, customers, and beneficiaries with funds due to them. Direct Deposit is often used for the deposit of payroll, but can also be used to distribute funds for Social Security payments, commissions, annuities/IRAs, dividends/interest, expense

---

[7] For this information and more, see http://www.newyorkfed.org/

reimbursements, healthcare/prescriptions, benefits, and pensions.

Direct Payments (which you may know as "automatic withdrawals") are created when a consumer gives the originating institution or corporation (Originator) authorization to debit his/her account on a regular basis. Direct Payment can be used to pay utility, mortgage/rent, or automobile loan payments; charitable contributions; insurance premiums; membership dues; tuition payments; and nonprofit organization fees.[8]

Many corporations have been able to realize significant savings by collecting recurring consumer payment obligations by debiting consumers' bank accounts electronically after obtaining approval of the bill payer to debit his or her bank account periodically for the amount owed. Insurance companies, securities dealers, loan processors, and others have successfully used this application.

A consumer or a corporation can make an electronic credit payment instead of issuing a paper check. Using a telephone service, a personal computer interface, or written authorization, the consumer instructs a bank to debit his or her account and to issue a credit to the bank account of the payee. A corporation typically creates a computer file of payment instructions and delivers the file to its servicing bank. The servicing bank will debit its customers' accounts and deliver to the ACH an

---

[8] For this information and more, see http://www.frbservices.org.

electronic file of all the payment instructions it has received from all of its customers.

The ACH processor receives the payment file from the depository institution serving the consumer or corporation. The individual debit and credit items are sorted to create a separate output file for each depository institution, and are delivered to the depository institution electronically. The ACH processor then posts the net amount for each of the depository institutions to its account. The depository institution processes the file and posts the individual entries to the accounts of its customers.[9]

E. HOW YOUR ACH TRANSACTION WORKS

Suppose you are a third-year law student. You seldom attend classes and read very little . . . saving yourself for the upcoming bar exam. You decide the time is right to move up from the old, reliable bike. Using your signing bonus as a down payment, you buy a new car: a Ford SUV. The payment is $750 a month. (The signing bonus was nice but not too big.)

You can write a check every month and mail it to Ford Credit.

Alternatively, you can direct your bank automatically to debit your checking account every month in the amount of $750 and send the money to Ford Credit. Your bank has many customers following this same process to pay Ford Credit and lots of other creditors every month. The bank

---

9 Id.

regularly consolidates all these payment orders and electronically sends them directly or indirectly to an ACH operator and through the ACH network. The network collects similar batches from many banks, sorts them by the identities of the intended recipients, and pushes the total to them.

A variation is your bank getting the instruction from Ford Credit, not from you directly. Ford Credit asks your permission to make your monthly payment as an ACH transfer. You agree and fill out a form giving Ford Credit your bank and account information. Ford Credit gets lots of customers to agree to this method of payment and regularly sends batches of payment orders through the ACH network to the various banks of its customers. These banks debit their customers' account and remit back to Ford Credit through the ACH network.

ACH transfers are now the preferred, principal means by which the federal government pays employees and recipients of all kinds of federal payments and other benefits. This method of payment is quickly growing in the private section. You, too, may get paid through the ACH network after you pass the bar (and you surely will pass.) and join the firm. Here's how.

The firm (as *originator*) instructs its bank (known as the Originating Depository Financial Institution (*ODFI*)) to pay regularly the designated salaries of all lawyers and staff who have agreed to direct deposit payment of these salaries. These instructions will include the payees' banks and account numbers. Every month (or by some other schedule) the law firm's bank debits the firm's account for the total and sends the separate credits in batch form through the ACH network. The credits end up at the respective banks of the payees. Each of these banks is known as the Receiving Depository Financial Institution (*RDFI*). These banks then channel the money into the respective accounts of the payees, each of whom is the *receiver*. The principal players can be diagrammed like this:

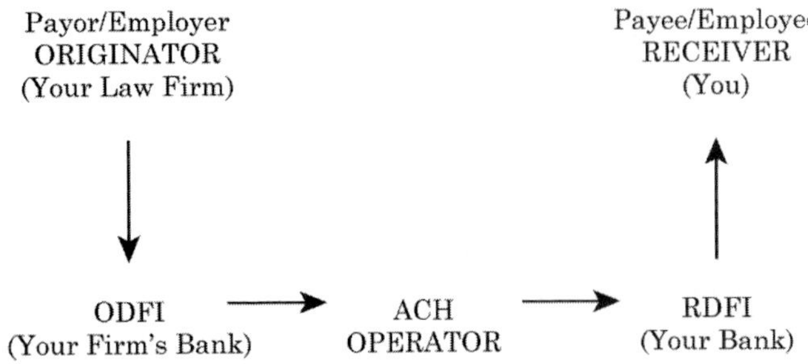

2. ELECTRONIC FUND TRANSFER ACT (EFTA)

The Electronic Fund Transfer Act (EFTA), 15 U.S.C.A. § 1693 et seq., "establishes the basic rights, liabilities, and responsibilities of consumers who use electronic fund transfer . . . services and of financial institutions or other persons that offer these services." 12 C.F.R. § 1005.1(b). The primary objective "is the protection of individual consumers engaging in electronic fund transfers. . . ." Id. To implement the statute, the Federal Reserve Board originally promulgated Regulation E, 12 C.F.R. part 205. Pursuant to the Dodd-Frank Wall Street Reform and Consumer Protection Act of 2010, Pub. L. 111–203, Title X, § 1022, 124 Stat. 1376 (July 21, 2010), however, consumer financial protection functions were transferred to the newly created Consumer Financial Protection Bureau (CFPB). The CFPB thereafter promulgated its own version of Regulation E, set out at 12 C.F.R. Part 1005.[10] Regulation E is amended from time to time to deal with issues arising under EFTA. The CFPB also issues official commentary to Regulation E to address in detail specific problems faced by the institutions that are subject to EFTA.

To date, there is very little litigation with respect to EFTA and the courts have played only a minor role in interpreting EFTA. A possible, contributing reason is the growing use of arbitration in agreements between banks and customers respecting checking and other accounts, which can legally include disputes over compliance with Regulations E and Z. *Johnson v. West Suburban Bank*, 225 F.3d 366 (3d Cir. 2000); *American Express Co. v. Italian Colors Restaurant*, 133 S.Ct. 2304, 81 U.S.L.W. 4483 (2013).

Some states have laws that also govern consumer electronic fund transfers. These laws are preempted to the extent inconsistent with the EFTA and Regulation E. 12 C.F.R. § 1005.12(b) & 12 C.F.R. pt. 1005, Supp. I, Official Staff Interpretations 12(b). The Bureau is given the power to determine whether

---

[10] Citing references will therefore be made only to the CFPB recodification of Regulation E. Corresponding cites to the FRB Regulation E are generally similarly numbered in 12 C.F.R. Part 205.

state law is pre-empted, and can also grant exemption from preemption. 12 C.F.R. § 1005.12(b–c). To some extent, however, other federal laws governing banks are more stringently preemptive and can completely trump state law touching aspects of fund transfers. *Bank One, Utah v. Guttau*, 190 F.3d 844 (8th Cir. 1999) (state laws on the placement and operation of ATMs completely preempted by the National Bank Act notwithstanding the EFTA).

A. SCOPE OF APPLICATION

EFTA and Regulation E govern "electronic fund transfers" defined by Regulation E to mean "any transfer of funds that is initiated through an electronic terminal, telephone, computer, or magnetic tape for the purpose of ordering, instructing, or authorizing a financial institution to debit or credit a consumer's account." 12 C.F.R. § 1005.3(b). Specifically, the five primary consumer electronic fund transfer transactions governed by the legal framework are:

- Automated Teller Machine (ATM) transactions such as cash withdrawals, deposits, transfers between accounts, and payments through an ATM;
- Debit cards and point-of-sale (POS) transactions involving transfers of funds from the customer's account to the merchant's account in payment for goods or services;

- Telephone bill-paying services where the customer directs payment by her bank or financial institution to designated creditors for recurring expenditures;
- Consumer wire service transfers such as that conducted by Western Union; and
- ACH transactions governing preauthorized payments from the customer's account to a third party, or direct deposit of wages, government benefits, dividends or other payments to the customer's account.

Very often, an EFT starts from or ends in a consumer account with a business on the other side of the transaction. For example, a consumer transfers funds to a creditor to pay a bill, or an employer directly deposits the consumer's salary through an ACH transfer. EFTs involving businesses are usually governed by UCC Article 4A. This statute, however, excludes from its scope "a funds transfer any part of which is governed by the Electronic Fund Transfer Act." 4A–108.

Regulation E reciprocally excludes "[a]ny transfer of funds through Fedwire or through a similar wire transfer system that is used primarily for transfers between financial institutions or between businesses." 12 C.F.R. § 1005.3(c)(3). Yet, somewhat in tandem with 4A–108, Regulation E's Official Interpretations add: "If a financial institution makes a fund transfer to a consumer's account after receiving funds through Fedwire or a similar network, the transfer by ACH [to the consumer's account] is covered by the regulation even though the Fedwire or network transfer is exempt [from Regulation E]." 12 C.F.R. pt. 1005, Supp. I, Official Staff Interpretations 3(c)(3)(1.).

This comment brings within Regulation E only the piece of the transfer from the consumer's bank to the consumer's account. It doesn't cover the earlier piece or pieces of the transfer: from the business (the originator), to the bank the business uses (the originator's bank); to the consumer's bank (the beneficiary's bank). Yet 4A–108 excludes from Article 4A "any funds transfer that is governed in any part by EFTA." 4A–108 comment 1. So, does this mean that no law governs the earlier pieces of the funds transfer? Contract law applies, of course, and probably also other federal regulations when Fedwire is involved. See Regulation J, 12 C.F.R. part 210; cf. 12 C.F.R. pt. 1005, Supp. I, Official Staff Interpretations 3(c)(3). Appropriate principles of Article 4A, if not the statute itself, might apply too. An issue related to *what* the regulation covers is *whom* it covers. Regulation E imposes various kinds of requirements for protecting consumers. The question is who must obey them. Banks and other financial institutions that are usually and generally within the Board's or Bureau's authority clearly must comply.

The Board has long argued that its authority under Regulation E extended, as well, to merchants and other payees who are not banks, but the Board rarely exercised its putative authority under Regulation E over non-banks to require them directly to act or refrain from acting. However, the Dodd-Frank Act of 2010 specifically authorizes the Bureau to supervise nonbank covered persons whose conduct "poses risks to consumers with regard to the offering or provision of consumer financial products or services." Dodd-Frank Wall Street Reform and Consumer Protection Act of 2010, PL 111–203, Title X, § 1024(a)(1)(C), 124 Stat. 1376 (July 21, 2010). The Bureau has therefore begun the process of supervision of nonbanks by issuing initial procedural rules. *See* http://www.consumerfinance.gov/newsroom/the-cfpb-issues-procedural-rule-on-supervising-nonbanks-that-pose-risks-to-consumers/ (last visited Oct. 29, 2014), and 12 C.F.R. pt. 1091.

B. MAJOR PROTECTIONS

1. Disclosures

To a large extent Regulation E is a disclosure statute. It requires a bank to disclose the terms of a consumer's account that provides for EFT services to and from the account. So, when a customer opens a checking or other asset account and the agreement provides for EFT credits or debits, the Regulation E disclosure requirements apply to the account. 15 U.S.C.A. § 1693c–e. The requirements include:

- Initial disclosures when the consumer contracts for an EFT service or before the first EFT is made involving the consumer's account;
- Disclosures when certain terms of EFT service are changed;

- Receipts when a consumer initiates an EFT at an electronic terminal, such as an ATM;
- Periodic statements reporting EFTs affecting the consumer's account; and
- Notices of preauthorized transfers to the consumer account, and written authorizations by the consumer for preauthorized transfers from the account.

The initial disclosures must include explanations of the two most important substantive provisions of Regulation E: liability for unauthorized EFTs and the procedures for error resolution.

2. Unauthorized Transfers

Banks have great incentives to comply with the disclosure requirements of Regulation E, including the rule that absent certain disclosures a consumer has no liability for unauthorized electronic fund transfers involving the consumer's account. Even with the necessary disclosures, the consumer's liability is limited but not as generously as the limits on liability for unauthorized use of credit cards. See Chapter 11 *supra*.

Suppose, for example, that Gordon Brumwell is in possession of a bank card he applied for and got from Issuing Bank. The card permits Gordon to withdraw cash from an ATM machine from an account with Issuing Bank. The card also acts as a debit card, allowing Gordon to purchase goods at the point of sale by using the card to transfer funds electronically from his checking account to the merchant's account.

This card is known as an "access device," which means "a card, code, or other means of access to a consumer's account, or any combination thereof, that may be used by the consumer to initiate electronic fund transfers." 12 C.F.R. § 1005.2(a)(1). There are other means to effect EFTs that don't require or involve an access device, but using such a device is the most familiar means of causing an electronic fund transfer from a consumer's account.

So, if Gordon's bank card is stolen and used by a thief, then he has *no liability* for unauthorized use unless (1) the card was accepted and (2) Issuing Bank has provided a means whereby the user of the card "can be identified as the person authorized to use it." 15 U.S.C.A. § 1693g(a). This means is normally a personal identification number (PIN). Practically speaking, these two conditions are routinely always satisfied.

So, in the typical case Gordon IS liable. His liability is initially limited but expands depending on a three-tier analysis: $50 limit; $500 limit: and unlimited liability.

Here are the rules as stated in Regulation E:

> A consumer's liability for an unauthorized electronic fund transfer or a series of related unauthorized transfers shall be determined as follows:
>
> (1) Timely notice given. If the consumer notifies the financial institution within two business days after learning of the loss or theft of the access device, the consumer's

liability shall not exceed the lesser of $50 or the amount of unauthorized transfers that occur before notice to the financial institution.

(2) Timely notice not given. If the consumer fails to notify the financial institution within two business days after learning of the loss or theft of the access device, the consumer's liability shall not exceed the lesser of $500 or the sum of:

(i) $50 or the amount of unauthorized transfers that occur within the two business days, whichever is less; and

(ii) The amount of unauthorized transfers that occur after the close of two business days and before notice to the institution, provided the institution establishes that these transfers would not have occurred had the consumer notified the institution within that two-day period.

(3) Periodic statement; timely notice not given. A consumer must report an unauthorized electronic fund transfer that appears on a periodic statement within 60 days of the financial institution's transmittal of the statement to avoid liability for subsequent transfers. If the consumer fails to do so, the consumer's liability shall not exceed the amount of the unauthorized transfers that occur after the close of the 60 days and before notice to the institution, and that the institution establishes would not have

> occurred had the consumer notified the institution within the 60-day period. When an access device is involved in the unauthorized transfer, the consumer may be liable for other amounts set forth in paragraphs (b)(1) or (b)(2) of this section, as applicable.

12 C.F.R. § 1005.6(b).

Now, here's an explanation aided and informed by the Official Staff Interpretations, which supplement Regulation E. *The basic liability limit is $50 and applies only if the consumer gives timely notice of the loss or theft.* "For example, the consumer's card is lost or stolen on Monday and the consumer learns of the loss or theft on Wednesday. If the consumer notifies the financial institution within two business days of learning of the loss or theft (by midnight Friday), the consumer's liability is limited to $50 or the amount of the unauthorized transfers that occurred before notification, whichever is less." 12 C.F.R. pt. 1005, Supp. I, Official Staff Interpretations 6(b)(1)(1.).

For purposes of this rule, "[t]he two-business-day period does not include the day the consumer learns of the loss or theft or any day that is not a business day. The rule is calculated based on two 24-hour periods, without regard to the financial institution's business hours or the time of day that the consumer learns of the loss or theft. For example, a consumer learns of the loss or theft at 6 p.m. on Friday. Assuming that Saturday is a business day and Sunday is not, the two-business-day period begins on Saturday and expires at 11:59 p.m. on Monday, not at the end of the financial institution's business day on Monday." Id. at (3.).

The second tier of liability is $500 and applies when timely notice of the loss or theft is not given. "For example, the consumer's card is stolen on Monday and the consumer learns of the theft that same day. The consumer reports the theft on Friday. The $500 limit applies because the consumer failed to notify the financial institution within two business days of learning of the theft (which would have been by midnight Wednesday). How much the consumer is actually liable for, however, depends on when the unauthorized transfers take place."

"In this example, assume a $100 unauthorized transfer was made on Tuesday and a $600 unauthorized transfer on Thursday. Because the consumer is liable for the amount of the loss that occurs within the first two business days (but no more than $50), plus the amount of the unauthorized transfers that occurs after the first two business days and before the consumer gives notice, the consumer's total liability is $500 ($50 of the $100 transfer plus $450 of the $600 transfer, in this example). But if $600 was taken on Tuesday and $100 on Thursday, the consumer's maximum liability would be $150 ($50 of the $600 plus $100)." Id. at 6(b)(2).

The third and final tier is unlimited liability and applies when the consumer fails to report unauthorized transfers revealed in the periodic statement of account that the bank sends the consumer. "If a periodic statement shows an unauthorized transfer made with a lost or stolen debit card, the consumer must notify the financial institution within 60 calendar days after the periodic statement was sent; otherwise, the consumer faces unlimited liability for all unauthorized transfers made after the 60-day period. The consumer's liability for unauthorized transfers before the statement is sent, and up to 60 days following, is determined based on the first two tiers of liability: up to $50 if the consumer notifies the financial institution within two business days of learning of the loss or theft of the card and up to $500 if the consumer notifies the institution after two business days of learning of the loss or theft." Id. at 6(b)(3)(1.).

Some important definitions and other details inform these rules of liability:

1. A consumer has no liability whatsoever for erroneous or fraudulent transfers initiated by an employee of a financial institution. Id. at 2(m)(1.).

2. Any transfer initiated by someone to whom the customer has furnished her card and PIN is not considered unauthorized until the consumer notifies the financial institution that the person no longer has permission to use the card. Id. at 2(m)(2.). However, the consumer need not recover the card and, based on the "mailbox" rule, the financial institution need not receive the notification, which is effective when sent.

3. An unauthorized EFT includes a transfer initiated by a person who obtained the access

device from the consumer through fraud or robbery, and also includes an EFT at an automated teller machine (ATM) if the consumer is induced by force to initiate the transfer. Id. at 2(m)(3.–4.).

4. The extent of the consumer's liability is determined solely by the consumer's promptness in reporting the loss or theft of an access device. Therefore:

    a. Negligence by the consumer cannot be used as the basis for imposing greater liability than is permissible under Regulation E. Thus, consumer behavior that may constitute negligence under state law, such as writing the PIN on a debit card or on a piece of paper kept with the card, does not affect the consumer's liability for unauthorized transfers. Id. at 6(b)(2.) (However, *see* Id. at 2(m)(2.) regarding termination of the authority given by the consumer to another person.)

    b. Similarly, no agreement between the consumer and an institution may impose greater liability on the consumer for an unauthorized transfer than the limits provided in Regulation E. Id. at 6(b)(3.).

Effecting EFT's from a consumer's account does not always require an access device, as is true when an electronic check is used. See discussion below. In case of unauthorized transfers not involving access devices, "[t]he first two tiers of liability do not apply. . . . If, however, the consumer fails to report such unauthorized transfers within 60 calendar days of the financial institution's transmittal of the periodic statement, the consumer may be liable for any transfers occurring after the close of the 60 days and before notice is given to the institution. For example, a consumer's account is electronically debited for $200 without the consumer's authorization and by means other than the consumer's access device. If the consumer notifies the institution within 60 days of the transmittal of the periodic statement that shows the unauthorized transfer, the consumer has no liability. However, if in addition to the $200, the consumer's account is debited for a $400 unauthorized transfer on the 61st day and the consumer fails to notify the institution of the first unauthorized transfer until the 62nd day, the consumer may be liable for the full $400." Id. at 6(b)(3)(2.).

3. Error Resolution

EFTA and Regulation E, moreover, provide a set of detailed rules for resolving alleged account errors. See 12 C.F.R. § 1005.11. Possible errors include:

- an unauthorized transfer,
- an incorrect transfer to or from the consumer's account,
- the omission of a transfer from a periodic statement,
- a math error made by the bank, or

- the consumer's receipt of an incorrect amount of money from an electronic terminal.

Pursuant to the relevant EFTA provisions, if a consumer believes an error has been made she must notify the financial institution orally or in writing within sixty days after the documentation has been transmitted to her. The institution must then correct the error within ten business days of receiving the notice or, alternatively, give the consumer a provisional credit within ten business days of receiving notice and correct the error within forty-five days of receipt of the notice. If, however, the institution determines that no error has occurred, it must explain its conclusion to the consumer within three business days after completing the investigation. If the institution has provisionally credited the customer's account pending investigation and finds no error, it may debit the account after properly investigating and explaining to the consumer.

4. Preauthorized Debits

A very common EFT is a scheduled, single or recurring debit that the consumer authorizes her bank to make in favor of a creditor. It happens, for example, by the customer using the bank's Web site to schedule an EFT payment,[11] or by the consumer

---

[11] Regulation E will not apply, however, if the customer uses the same system or another system but instructs the bank to issue a check chargeable to the consumer's account. 12 C.F.R. pt. 1005, Supp. I, Official Staff Interpretations 3(b)(1)(2.)(iii).

arranging with a creditor to pull regular payments from the consumer's account via EFT. In either case the consumer must authorize the scheduled EFT by a writing signed or similarly authenticated by the consumer. In the latter case the creditor who obtains the authorization must provide a copy to the consumer. 15 U.S.C.A. § 1693e(a); 12 C.F.R. § 1005.10(b).

If the bank fails to make a scheduled payment, the bank is liable, much as a bank is liable for dishonoring a check that is properly payable against a customer's account. See Chapter 3 *supra*. In this case, however, the liability is based on the EFTA, not the UCC. The statute provides that "a financial institution shall be liable to a consumer for all damages proximately caused by:

> 1) the financial institution's failure to make an electronic fund transfer, in accordance with the terms and conditions of an account, in the correct amount or in a timely manner when properly instructed to do so by the consumer, except where—
>
> > a) the consumer's account has insufficient funds;
> >
> > b) the funds are subject to legal process or other encumbrance restricting such transfer;
> >
> > c) such transfer would exceed an established credit limit;
> >
> > d) an electronic terminal has insufficient cash to complete the transaction; or

> e) as otherwise provided in regulations of the Bureau;
>
> 2) the financial institution's failure to make an electronic fund transfer due to insufficient funds when the financ[i]al [sic] institution failed to credit, in accordance with the terms and conditions of an account, a deposit of funds to the consumer's account which would have provided sufficient funds to make the transfer. . . ."

15 U.S.C.A. § 1693h(a). The bank gets a break, however, and avoids liability if the failure to pay is attributable to:

> an act of God or other circumstance beyond its control, that it exercised reasonable care to prevent such an occurrence, and that it exercised such diligence as the circumstances required; or
>
> a technical malfunction which was known to the consumer at the time he attempted to initiate an electronic fund transfer or, in the case of a preauthorized transfer, at the time such transfer should have occurred.

15 U.S.C.A. § 1693h(b). Also, if the failure to pay "was not intentional and . . . resulted from a bona fide error, notwithstanding the maintenance of procedures reasonably adapted to avoid any such error, the financial institution shall be liable for actual damages proved." Id. 1693h(c).

What happens if the consumer changes her mind? Regulation E gives the consumer a right to stop payment.

> A consumer may stop payment of a preauthorized electronic fund transfer from the consumer's account by notifying the financial institution orally or in writing at least three business days before the scheduled date of the transfer.
>
> * * * The financial institution may require the consumer to give written confirmation of a stop-payment order within 14 days of an oral notification. An institution that requires written confirmation shall inform the consumer of the requirement and provide the address where confirmation must be sent when the consumer gives the oral notification. An oral stop-payment order ceases to be binding after 14 days if the consumer fails to provide the required written confirmation.

12 C.F.R. § 1005.10(c)(1) & (2). The financial institution is liable for all damages proximately caused by failing "to stop payment of a preauthorized transfer from a consumer's account when instructed to do so in accordance with the terms and conditions of the account." 15 U.S.C.A. § 1693h(a)(3). In this case, too, the liability is limited to actual damages proved if ignoring the stop order was unintentional and resulted from a bona fide error in the face of procedures reasonably adapted to avoid the mistake. 15 U.S.C.A. § 1693h(c).

So, what's the difference between "all damages proximately caused" in the case of an intentional conduct (failing to pay or paying over a stop order) under subsection 1693h(a) and "actual damages proved" for unintentional conduct under 1693h(c)? Arguably, the former allows damages per se or presumed without specific proof of loss.[12]

The EFTA also provides more generally for liability for violating any provision of the statute or regulations. See 15 U.S.C.A. § 1693m, which is discussed immediately below. These provisions apply to 1693h cases, too, except in a few instances where the more specific provisions of 1693h are more generous or particular parts of 1693m explicitly state inapplicability to 1693h cases.

5. Debit Card Overdraft Fees

Just as we discussed with regard to checks, the account agreement with a bank may permit the holder of a debit card to use that card to overdraft her account. In 2010, Regulation E was amended to protect debit card holders from unknowingly agreeing to pay fees for that privilege. The new rule prohibits a bank from charging overdraft fees "for paying an ATM or one-time debit card transaction" unless the consumer has affirmatively consented ("opted-in") to such charges. 12 C.F.R § 1005.17(b)(1). The bank must also notify the consumer of her right

---

[12] Robert D. Cooter & Edward L. Rubin, A Theory of Loss Allocation for Consumer Payments, 66 Tex. L. Rev. 63, 111–12 & n. 180 (1987).

to revoke that consent if she so desires. Id. at (b)(1)(iv).

Consumers have also attempted to attack debit card overdraft charges through the courts. In *Gutierrez v. Wells Fargo Bank, N.A.*, 704 F. 3d 712 (9th Cir. 2012), for example, card holders claimed that the practice of high to low posting of debit charges in order to increase overdraft fees was unfair and fraudulent in violation of California's Unfair Competition Law.[13] The Ninth Circuit held that the practice itself was not "unfair" due to pre-emptive federal banking law, but affirmed the district court's finding that the bank's misleading statements in regard to its posting practices were fraudulent. On remand, the district court enjoined Wells Fargo from making future misleading statements, and reinstated a restitution award of over $200 million on the basis of the fraud claim alone. 944 F. Supp. 2d 819 (N.D. Calif. 2013).

6. Regulation of Debit Card Interchange Fees

Merchants had long resented high debit card interchange fees, particularly because fees charged by signature-based networks were similar to the higher fees charged for credit card transactions. Merchants argued that the risks of debit card transactions (where the money is in the account) were unlike the risks of credit card transactions

---

[13] Similar arguments with respect to checks have generally been unsuccessful due to 4–303(b), which states that "items may be accepted, paid, certified, or charged to the indicated account of its customer in any order."

(where the money is being borrowed). In 1996, numerous retailers including Wal-Mart and Sears brought a class action against Visa and MasterCard, claiming illegal tying arrangements in violation of antitrust laws. The case was settled in 2003 for the "largest antitrust settlement in history." *In re Visa Check/MasterMoney Antitrust Litigation*, 297 F. Supp. 2d 503, 508 (2003). Among other things, Visa and MasterCard agreed to a $3.05 billion settlement, to terminate their "honor all cards" policies by which merchants who accepted their credit cards were required to accept their debit cards, and to lower their debit card interchange fees by roughly one-third for a short period of time. Id.

A second class action comprised of approximately 12 million merchants alleging conspiracy to fix interchange fees settled in 2013. *In re Payment Card Interchange Fee and Merchant Discount Antitrust Litigation*, 986 F. Supp. 2d 207 (E.D.N.Y. 2013). That settlement agreement included a total cash fund of up to $7.25 billion, rule changes permitting merchants to impose surcharges on Visa and MasterCard credit card transactions, and an obligation of Visa and MasterCard to negotiate interchange fees in good faith with merchant buying groups. Id.

Meanwhile, further relief to merchants was provided by the "Durbin Amendment" to the Dodd-Frank Wall Street Reform and Consumer Protection Act of 2010, codified at 15 U.S.C.A. § 1693o–2. For any issuer with over $10 billion in assets, the statute requires that any interchange fee "be reasonable and proportional to the cost incurred by the issuer with respect to the transaction." 15 U.S.C.A § 1693o–2(a)(2). Implementing regulations have adopted a safe harbor of 21 cents, plus "5 basis points multiplied by the value of the transaction." 12 C.F.R. § 235.3(b).[14] Regulations were further adopted to prevent networks from designating their own network as the exclusive one over which the transactions could be processed, so that merchants may be able to encourage debit card holders to select a network cheaper for the merchant. 12 C.F.R. § 235.7(a)(1).

3. CIVIL LIABILITY FOR EFTA VIOLATIONS

The discussion of liability in Section B(4) *supra* was limited to liability under section 1693h. It is a specific provision that deals only with the wrongs of not paying a funds transfers or violating an effective order to stop payment of a funds transfer.

Another section, 15 U.S.C.A. § 1693m, describes liability for any other violations of the EFTA and Regulation E and, to some extent, governs 1693h cases, too. Section 1693m(a) provides that *"[e]xcept as otherwise provided by this section and section 1693h,"* any bank, other financial institution, or any other person who fails to comply with the EFTA with respect to any consumer is liable to such consumer in an amount equal to the sum of any actual damage sustained by such consumer as a result of such

[14] An additional penny was added to compensate the issuer for fraud prevention. 12 C.F.R. § 235.4(a).

failure and statutory damages in an amount not less than $100 nor greater than $1,000. 15 U.S.C.A. § 1693m(a).

Class actions are possible, too. Damages are allowed in such amount as the court may allow, except that (i) as to each member of the class no minimum recovery shall be applicable, and (ii) the total recovery under this subparagraph in any class action or series of class actions arising out of the same failure to comply by the same person shall not be more than the lesser of $500,000 or 1 per centum of the net worth of the defendant. Id.

Plus, and this provision is very important, in the case of any successful individual or class action, the damages include the costs of the action, together with a reasonable attorney's fee as determined by the court. Id.

In determining damages in an individual action the court must consider the frequency and persistence of noncompliance, the nature of such noncompliance, and the extent to which the noncompliance was intentional; and in a class action must also consider the resources of the defendant and the number of persons adversely affected. Id. at (b).

Presumably, with an important exception, all of the foregoing provisions apply to 1693h cases, which involve a bank failing to make a scheduled funds transfer or failing to obey a consumer order to stop payment of a transfer. (See the discussion in the preceding section above.) The exception is that the measure of damages stated in 1693m(a) (actual damages) is different under 1693h when the bank's conduct is intentional and damages are per se or presumed.

There is an exception to civil liability under 1693m(a) for mistakes the bank makes that are resolved in accordance with the procedure the law outlines for error resolution (15 U.S.C.A. § 1693f). Plus, the statute creates four, important, absolute defenses if the violation:

- was not intentional and resulted from a bona fide error notwithstanding the maintenance of procedures reasonably adapted to avoid any such error [but this defense explicitly does not apply in 1693h cases];
- involved any act done or omitted in good faith in conformity with any rule, regulation, or interpretation thereof by the Bureau or the Board or in conformity with any interpretation or approval by an official or employee of the Bureau or the Federal Reserve System duly authorized by the Bureau or the Board to issue such interpretations or approvals under such procedures as the Bureau or the Board may prescribe therefor;
- is based on any failure to make disclosure in proper form if a financial institution utilized an appropriate model clause issued by the Bureau or the Board, or
- is admitted prior to suit and the defendant notifies the consumer concerned of the

> violation, complies with the requirements of this subchapter, and makes an appropriate adjustment to the consumer's account and pays actual damages or, where applicable, damages in accordance with section 1693h of this title [and thereby explicitly does apply in 1693h cases].

Moreover, as if further deterrence to consumer lawsuits is necessary, the statute punishes some unsuccessful actions: "On a finding by the court that an unsuccessful action under this section was brought in bad faith or for purposes of harassment, the court shall award to the defendant attorney's fees reasonable in relation to the work expended and costs." 15 U.S.C.A. § 1693m(f).

Jurisdiction of actions is given the federal district courts, without regard to amount in controversy, or any other court of competent jurisdiction. The statute of limitations requires bringing an action within one year from the date of the occurrence of the violation. Id. § 1693m(g).

4. EFTA AND CHECKS

Article 3 checks are, of course, paper. In the check collection process, however, checks often trigger electronic effects on the accounts of consumer customers. Nevertheless, Regulation E generally does not apply because "[a]ny transfer of funds *originated* by check, draft, or similar paper instrument" is explicitly excluded from coverage. 12 C.F.R. § 1005.3(c)(1) (emphasis added). So, Regulation E does not apply to truncated and represented checks but makes an exception for and covers electronically converted checks.

A. ARTICLE 3 "TRUNCATED" CHECKS

Paper checks are very often processed through the Federal Reserve System's "check collection services," which is a network separate from the FED ACH. The Federal Reserve check collection system involves "collecting banks" sending all of their deposited checks to the local Federal Reserve Bank, which, in turn, sends the checks to the "paying banks." (Article 4 uses the term "Payor bank."). Traditionally, this process has commonly been accomplished using actual paper items. See Chapter 3 *supra*.

Increasingly, paper checks are "truncated," which means the information in the check is captured and put in electronic form by the payee or depositary bank and collected through the ACH network. These truncated, "electronic drafts or checks" are commonly called "items", "transactions", "debits", "ach's", and "checks". Technically, a check that has been converted into an electronic draft is no longer a check; however, colloquial language often still uses the term "check" to describe these transactions. The ACH network serves as intermediary between the depositary bank and the paying bank for processing "truncated checks" and other "electronic items."[15]

These truncated checks are not covered by EFTA even if they are drawn against a consumer's account.

---

[15] For this information and more, see http://www.frbservices.org/.

True, the account in the end is accessed and debited electronically. The key to applying EFTA, however, is debiting or crediting a consumer's account by a transfer of funds *initiated* by electronic means. A truncated check ends up electronically transferring funds but the process was not initiated by electronic means. EFTA does not apply. UCC Articles 3 and 4 apply.

B. RE-PRESENTED CHECKS

You know the rights and remedies available to a depositary bank when a dishonored check is returned. The most basic, easiest, and cheapest remedy is to charge back the item against the account of the customer who deposited the check. See the discussion Chapter 3 *supra*.

Businesses, however, often authorized their depositary bank to re-present the dishonored check, that is, run it through again in the hope that the check will "clear" (be paid) on the second trip to the drawee-payor bank. This second trip is called re-presentment.

Typically, the re-presentment is accomplished purely electronically. The data from the check is presented the second time instead of the check itself. Arguably, this re-presentment, standing alone, is an electronic fund transfer that is not originated by check. On this reasoning, Regulation E applies.

The regulation, however, looks at the overall transaction, which was originated by a paper check, and explicitly excludes electronically re-presented checks:

> The electronic re-presentment of a returned check is not covered by Regulation E because the transaction originated by check. Regulation E does apply, however, to any fee debited via an EFT from a consumer's account by the payee because the check was returned for insufficient or uncollected funds. The person debiting the fee electronically must obtain the consumer's authorization.

12 C.F.R. pt. 1005, Supp. I, Official Staff Interpretations 3(c)(1)(1.).

C. ELECTRONIC CHECK CONVERSION ("E-CHECKS")

Never heard of **electronic check conversion** (a/k/a "**e-checks**")? This is a relatively new but increasingly used process.[16] A check is used for the purpose of capturing information for initiating a one-time-ACH debit from the consumer's account.

Here is an explanation of check conversion from the Federal Reserve Board:[17]

> Electronic check conversion is a process in which your check is used as a source of information—for the check number, your account number, and

[16] The 2010 Federal Reserve Payments Study at p. 14 indicates that 3.3 billion checks were converted in 2009.

[17] Federal Reserve Board, When Is Your Check Not a Check? Electronic Check Conversion, available at http://www.federalreserve.gov/pubs/checkconv/.

> the number that identifies your financial institution. The information is then used to make a one-time electronic payment from your account—an electronic fund transfer. The check itself is not the method of payment. * * * When you provide your check, you must be given notice that information from your check may be used to make an electronic payment from your account. * * * If you pay with a check at a store . . . a merchant must post a sign—typically at the register—notifying you that if you pay by check, you are agreeing to let the merchant make an electronic fund transfer from your account. Second, you will be given a copy of the posted notice (or a similar notice) that you can keep for your records. This notice usually appears on your sales receipt. * * *
>
> Your electronic transaction may be processed faster than a check. Be sure you have enough money in your account at the time you make a purchase. Your financial institution will not return any checks that are converted, even if you normally receive your original checks or images of those checks with your statement. * * * When you provide your check, you have the right to receive notice of any fee . . . , the right to receive a receipt . . . [and] the right to have this same transaction information included as part of the regular account statement from your financial institution.

Regulation E covers this form of check conversion:

> A transfer via ACH where a consumer has provided a check to enable the merchant or other payee to capture the routing, account, and serial numbers to initiate the transfer, whether the check is blank, partially completed, or fully completed and signed; whether the check is presented at POS or is mailed to a merchant or other payee or lockbox and later converted to an EFT; or whether the check is retained by the consumer, the merchant or other payee, or the payee's financial institution.

12 C.F.R. pt. 1005, Supp. I, Official Staff Interpretations 3(b)(1)(1.)(v). Electronic check conversion can also happen when you pay a bill by drawing and sending a check to the payee who captures the account information and collects electronically instead of sending the instrument itself through the check collection process. Regulation E applies in this case, too. Arguably, the UCC also applies to some extent, except where the federal law preempts. The protection these laws provide, however, against possible double dipping is not entirely clear and certain.

Suppose you send the check and the amount is collected electronically. The payee, however, also deposits the check for collection. It's tacky, of course, and illegal but nevertheless happens. If you are lucky enough to stop payment of the check, the instrument will bounce back to the payee. You've got a good defense against her. If the payee's account is empty, however, the check will stop with the depositary bank, which is likely a holder in due course and takes free of your defense.

If the check is paid, a basis for forcing your bank to re-credit your account is hard to find under Article 4. The check was properly payable in terms of the deposit agreement between you and the bank.

Regulation E provides only a slightly clearer basis for remedying the double debit. The EFT debit in this case may be (though not certainly) the kind of "error" the regulation protects against. (See the related discussion above.) Another theory may be that in light of the duplicity, the electronic debit was "unauthorized" within the meaning of Regulation E, and thus the loss can be shifted to the bank on this basis within the limits the regulation provides. If so, the consumer is favored by the liability rules of Regulation E. The limitations on liability are more generous when unauthorized use happens without an "access device," see discussion above; and a check used to capture account information is not an access device. 12 C.F.R. pt. 1005, Supp. I, Official Staff Interpretations 2(a)(2.).

Another uncertainty in Regulation E's coverage of check conversion is the case of a consumer who, on line or by telephone, provides information about her account that the payee will use to effect an electronic fund transfer. These transfers are known, respectively, as WEB and TEL check conversion transactions. The regulatory provisions dealing specifically with check conversion assume that the consumer provides "a check" from which the information is extracted. In this case, the customer is using the Internet or telephone; is remote from the payee; and provides the information herself and directly but not the check form itself. Also, the regulation flatly excludes "telephone-initiated transfers" between a consumer and a financial institution; but the exclusion does not reach such transfers between a consumer and a merchant or other nonbank person.

The WEB or TEL check conversion transaction, which may be an EFT covered by Regulation E, should be distinguished from a transaction in which the payee (often a telemarketer) simply creates a physical check long distance. If the consumer, on line or by telephone, provides information about her account (generally from the MICR line) that the payee then uses to create an actual check collected through traditional banking channels, the transaction should instead be covered by good old Articles 3 and 4. The payee will simply be an agent authorized to sign on behalf of the drawer, and the signature (if the check is signed at all) should so indicate. Article 3 was amended in 2002 to acknowledge this type of instrument, labeled a "**remotely-created consumer item.**" 3–103(a)(16). Both Articles were then amended to create warranties on the part of persons who transfer or present such items, promising that the items are authorized for the designated dollar amounts. 3–416(a)(6); 3–417(a)(4); 4–207(a)(6); 4–208(a)(4).

Regulation E does explicitly cover bill paying available to a consumer "via computer or other electronic means." This coverage, however, is limited to payments made by a "bill payer under a bill-payment service. . . ." 12 C.F.R. pt. 1005, Supp. I, Official Staff Interpretations 3(b)(1)(1.)(vi). It's possible, however, that buying something on line by providing your checking account information to effect an EFT (which the ACH codes refer to as a WEB transaction) is brought within the scope of Regulation E by the general definition of electronic fund transfer, which includes any transfer of funds initiated by computer.

Recurring payments are less troublesome. Regulation E undoubtedly applies where a consumer has authorized a creditor, on a recurring basis, to pull money from her bank account on a regular basis via ACH or has authorized her bank to push money to the creditor on the same basis. It makes no difference to trigger application of Regulation E whether the arrangement is initiated by the customer providing a check form or the information from the check.

5. FUNDS TRANSFERS BEYOND EFTA

A. MULTI-PURPOSE CARDS USED FOR CREDIT

Credit cards used as such are not within the scope of EFTA. The statute applies only to consumer checking, savings, or other asset accounts, not lines of credit.

These days, however people commonly carry multi-purpose cards that can access credit lines and also checking and other asset accounts via ATM machines, point-of-sale terminals and other means.

People still tend to call them credit cards, often because they carry the logos of Visa or MasterCard.

What decides the applicable law is not what anybody calls these cards or how the cards are marketed. The key is how they are used, and it depends on the particular use in each transaction.

- EFTA *does not* apply whenever the card is used solely to charge the price of property or services to a line of credit with Visa or MasterCard or somebody else. The applicable law on the consumers' rights is mainly the contract with the card issuer and other federal law, mainly Regulation Z (12 C.F.R. part 1026). See Chapter 11 *supra*.

- EFTA and Regulation E do apply, and not Regulation Z, whenever a consumer uses the very same card solely to initiate a funds transfer affecting her checking or savings account whether by ATM, point-of-sale terminal, or other means.

The main reason this subject is important is to decide which law's limitations of liability apply. So, suppose a consumer's ATM or debit card (the access device for Regulation E purposes) is also a credit card. The card is stolen and used to make unauthorized withdrawals from a checking account and also to obtain unauthorized cash advances directly from the credit card, which is separate from the checking account. Which law applies?

The Bureau's answer is: "both Regulation E and Z apply." 12 C.F.R. pt. 1005, Supp. I, Official Staff

Interpretations 12(a)(1.). Fortunately, they provide examples to illustrate:

> A consumer has a card that can be used either as a credit card or a debit card. When used as a debit card, the card draws on the consumer's checking account. When used as a credit card, the card draws only on a separate line of credit. If the card is stolen and used as a credit card to make purchases or to get cash advances at an ATM from the line of credit, the liability limits and error resolution provisions of Regulation Z apply; Regulation E does not apply.
>
> In the same situation, if the card is stolen and is used as a debit card to make purchases or to get cash withdrawals at an ATM from the checking account, the liability limits and error resolution provisions of Regulation E apply; Regulation Z does not apply.
>
> In the same situation, assume the card is stolen and used both as a debit card and as a credit card; for example, the thief makes some purchases using the card as a debit card, and other purchases using the card as a credit card. Here, the liability limits and error resolution provisions of Regulation E apply to the unauthorized transactions in which the card was used as a debit card, and the corresponding provisions of Regulation Z apply to the unauthorized transactions in which the card was used as a credit card.

Assume a somewhat different type of card, one that draws on the consumer's checking account and can also draw on an overdraft line of credit attached to the checking account. There is no separate line of credit, only the overdraft line, associated with the card. In this situation, if the card is stolen and used, the liability limits and the error resolution provisions of Regulation E apply. In addition, if the use of the card has resulted in accessing the overdraft line of credit, the error resolution provisions of § 1026.13(d) and (g) of Regulation Z also apply, but not the other error resolution provisions of Regulation Z.

B. TELEPHONE REQUESTS FOR TRANSFERS

Consumers sometimes telephone their banks and ask to debit funds from their checking or savings accounts and "wire" the funds to somebody, such as a kid in law school somewhere. This wire transaction is an EFT but is probably not covered by Regulation E, which excludes "[a]ny transfer of funds that is initiated by a telephone communication between a consumer and a financial institution making the transfer and does not take place under a telephone bill-payment or other written plan in which periodic or recurring transfers are contemplated." 12 C.F.R. § 1005.3(c)(6).

Article 4A might govern. It excludes funds transfers covered by the EFTA. 4A–108, but the general scope of the statute is not limited to commercial funds transfers. So, consumer transfers kicked out of the EFTA would seem to fall within

Article 4A. It's likely, though, if the bank uses Fedwire, that all or a part of the applicable law is Regulation J, 12 C.F.R. part 210, which controls funds transfers through Fedwire. 12 C.F.R. pt. 1005, Supp. I, Official Staff Interpretations 3(c)(3).

CHAPTER 14

FUNDS TRANSFERS WHICH DO NOT DEBIT A CONSUMER BANK ACCOUNT

1. INTRODUCTION

As we discussed in Chapter 13, the **Electronic Fund Transfer Act** protections as drafted apply only to EFTs which debit an "account." 15 U.S.C.A. § 1693a(7). An "account" is defined to mean "a demand deposit (checking), savings, or other consumer asset account * * * held directly or indirectly by a financial institution and established primarily for personal, family, or household purposes." 12 C.F.R. § 1005.2(b)(1). The problem is that the funds which are being debited by many of the electronic payment devices currently being used (or developed) are held by nonconsumers (e.g. governmental entities, retailers, employers or other businesses), and may be held in "pooled" or master bank accounts which have NOT been established for personal, family, or household purposes.

So the issue is whether courts, legislatures and regulators should interpret or modify the current protections to include the new devices, should adopt alternative protections, or should leave the new devices unregulated.

A. WHY OTHER PAYMENT DEVICES?

So why are other payment devices necessary? Don't we have enough already? The answer is that the current devices may leave certain gaps.

One gap is for sellers who are unwilling to take the risks inherent in checks (insufficient funds, stop orders) but who are not equipped to take debit or credit cards. Sometimes labeled person-to-person payments (P2P), these sellers may be occasional sellers like those selling over eBay.

Another gap is for the unbanked. Maintenance of a bank account may be beyond the means, comfort level, or desire for privacy, of many people. Or perhaps an issuer wants to create a payment device that combines a variety of functions—access to buildings, the retention of health information, or the ability to receive rewards or coupons.

The market for prepaid cards has been described as "a market of niches."[1] Such cards may be marketed as a checking account substitute, a spending tool for college students, a special payment device for health-care expenses or mass transit fares, or as a teen-spending device.

B. HOW TO REGULATE

As new devices developed, the urge to regulate was offset by a reluctance to stifle potentially beneficial

---

[1] Philip Keitel, Federal Regulation of the Prepaid Card Industry: Costs, Benefits and Changing Industry Dynamics, 15 No. 8 Elec. Banking L. & Com. Rep. 1 (2012).

fledgling devices. The tremendous diversity of new devices, and disagreement on policy, also hampered regulation. For example, a UCC committee formed in 2008 to study payment systems was disbanded in 2011 due to "insufficient consensus for moving forward at this time."[2] Over time, different regulatory approaches are being developed for different devices. For some, the EFTA has been specifically amended to apply to the particular device. For others, piecemeal legislation has been adopted to regulate particular abuses. And as to others, regulation is still in the process of study, investigation, or proposal.

2. REGULATION BY AMENDMENT OF THE EFTA OR REGULATION E

A. ELECTRONIC BENEFIT TRANSFERS (EBTS)

Today, federal and state agencies frequently provide access to governmental benefits—assistance to needy families, nutrition programs or other social programs—by electronic means. The relevant agency establishes an account for the beneficiary, which is then generally accessed by a plastic EBT card and PIN at a point of sale terminal or ATMs. The electronic transfer of those benefits to the recipient is known as an electronic benefit transfer (EBT).

In 1994, Regulation E was amended to extend coverage of the EFTA to EBTs issued by

---

[2] Fred H. Miller, UCC Study Committee on Payment Systems Postponed, 65 Consumer Fin. L. Q. Rep. 437, 438 (2011).

governmental agencies. 59 FR 10678–01 (March 7, 1994). EBTs are therefore subject to many of the EFTA protections, although with significant modifications. 12 C.F.R. § 1005.15. For example, governmental agencies need not provide periodic statements so long as the account balance and history are accessible by specified other means. 12 C.F.R. § 1005.15(d).

B. PAYROLL CARDS

Employers have also recently begun to pay wages and salaries to employees by electronic means. If the employee maintains no bank account, the employer may itself establish a pooled payroll card account—generally at a federally insured financial institution. The account is then accessed by the employee through some device, generally a plastic payroll card and PIN.

In 2006, Regulation E was further amended to extend coverage of the EFTA to such payroll card accounts. 71 FR 51437–01 (Aug. 30, 2006). Similarly to EBTs, however, the protections were modified to remove some of the administrative burden on employers. 12 C.F.R. § 1005.18.

C. GIFT CARDS

Prepaid gift cards are the modern form of the old-fashioned gift certificate. These cards generally carry a magnetic stripe that records a dollar value, which is either a set amount or determined by the consumer when the card is purchased. The dollar value of each transaction is deducted until the balance reaches zero, and the card is discarded or reloaded. Gift cards may be sold by merchants at checkout counters for use in the store, or can be purchased online or in some other manner from issuers such as Visa or MasterCard.

In response to consumer complaints about unfair gift card practices, Congress in 2009 amended the EFTA to address prepaid cards, gift cards, and gift certificates for the first time. 15 U.S.C.A. § 1693l–1. The definition of covered devices includes any card, code, or other device (excluding those only in paper form) which is issued to a consumer on a prepaid basis primarily for personal, household, or family purposes, and which is honored on presentation for goods or services. 15 U.S.C.A. § 1693l–1(a); 12 C.F.R. § 205.20. Congress made clear, however, that the new protections did not apply to reloadable cards that were not marketed or labeled as gift cards. 15 U.S.C.A. § 1693l–1(a)(2)(D)(ii). Congress was not yet ready to address general purpose reloadable cards that were used as substitutes for traditional bank accounts.

Even the gift cards and devices that were addressed were not subjected to the full range of EFTA protection, however, as the amendments only addressed particular abuses. Consumers had mostly complained about fees for nonuse that "ate up" the card, and short expiration dates. Under the EFTA amendments, therefore, issuers are now prohibited from charging inactivity (dormancy) fees until the card has been inactive for one year, and then only if the fee is clearly disclosed. 15 U.S.C.A. § 1693l–1(b).

Furthermore, issuers may not issue gift cards or certificates which expire before five years from the date of issue or last loading with funds. 15 U.S.C.A. § 1693l–1(c)(2)(A).

D. OTHER PREPAID CARDS

1. Definition

The term "prepaid card" (a/k/a "stored value card") covers a wide variety of products and purposes—including the gift cards that were singled out for regulation as just described above. The Consumer Financial Protection Bureau (CFPB) describes such a payment device as follows:

> A prepaid card is a card that you use to access money you have paid in advance. A prepaid card can refer to a number of different types of cards. For example, gift cards are prepaid cards that typically are used up after you deplete the value on the card. But you can also buy a prepaid debit card that you can add money to and continue using over and over. You "load" money on the card by paying in advance, and then you spend that money by using the card. Some types of prepaid cards also allow you to take money out at an ATM.

What is a prepaid card? www.consumerfinance.gov/askcfpb/379/what-prepaid-card.html (last visited Sept. 30, 2014).

The CFPB further explains their difference from a traditional debit card:

> Even though it's called a debit card, a prepaid debit card is very different from a bank account debit card. A bank account debit card is linked to your checking account; a prepaid debit card is not. Instead, you pay in advance to load funds onto a prepaid card, and then use the money you have loaded onto the card.

What is the difference between a debit card and a prepaid debit card? www.consumerfinance.gov/ask cfpb/435/what-difference-between-debit-card-and-prepaid-card.html (last visited Sept. 30, 2014).

Although the funds are described as being "stored" or "loaded" on the card, of course, the actual funds are likely to be held by the issuer in a bank account maintained by the issuer. The funds are then generally accessed by the consumer by means of a plastic card, which may require a PIN.

The first generation of prepaid cards consisted of simpler devices for making copies, paying fares on public transit systems, making telephone calls, or paying highway tolls. These were followed by more sophisticated cards with imbedded microchips that could be used to buy goods or services in "closed loop systems" like college campuses or military bases. Those cards could only be used for certain transactions in specific locations.

More recent products include "open loop system" cards. Open system cards "may have a single issuer or multiple issuers. They are considered 'open' in the sense that they may be used for a wide variety of transactions, with the issuer of the value not necessarily being the entity providing the good or service. In the case of the single-issuer model, one firm would develop the product and issue the 'value' used on the cards but would employ other firms as members of its distribution and marketing network. The firms in the distribution network, and third party merchants and vendors, would accept the 'value' stored by users of the product and ultimately redeem that 'value' from the issuing institution. . . . In an open system that has multiple issuers, the issuers adopt a common technology (standard) for cards, establish a distribution and marketing network, and arrange a mechanism for clearing and settlement."[3] Visa, for example, currently lists on its website a choice of almost forty prepaid card options. http://usa.visa.com/personal/personal-cards/prepaid-cards/buy-online.jsp (last visited Nov. 4, 2014).

2. Consumer Protection Regulation of Prepaid Cards

Since prepaid cards do not clearly access a consumer asset account, the extent of their coverage by the EFTA and Regulation E remains murky. It is clear, however, that they have no application to prepaid cards used for business purposes, as the EFTA is limited to consumer transactions.

Unless the EFTA (or scattered state statutes) are interpreted to cover the particular prepaid card, the

---

[3] American Bar Association Task Force on Stored-Value Cards, A Commercial Lawyer's Take on The Electronic Purse: An Analysis of Commercial Law Issues Associated with Stored-Value Cards and Electronic Money, 52 Bus.Law. 653, 658–59 (1997).

extent of the holder's protection therefore depends on the contract drafted by the issuer. Some industry participants have adopted pieces of regulatory schemes to play it safe and stave off clearer governmental rules. In general, prepaid card contracts were influenced less by individual bargaining than by market forces and industry precaution.

The Federal Reserve Board first attempted to regulate prepaid cards in 1996. 61 FR 19696–01 (1996). The Board proposed to divide stored value cards into categories, depending on whether balance and transaction data were maintained only on the card itself, or by communication with a bank or central data facility. The latter types of cards were viewed as the functional equivalent of bank accounts, and the Board therefore proposed that such cards be covered by the EFTA. After adverse reaction, however, the proposed regulations were withdrawn and the effort was abandoned.[4]

When amending Regulation E to address payroll cards in 2006, the Federal Reserve Board again declined to extend its protections to general spending cards. The Board at that time reasoned that such cards may only be "used for limited purposes or on a short-term basis, and * * * may hold minimal funds." 71 FR 51437–01, 51441 (Aug. 30, 2006). Based on that premise, the Board concluded that "[c]onsumers

---

[4] *See* Report to the Congress on the Application of the Electronic Fund Transfer Act to Electronic Stored-Value Products (March 1997), *available at* http://www.federalreserve.gov/board docs/rptcongress/efta_rpt.pdf (last visited Nov. 4, 2014).

would derive little benefit from receiving full Regulation E protections * * * while the issuer's cost of compliance with Regulation E might be significant." Id.

The first specific federal protection provided to holders of general use prepaid cards therefore arose out of the complaints about exorbitant interchange fees charged for debit card transactions (*see* Chapter 13 *supra*). The resulting Congressional mandate that interchange fees charged for debit card transactions be "reasonable and proportional to the cost incurred by the issuer" extends to interchange fees charged for general use prepaid card transactions as well. 15 U.S.C.A. § 1693o–2(a)(2); 1693o–2(c)(2)(B).

More recently, the Bureau of Consumer Financial Protection has begun the process of extending the EFTA and Regulation E to at least some types of prepaid cards. In 2012, the Bureau provided advance notice of proposed rulemaking (ANPR), seeking both comment and information from the public regarding a specific type of prepaid card known as a "general purpose reloadable (GPR) prepaid card." 77 FR 30923–01 (May 24, 2012). Such a card is described by the CFPB notice as follows:

> A GPR card is issued for a set amount in exchange for payment made by a consumer. A GPR card is reloadable, meaning the consumer can add funds to the card. While this ANPR refers to a "card," these devices may include other mechanisms, such as a key fob or cell phone application, that access a financial account. This ANPR does not seek information

about "closed loop" cards, debit cards linked to a traditional checking account, non-reloadable cards, payroll cards, electronic benefit transfers (EBTs), or gift cards.

The CFPB notice characterized the GPR card market as "one of the fastest growing segments of the overall prepaid market," and noted that many issuers "voluntarily provide some protections for consumers." However, the notice stated that the Bureau was gathering information about GPR cards "in order to ensure that consumers are protected regardless of the economic environment." The notice takes the form of questions designed to solicit information regarding the appropriate definition of GPR cards, the applicability and extent of various EFTA protections, the ability to compare products, the extent of disclosure, etc. Meanwhile, the CFPB has begun testing potential disclosures that may be proposed for use on the packaging of prepaid cards. *See* Kelly Cochran, *Spring 2014 rulemaking agenda,* http://www.consumerfinance.gov/blog/spring-2014-rulemaking-agenda/ (last visited Nov. 3, 2014).

3. Current Lack of Regulation of Prepaid Cards

Until such rules are adopted, of course, prepaid cards which cannot be interpreted to fall within the EFTA and Regulation E remain largely unregulated. So what is likely to happen in the following situations?

a. Loss or Theft of a Prepaid Card

So, what happens if you lose a prepaid card and somebody else finds it and uses the card to pay for property or services? Between you and the issuer, who bears the loss depends on the terms of your card contract. As the CFPB website says, "Your rights to recover money taken from your prepaid card account depend on what type of card it is, what your contract promises, and how quickly you report the loss after you discover it." Commonly Asked Questions, http://www.consumerfinance.gov/askcfpb/425/what-should-i-do-if-my-prepaid-card-or-card-pin-lost-or-stolen.html (last visited Nov. 4, 2014). For example, the current cardholder agreement for the Wal-Mart Basic MoneyCard adopts a modified version of the $50/$500/unlimited liability scheme for unauthorized use applicable to debit cards under the EFTA. Cardholder Agreement, 3–4, available at www.walmartmoneycard.com/walmart/account/legal info-page?doc=cha&productn. Some issuers may even extend their "zero liability" policy to their prepaid card products. The bottom line—read your contract!

What about your rights against the person who got the funds? This situation conjures the possibility of new life for an old precedent, *Miller v. Race*, which is central to the discussion of currency in Chapter 1 *supra*. Lord Mansfield said in *Miller* that you cannot follow money that in ordinary course has passed in currency. *Miller*, which is so old that it involved money in the form of a bank note, might very well decide this case as a matter of common law, absent otherwise applicable statutes or regulations to the contrary. Significantly and ironically, a couple of Federal Reserve economists have compared stored-value cards for other purposes to bank notes of past centuries.[5]

b. Finality of Payment

Unless the particular card contract provides a means of reversal or chargeback, payment is likely to be deemed final when value is spent. There will generally be no means for stopping payment or otherwise reversing the transaction. The very stingy, expensive remedy of common-law restitution against the person who received payment is likely to be the only recourse.

c. Risk of Issuer Insolvency

Remember that funds for a prepaid card are paid in advance. Although the holder may think of those funds as being held "on the card," they are most likely actually held in a bank account maintained by the issuer. In effect, therefore, any remaining value on that prepaid card represents a *claim* against the issuer.

If the issuer is a bank, the consumer probably feels relatively safe—she knows that the bank is financially backed in various ways by the Federal

---

[5] William P. Osterberg & James B. Thomson, Bank Notes and Stored-Value Cards: Stepping Lightly into the Past, Federal Reserve Bank of Cleveland (Sept. 1998), *available at* http://www.clevelandfed.org/research/commentary/1998/0901.pdf (last visited Nov. 4, 2014).

Reserve, including borrowing rights. The funds may even be insured up to the insurance limits by the FDIC. A General Counsel's opinion issued by the FDIC in 2008 permits stored value funds to be treated as deposits if held by an insured depository institution.[6] In order for the holder of a prepaid card to qualify for that insurance if the funds are held in a pooled account, however, the bank's records must disclose the custodial relationship, certain designated records must disclose the identity of the owner and the amount, and the deposits must actually be owned by the claimant under the terms of their agreement.

If the issuer is not a bank, the holder of a prepaid card lacks the protection of that powerful, deep-pocketed surety. Since she would generally be classified as an unsecured creditor, she would be dependent upon the continuing financial stability of the issuer and the terms of her contract with it. As the CFPB warns, "If your prepaid debit card issuer is not a bank, you cannot have any FDIC insurance, and whether you will get your money back depends on the issuer's rules."

Is the money on my prepaid debit card FDIC-insured? http://www.consumerfinance.gov/askcfpb/529/money-my-prepaid-debit-card-fdic-insured.html (last visited Nov. 4, 2014).

---

[6] Insurability of Funds Underlying Stored Value Cards and Other Nontraditional Access Mechanisms, New General Counsel's Opinion No. 8, 73 FR 67155–01 (Nov. 13, 2008).

Even should Regulation E protections be applied to prepaid cards, consumers would not be protected from issuer insolvency. As recognized by the Board in its report to Congress in 1997, " * * * Regulation E does not cover some important risks faced by consumers using stored-value products, such as loss (where no unauthorized use occurs) or expiration of the instrument or insolvency of the issuer."[7] However, such nonbank issuers are likely to be subject to federal or state laws regulating money transmitters, a few of which are based on the **Uniform Money Services Act (UMSA).** Those statutes license and regulate money transmitters in regard to security and net worth requirements, and therefore provide at least a limited degree of financial protection. In fact, one of the goals stated in the Prefatory Note to the UMSA is to provide "a consistent approach to the licensing and regulation of *stored value and other forms of emerging Internet and electronic payment mechanisms.*" (emphasis added).

The purposes of money transmitter laws are to guard entry into the business, to aid law enforcement in the prevention of money laundering, and to standardize reporting and record keeping requirements. Such statutes therefore not only protect the public welfare but to a certain extent protect parties using prepaid cards.

---

[7] Report to the Congress, *supra* note 4 at 4.

d. Lack of Disclosure

One of the major complaints of consumers in regard to prepaid cards are fees which deplete the value loaded on the card—out-of network ATM fees, balance inquiry fees, fees for customer service, etc.,[8] and some Congressional proposals have been made to at least address the disclosure of such fees.[9] Until disclosure is mandated, however, fees may remain hidden and consumers may lack the ability to make comparisons between various products.

As this discussion illustrates, in the absence of specific contract protections, the risks of using prepaid cards are more similar to those of cash than checks, credit cards, or other electronic fund transfers.

E. REMITTANCE TRANSFERS

The most recent amendment of Regulation E added a new subpart B to govern "remittance transfers." 12 C.F.R. § 1005.30–36 (effective Oct. 28, 2013); 78 FR 30662–01 (May 22, 2013). The amendment extends EFTA protections to electronic transfers made to recipients in foreign countries. Such transfers are often low value transfers made by

---

[8] Monica C. Platt, An Uncertain Regulatory Future for Prepaid Cards, 31 No. 7 Banking & Fin. Services Pol'y Rep.1, 2 (July 2012).

[9] *See, e.g.*, the "Prepaid Card Disclosure Act of 2014" [S. 1903, 113th Congress, 2d Sess. (2014)].

workers for the purpose of supporting families in their home countries.[10]

3. ALTERNATIVE PAYMENT SYSTEMS

Existing payment devices still fail to address the need for person-to-person payments (P2P) between parties lacking the technological structure for traditional cards, or desiring a level of privacy not provided by the traditional networks. Innovations continue to try to fill that gap.

A. PAYMENT INTERMEDIARIES

A variety of intermediaries have attempted to provide a communication and settlement structure between buyers and sellers to facilitate online payment for goods and services.[11] PayPal, Inc. is the most significant player. Founded in 1998 and acquired by eBay, Inc. in 2002,[12] PayPal currently has 157 million active digital wallets utilizing more than 100 international currencies. PayPal, https://www.paypal-media.com/about (last visited Nov. 4, 2014).

---

[10] *See* Laura H. Brown, Candace M. Davis, Lois S. Woodward, & Ryan S. Stinneford, Current Developments in Deposit Products and Payment Systems, 68 Bus. Law. 603 (Feb. 2013).

[11] Other systems include Google Wallet, http://www.google.com/wallet/shop-in-stores/?gclid=CPbB6NS388ECFZKLaQod_ywA2A; Amazon, www.amazon.com; Square, www.squareup.com, and Apple Pay, http://www.apple.com/apple-pay/.

[12] eBay, Inc. has announced plans to separate eBay and PayPal into independent publicly traded companies in 2015.

In order to establish a PayPal account, customers agree to the terms of an extensive user agreement. The customer then funds the account, usually by traditional means such as a credit card, debit card, ACH transfer, etc. When the customer makes a purchase, PayPal debits funds from the buyer's account and credits them to the seller's account.

The exact legal status of intermediaries like PayPal remains unclear. PayPal maintains that it is not a bank. One federal court that considered the issue in regard to Facebook credits agreed that Facebook was not acting in the capacity of a bank as to those credits—at least for the purpose of coverage of the EFTA. In the case of I.B. by *Fife v. Facebook, Inc.*, 2013 WL 6734239 (D.N.D. Calif. 2013), minors used their parents' debit cards without permission to buy "Facebook Credits" to make purchases on the Facebook website. Although the plaintiff parents tried to characterize the purchases as unauthorized electronic fund transfers covered by the EFTA, Facebook asserted that the relevant sections applied only *to a financial institution*. The court agreed, dismissing the claim on the basis that the relevant sections "cannot be applied to an entity such as Facebook, which is not a financial institution." Id. at 6.

However, payment intermediaries like PayPal are likely to fall within federal or state money transmitter laws.[13] Those statutes may therefore

---

[13] *See* M. MacRae Robinson, Easing the Burden on Mobile Payments: Resolving Current Deficiencies in Money Transmitter Regulation, 18 N.C. Banking Inst. 553, 561 (2014).

provide some limited oversight and solvency protection.

So what exactly is the relationship between PayPal and its customers? By the terms of its user agreement prior to 2012, PayPal held its customers' funds as an agent or custodian. In 2012, however, PayPal changed the terms of that agreement. PayPal's relationship with its customers is instead currently described in the PayPal User Agreement as follows:

> PayPal is Only a Payment Service Provider * * * and is not your agent. * * * If you do hold a Balance, that Balance represents an unsecured claim against PayPal and is not insured by the FDIC. PayPal will combine your Balance with the Balances of other Users and will invest those funds in liquid investments in accordance with State money transmitter laws. PayPal will own the interest or other earnings on pooled Balances.

PayPal User Agreement, § 1.1 and 5.1 http://www.paypal.com/us/webapps/mpp/ua/useragreement-full. (last visited Nov. 4, 2014).

If the funds in the various accounts are owned by PayPal rather than its customers, the transfer of funds *between* PayPal accounts would *not* debit or credit a consumer asset account. Therefore, the EFTA should not apply to that portion of the transaction. On the other hand, the EFTA should still apply to transfers *into* or *out of* a customer's PayPal account, if those transfers involve an EFT coming from, or going into, that customer's consumer bank account.

The result is that internal disputes between customers and PayPal, Inc. are currently left to resolution on the basis of traditional common law or statutory grounds—unconscionability of arbitration clause (*Comb v. PayPal, Inc.*, 218 F. Supp. 2d 1165 (D.N.D. Cal. 2002) (clause invalidated)); antitrust violations (*In re eBay Seller Antitrust Litigation*, 545 F. Supp. 2d 1027 (D.N.D. Cal. 2008); *Smith v. eBay Corp.*, 2012 WL 1951971 (D.N.D. Cal. 2012)); breach of contract, good faith or fiduciary duty (*Zepeda v. PayPal, Inc.*, 2014 WL 718509 (D.N.D. Cal. 2014) (improper holds on account funds)).

B. VIRTUAL CURRENCIES

1. Description

"Virtual currencies" as used here means currency that is stored and transferred in electronic form. Virtual currencies have a variety of labels—"digital cash," "digital currency," "online currency," "digital coins," etc. As described by one authority:

> Digital currency is an electronic version of money, which may be purchased with a credit card or bank transfer and used like cash online. Digital cash products such as Digicash's ecash or CyberCash's CyberCoin provide consumers with electronic tokens containing encrypted data that is recognized as valid by special software and may be freely exchanged by people online

> without any need for obtaining authorization from a credit card issuer or bank.[14]

Although most attempts to launch virtual currencies have failed (both Digicash and CyberCash went bankrupt), consumers today are becoming more comfortable with conducting financial transactions online.

Most virtual currencies are managed by some central authority that acts as issuer and intermediary. However, in 2009 the first decentralized virtual currency was created in the form of Bitcoin.[15] That type of virtual currency was recently described as follows:

> A final type of convertible virtual currency activity involves a de-centralized convertible virtual currency (1) that has no central repository and no single administrator; and (2) that persons may obtain by their own computing or manufacturing effort.[16]

As one commentator put it, "Bitcoin is not an institution, business, or person—it is not even an entity. Bitcoin is essentially a collection of users

---

[14] Lawrence D. Kaplan and Todd W. Beauchamp, *E-Commerce & Internet Law* § 31.08[10].

[15] For a description of the technology that supports Bitcoins, see Nikolei M. Kaplanov, Nerdy Money: Bitcoin, the Private Digital Currency, and the Case Against Its Regulation, 25 Loy. Consumer L. Rev. 111, 116–127 (2012).

[16] Application of FinCEN's Regulations to Persons Administering, Exchanging, or Using Virtual Currencies, at (c) (Mar. 18, 2013), available at http://www.fincen.gov/statutes_regs/guidance/pdf/FIN-2013-G001.pdf (last visited Nov. 5, 2014).

embracing a payment mechanism. * * * Once acquired, there is no expectation that the users ever repay the bitcoin system."[17]

So why use a virtual currency instead of the other payment devices we have discussed so far? One reason is to avoid the costs associated with checks, debit or credit cards. Micropayment of a few dollars or cents for the purchase of music or online information would be overburdened by the cost of maintaining a bank account or paying the transaction fees required by a debit or credit card network.

A second major advantage is at least relative anonymity. Buyers therefore often use virtual currencies for purposes of privacy (e.g. the purchase of pornography), or for engaging in a variety of illegal activities. A third advantage is that internet currencies are generally simple to use and accessible worldwide with a simple Internet connection. Finally, users of digital currencies may simply have a distrust of government, or seek a device that supersedes or is more reliable than the available currency.

On the other hand, virtual currencies are subject to a variety of risks. As one commentator explained in regard to Bitcoins:

> Bitcoins are computer files * * * and can be destroyed or lost just like cash. They are stored either on a personal computer or entrusted to an

---

[17] Kaplanov, *supra* note 15 at 151, 153.

> online service. Since the coins are simple files stored on a computer, spending them is as easy as sending an e-mail over the internet. In order to spend and accept bitcoins, all transactions must be logged on a public ledger. The public ledger is a decentralized network operated and maintained by thousands of home computers—similar to a peer-to-peer music-sharing network—rather than a central server. Once the transaction has been cleared by another bitcoin user on the network, the transaction is complete, and the bitcoins have transferred from one user to another.[18]

Generally like cash, therefore, digital cash stored in an online wallet or on a personal computer may be stolen by a hacker[19] or lost if the computer suffers a virus or physical damage.

2. Consumer Protection Regulation of Digital Cash

At the current time, digital cash remains largely unregulated. One of the major reasons has been a governmental policy of giving the private sector flexibility to develop new forms of payment. As Federal Reserve Board Chairman Greenspan commented as long ago as1996:

---

[18] Kaplanov, *supra* note 14 at 116.

[19] *See also* Derek Dion, I'll Gladly Trade You Two Bits on Tuesday for a Byte Today: Bitcoin, Regulating Fraud in the E-conomy of Hacker-Cash, 2013 U. Ill. J.L Tech. & Pol'y 165, 184–185 (Spring 2013).

> In the current period of change and market uncertainty, there may be a natural temptation for us—and a natural desire by some market participants—to have the government step in and resolve this uncertainty, either through standards, regulation, or other governmental policies. In the case of electronic money and banking, the lesson from the ACH [automated clearing house] is that consumers and merchants, not governments, will ultimately determine what new products are successful in the marketplace. Government action can retard progress, but almost certainly cannot ensure it.[20]

As the use of virtual currencies expands—particularly its use for illegal activities—that approach appears to be changing. In 2013, for example, the FBI cracked down on the online drug marketplace, the Silk Road, and arrested its owner. That same year, the Senate Committee on Homeland Security and Governmental Affairs conducted hearings on the benefits and risks of virtual currency. As the Chair stated in his opening remarks:

> Virtual currencies, perhaps most notably Bitcoin, have captured the imagination of some, struck fear among others, and confused the heck out of many of us. Indeed . . . it is clear that the

---

[20] Remarks by Chairman Alan Greenspan, Regulation of Electronic Payment Systems, U.S. Treasury Conference on Electronic Money & Banking: The Role of Government (Sept. 19, 1996), available at http//www.federalreserve.gov/boarddocs/speeches/1996/19960919.htm (last visited Nov. 5, 2014).

> knowledge and expectation gaps are wide. Fundamental questions remain about what a virtual currency actually is, how it should be treated, and what the future holds.[21]

At the current time, there appears to be widespread disagreement as to the need for, and extent of, regulation of virtual currencies.[22] Any such regulation therefore appears to be proceeding on a piecemeal basis.

For example, in March of 2013 FinCEN[23] issued a set of guidelines regarding the application of the Bank Secrecy Act to the users of virtual currencies.[24] The guidelines provide that persons obtaining virtual currencies and using them to purchase real or virtual goods or services are *not* money service businesses (MSBs) subject to a variety of registration, reporting and record keeping requirements. However, businesses that issue or redeem virtual currencies, or exchange them for real currency, are likely to be classified as MSBs (specifically, money transmitters).

A further example of potential regulation came in the area of securities law. Enticements to invest in Bitcoin-related investment opportunities have been

---

21 Opening Statement of Thomas R. Carper, Chairman, Senate Homeland Security and Governmental Affairs Committee. 2013 WLNR 29217367. (Nov. 20, 2013).

22 *See* Kaplanov, *supra* note 14; Paul H. Farmer, Jr., Speculative Tech: the Bitcoin Legal Quagmire and the Need for Legal Innovation," 9 J. Bus. & Tech. L. 85 (2014).

23 Financial Crimes Enforcement Network, a bureau of the United States Treasury Department.

24 *See supra* note 15.

classified by at least one federal district court as the sale of a security subject to regulation under federal securities law. *SEC v. Shavers*, 2013 WL 4028182 (D.E.D. Tex. 2013).

In the absence of specific regulation, the rights of holders of virtual currency are likely to be similar to those of holders of prepaid cards. That means that any protection will be largely dependent on the terms of any relevant contract, and on the continued solvency of the issuer, if one even exists.[25] So in many ways, what is old is new. In the absence of regulation or agreement, the law applicable to prepaid cards and virtual currency may very well be determined by the rules applicable to cash.

---

[25] As indicated *supra* at notes 14–15, no real issuer may exist for a decentralized virtual currency like Bitcoins.

INDEX

References are to Pages